LIVING LIGHTLY

Bring Happiness and Calm to Your Everyday

DALE CURD
KIMBERLY ALEXANDER

Collins

An imprint of HarperCollins*PublishersLtd*

Published by Collins, an imprint of HarperCollins Publishers Ltd

First edition

HarperCollins books may be purchased for educational, business,
or sales promotional use through our Special Markets Department.

HarperCollins Publishers Ltd
Bay Adelaide Centre, East Tower
22 Adelaide Street West, 41st Floor
Toronto, ON, M5H 4E3

www.harpercollins.ca

Library and Archives Canada Cataloguing in Publication

Title: Living lightly: bring happiness and calm to your everyday /
Dale Curd, Kimberly Alexander.
Names: Curd, Dale, 1963- author. | Alexander, Kimberly, 1968- author.
Identifiers: Canadiana (print) 20190213175 | Canadiana (ebook) 20190213183 |
ISBN 9781443457941 (hardcover) | ISBN 9781443457958 (ebook)
Subjects: LCSH: Devotional calendars. | LCSH: Self-actualization (Psychology) |
LCSH: Happiness. | LCSH: Calmness. | LCSH: Mindfulness (Psychology)
Classification: LCC BL624 .C87 2020 | DDC 204/.32—dc23

Printed and bound in the United States of America

LSC/C 9 8 7 6 5 4 3 2 1

For Evan and Molly.
We wrote *Living Lightly* with you two in our hearts.

Introduction

How Did We Get Here?

We carry inside us the wonders we seek outside us.
—Rumi

You may be looking at this book for yourself or for a friend. Why have you picked it up? What are you hoping for?

"How to begin?" or "Where to begin?" are the questions most of us ask when it comes to making changes in our lives. We start with a distant murmur or a hint that something isn't right, that we need to move away from—or towards—something. We're not happy; we're tired, over-whelmed, distracted, stressed, bored and lonely.

It wasn't supposed to be this way. We were going to be different. Yet somehow our lives just crept up on us, and now we're anxious to get away from it all and begin again. We are awakening to a deep need to make a fresh start. We can remember a time long ago when we felt like we were floating, and we want to feel light again.

So we start to search.

More often than not, I secretly wish that the coming year will be different, that *I* will be different. I long for lightness and freedom, yet the idea of "doing" more or willing myself to change produces a whisper inside of me asking, "Am I not enough already?"

This is a chronic condition in our modern world; so many people are searching for an answer—*the* answer—or the master, guru or self-help expert who can fix them and help them get their lives back on track. As therapists, my partner and I are part of that group of experts—along with counsellors, psychologists, psychiatrists, social workers, and life and success coaches—that others reach out to for help when they need or want to make a life change. They come to all of us looking for answers or solutions, support and help. And what most discover over time is that what they were looking for was always inside of them—it was just tucked away, ignored or forgotten.

Living Lightly is truly a "self-help" guide. The writing is steeped in our belief that *you* are the answer, that you always have been and always will be. If anything has been missing, it is your connection to, or communion with, your self. We want to see you build a strong belief in your self—to journey back into an intimate relationship with your self. Some pages in *Living Lightly* will feel like new terrain, featuring the latest thinking about being human, drawn from neuroscience and natural holistic therapies. Others invite you to explore the mechanics of how our psyches work, and still others offer tips on how to recognize, understand and express your feelings.

There are daily entries that evoke emotion through our personal sharing, through poetry and through instances of the sacred in everyday moments. And there are days when we park a thought or a perspective with you that we hope you'll be enticed to turn over and over in your mind like a Rubik's Cube. In the end, we hope you will find lightness and possibility while deepening your emotional intelligence and your intimacy with your self.

This year of living lightly offers opportunities for you to commune, in the deepest and most beautiful sense of that word, with your self and your life. For you to really get to know *you* through all of the many relationships that are available to us simply by being alive.

The simple truth is that we are always in relationship with something, everything and everyone around us; we are never completely alone. Indigenous peoples have known this for millennia—we are part of, and therefore always in relationship with, all that surrounds us, and being connected deeply to our self happens when we accept and embrace this truth. The most beautiful part of being alive is having a deep connection to who we really are—knowing ourselves. When we know who we are, it's almost impossible to become overattached or be in need of someone else to fix us, fill us up or make us whole. When we are connected to our self, we also see how we are a part of all that is around us, and we finally overcome our ego, which has tried to convince us we are separate.

Each day provides an opportunity to commune with our self via one of life's seven main relationship doorways: the nature around us, our inner nature, our work and purpose, our bodies, our minds, our community and our spirit. We are all in different places relative to each of these doorways, and reflecting on our relationship to one area can bring to the surface insights into the ways we relate to the whole of our lives. We have done our best to avoid being prescriptive. You have enough "to do" already. Thus, *Living Lightly* is ultimately an invitation. Whether you enact the specific scenarios we describe is secondary because the seed of possibility will be planted inside of you. Our hope is that you experience *Living Lightly* as both light and rich and that reading each day becomes a gift *to* you *from* you, as if you are planting seeds that nestle into the garden of your soul.

As guides who are with you every day, we too have waded into the waters of self. Like you, we are soul travellers. By opening our own hearts and offering therapeutic considerations from our journeys, we hope to inspire you to bear witness to the discoveries and learning of another as you progress towards living lightly—especially in those moments when life is not light.

So how do you work with this book? Again, the answer is deceptively simple. Form a connection with *Living Lightly* as you would any other relationship in your life. It makes no difference whether you read it all at once, a little every day, or pick it up and put it down occasionally: *Living Lightly* is always there for you, inviting you to connect. Feel free to doodle and dream in the margins and blank spaces, to ruminate and reflect. As you read and discover and experience new insights and awareness, you may become more self-assured, self-loving, open and accepting, and even grounded. The deeper your relationship to the book, the more aware of yourself you'll become. You'll feel a genuine relationship building within you—an intimate friendship like no other.

At times, *Living Lightly* also illuminates the paradox of being alive: that by living lightly, all that is not light within us is also revealed. We cannot escape such moments by distracting ourselves or chasing happiness. In these moments, we are with you, with guidance and presence, knowing that life can be hard—and sometimes, almost more painful than we think we can bear. At these times, we are here to remind you of the truth: that we are much, much stronger than we know. All of us are far more resilient than we might imagine, and we are all at various stages of entering or emerging from dark waters.

Living Lightly is not therapy, and yet you will read about our love of and belief in therapy. To hold space for another person while they journey back to themselves is an incredible offering, one that today is limited to professional listeners—therapists, healers and counsellors. We hope that holding space will one day become a way of life for all of us as we make the shift from aloneness to togetherness and from indifference to empathy.

You have our hearts with you in these pages, and we send you love and light for your own journey.

Much love,
Dale and Kim

What Is Living Lightly?

Kim's Journey

How is it that . . .

I can be in a heavy situation and feel light?

Or I can be in a light situation and feel heavy?

Living lightly, to me, is feeling free, regardless of what is happening outside of me.

I love exploring, and I love finding beauty. *Living Lightly* gave me 365 chances to explore and find beauty in my self, using interesting and beautiful life facts as doorways to reflection. The days' experiences proved to me that I can trust my self and love who I am.

You will find beauty and goodness inside of you, too, in these pages. And I am here with you because having a witness makes our experiences feel sacred and somehow more real. How wonderful to journey towards freedom together!

Dale's Journey

Writing *Living Lightly* has been about coming to terms and getting friendly with lightness as a discipline for me. As I sat down each day to consider and write an entry, I was alert to the reality that the world is both a fearsome and a friendly place, and that people are capable of so much kindness as well as causing so much pain. I couldn't bury my head in the sand and write niceties, pretending that suffering didn't exist—it does. I had to choose to rise above fear—transcend it as my default way of thinking and seeing the world—and let my mind redevelop the muscles of curiosity and empathy.

The discipline of writing every day anchored me and helped me turn my attention from the outside to the richness of my inner landscape. It has been—and, in a sense, remains—a mindfulness exercise, and I, the student, have come to it, formed a relationship with it and learned more about my self.

For me, there has also been a letting go of sorts. To walk the path back to myself, lowering my defences, I've had to reconsider much of what I grew up believing was manly. To be childlike in my curiosity and vulnerable enough to feel empathy, I've had to come to terms with and rewrite the conditioning I grew up with—that boyhood is something I must leave behind. Much of our "growing up" as men seems to be about shutting down our feelings, wants and needs, so much so that we lose our ability to recognize or describe what we feel, much less express our emotions fully and responsibly.

Writing *Living Lightly* reconnected me to the boy inside who would explore ponds, walk in the woods or make creations out of anything. I can see now how important it is for me to always maintain that bond in healthy ways, because it is he who leads me to live lightly. My inner adult, the responsible part of me, now needs that boy's lightness, curiosity and courage to guide me into aging, that next chapter, where I will again redefine my self.

January

✺ January 1

You're alive! This is a simple and beautiful thing to realize. Before we can change any aspect or the quality of our lives, we have to first appreciate and own that we *are* alive. From your first breath to the last one you just took, life is the most precious gift you have ever been given. Your life is your one true possession. Nothing else in our world can ever truly be owned—land, people, companies, even things have the potential to continue and live on when our lives come to an end. But your life ends when you stop breathing.

Life and breath are crucial to each other, and only you can ensure that they remain linked together. A friend once told me that it takes more muscle energy to resist the air around us rushing into our lungs than it does to breathe. The air around us wants to fill us up, and we are the ones who manage the way we breathe and how much air we take in.

How are you breathing? Are you letting the air in freely, without tension, without control? How deeply can you breathe? Can you fill your whole chest and lower abdomen with air and exhale with some force? Take a deep breath, savour it in your body, and then release it back into the world around you. You owned that breath. It was yours. Make it feel special. Try paying attention to your breathing, changing your posture to allow more air in, just as you'd open a window to let more fresh air into a room. Focus on breathing more easily with each breath. Make your breathing feel enjoyable.

Was that a good breath you just took? No? What about your next one? Try to appreciate that this simple process is what sustains life all around you, including *your* life.

You are alive!

January 2

One of the profoundest lessons I have learned in my life is about touch—literally, my sense of touch, and symbolically, the way I engage with the world around me. On our farm, I have had to practise so many different types of touch, from lifting and holding a draft horse's hoof so that it can be cleaned, to cradling day-old baby chicks and ducklings or feeling how much water is in a handful of soil. I marvel that the same hands are capable of so many different types of touch and of applying such a range of force—or gentleness.

I know that my hands are not only instruments of my mind, expressing my will and intention, but receivers for my brain, bringing enormous amounts of information about my world for me to consider, interpret and respond to. I've learned that my hands are listening tools. As a listener, my "touch" or presence with people is also developing. When I was younger, I treated most people similarly, meaning I had a limited selection of ways of being with and around others. I've learned how to have a light touch for shy, uncertain or cautious people and how to be firm yet open and empathetic with those folks who need to be reminded where my boundaries exist.

Touch is one of the ways we relate to the natural world and to ourselves, and it is a powerful avenue for learning, as it helps us sharpen our minds and expand our awareness.

How sensitive, how tuned in or developed, is your sense of touch?

January 3

For me, at this time of year I feel like I'm on the downward side of a massive wave of activity and get-togethers. Having come through the holidays, I'm often struck by how much pressure I've put on myself—and perhaps others—to make sure the holidays felt special, that people felt loved and seen, that there was laughter and closeness. In some cases, I look back and think perhaps I'm too emotionally invested in these moments occurring. The early-January hangover is my telltale sign that I've been overattached. Emotional attachment is important, even necessary, for togetherness and intimacy, and it certainly helps to enrich meaning in our lives. But overattachment is the major source of any disappointment we experience.

I've had to learn to be aware of when I'm investing too heavily in an event or a relationship happening in a certain way, and to pull back to let things happen naturally. We really are not in control of much in our lives except for ourselves, and it seems to me that this is the hardest lesson I've had to learn. It's taken me many years to really understand that attachment and control are both at the root of any heaviness in my life and relationships. So on this day I look back over the holidays and I can see where and with whom I was trying too hard, caretaking, holding back, even protecting—all to make sure the holidays were fun. Even as I write this, it sounds like so much work and effort.

Making a commitment to live lightly means that I welcome these moments to reflect on myself and become aware of my behaviours, and to make any adjustments that help me lighten up. These times yield incredible opportunities to remind myself that fun happens when people feel connected, free and comfortable. (Note for next year: lighten up.)

January 4

I was speaking with a young woman at the airport the other day about her relationship with her mother. Her aunt—her mother's sister—was set to arrive, and then the two planned to go to the hospital, where her mother was in a coma. "I regret never telling my mom how much I loved her," she said. "I'm going to carry that to my grave." I remember thinking how heavy a burden this guilt would be for her, and how long she would carry it. And as I was having this thought, I felt my shoulders slump forward and down as my stomach tightened. I wondered, "Is this how she feels every day of her life? And she is prepared to keep feeling this way forever. Why?"

I believe a big part of what makes regrets so powerful is that we feel helpless to remedy them. We limit our ability to process and learn from our regrets by being too literal about how to resolve and let go of them. We believe there's only one fix that will make the burden go away. For this woman, her mother had to wake from her coma; then there would be a moment of honesty, then forgiveness, then a hug. This was her vision, and with her mother in a deep unresponsive state, none of it could happen, so she felt trapped and stuck.

Being too fixated on a single resolution keeps us locked in the emotional tension and weight of the regret. Our minds are much more flexible than we believe them to be, and there are many ways to explore, unpack and heal a regret if we are just willing to try—to really want to let go and move on. Asking ourselves questions like "How can I feel lighter about this situation?" or "Where is the opening with this person?" or "What haven't I tried before?" can keep our minds agile and actively looking for ways to heal. I've seen and helped people heal regrets by writing letters they never send, making phone calls they were afraid to place, or telling a stranger their story. Regrets are like heavy emotional mud that will bog us down if we become too rigid in how they must be addressed. Your mind wants to be light, unburdened, energetic—this is its true natural state.

✳ January 5

You are about to slow down for a brief pause. Imagine your body is travelling at highway speed. Your heart is pumping hard. Your breathing is rapid and shallow, providing you with just enough air to keep the blood flowing, to keep your body running fast and hard. Now imagine there is a turnoff up ahead, and you have to slow down. Take a deeper breath, and another. You're now travelling along a road leading into a quiet, pretty town. Slow down even more—take deeper, slower breaths, bringing your body and mind into an easy, steady pace. Look around you; take in everything you see. Notice the colours, the shapes, the sounds, the sight of people walking. Feel the pace change and bring yourself into this peaceful place to align your body and mind into stillness. Slow down; slow right down. Steady your breath into deep, rolling inhales and exhales and be still.

❋ January 6

Do one thing, anything, really, really well.

In our modern Western culture, we tend to place significant value on being excellent or awesome across a broad range of endeavours. We want to be excellent in our work, but we also want to be perfect parents, incredible best friends, gifted at photography, hilariously funny, master chefs . . . and the list goes on and on. So great is our quest for general life mastery that many of us are burning out or tuning out, feeling less than adequate or highly anxious in our perfectionism. The mind trap for many of us is that we either have the time and the means to attempt so many different pursuits, or we have a moderate to high level of proficiency in most things we try, which leads us to believe we can be good at most things.

Let me state what used to be obvious: we can't be good at all things. We shouldn't even try. Being a generalist, an inch deep but a mile wide, creates a hunger within our psyches that can never be fed fully because what your mind truly craves is the experience of developing a deep, intimate relationship with something you work on with diligence and discipline. Our minds don't develop, and we don't grow as people, by rapidly consuming a constant supply of small morsels of interests. Becoming a specialist or mastering a craft requires us to fight distraction, focus our mind, apply effort, make mistakes and learn from them, and experience celebration and gratitude for what we're able to create. Specializing gives us the opportunity to be intimate with ourselves.

Look around you. How many things do you have on the go right now? How many parts of your life are you trying to perfect? Choose one thing to become really, really good at (hint: it will be the one that gives you the most personal "juice"); as for all the others, either let them go or reconcile yourself to the fact that you're okay with being average—or less than average.

But that one thing you choose? Make it your passion!

✺ January 7

It's unfortunate, and often painful, but other people will play mind games with you. In the early '60s, Canadian psychiatrist Eric Berne released his groundbreaking book *Games People Play*, which outlined the fundamentals of transactional psychology and revealed several key dysfunctional mind games and strategies we humans play with each other to satisfy our deeper needs. In Berne's book, which has sold over five million copies worldwide, he defines a game as "an ongoing series of complementary ulterior transactions progressing to a well-defined, predictable outcome. Descriptively, it is a recurring set of transactions . . . with a concealed motivation . . . or gimmick."

Taking place between people, a game involves a series of moments and interactions (words, body language, facial expressions) that follow a predictable pattern and flow towards an eventual payoff or goal for one party—and sometimes both. For the most part, we are unaware that we play these games with each other because they are rooted in our unconscious. Berne describes several predominant games, with names like "If It Weren't for You," "See What You Made Me Do" and "Ain't It Awful." I think one of Berne's greatest contributions to our understanding of the psychology of human relationships is the insight that much of the chronic, problematic behaviour we experience with each other is not random or spontaneous; rather, it is all connected and part of much larger, well-defined strategies.

The simplest way to stop playing or being involved in a game with another person is to work to become aware of what is happening in our interactions with each other. Being played, or being enrolled in a person's game, feels very repetitive and predictable. We feel "set up" or controlled, or manipulated and exploited. We tell ourselves things like "I can never win with him," "I always feel powerless when I'm with her," "I'm always the bad guy" or "She's always the good girl." These are expressions we use to underscore how constrained and scripted we feel in these relationships.

In this new year of being light, we can shed the costumes of roles we no longer want to play with others and resist the lures that entice us into another person's games. Remember, games are dysfunctional ways all of us have learned to get our needs and wants met—but we have the power to explore and practise new behaviours, ones in which we build intimacy, trust and lightness into our connections.

❀ January 8

Are you feeling heavy today? Does everything around you seem impossible? Are your shoulders weighed down with too much stress? Let's shift this burden. Think of an activity or a project you can start and finish in thirty minutes. It should be something that makes you move your whole body and gets your heart pumping. Shift your awareness to each task in the project and feel yourself working towards its completion, feel the light at the end of the tunnel nearing. Pour yourself into the activity, and perhaps even lose yourself in the actions and movement.

Maybe your activity is rooted in kindness—an act of service for someone who is not expecting it, one that makes them feel seen and loved. Or perhaps it's a job that needs completing, one you've been doggedly resistant or stuck about starting.

"Stuckness" is a point of view that can develop from a simple thought like "I can't do this right now" and set us on a general, murky, downward spiral towards seeing everything around us as impossible. Stuckness is a form of structural tension in our bodies, one that holds our emotional and mental well-being in a kind of anxious suspension. Action or movement is the only way out and forward from the tension.

🌺 January 9

Take a big full breath in. Now pause. Now let it out slowly.

How much do you genuinely love yourself? Not the false, narcissistic kind of ego love, but real gratitude and appreciation for who you are. When was the last time you fell in love with yourself? Imagine seeing yourself through a new lover's eyes. What do they see? What would they say about you in a letter—a love letter?

Conjure their voice in your head and sit down to write a love letter to yourself. Keep it short and adoring and full of descriptive, sensory words, as if you're falling in love with yourself for the first time. Put pen to paper for about twenty minutes, then stop, fold the letter and place it in an envelope with your name on the front. Then place it somewhere you will see it every day.

🌺 January 10

Caring and caretaking are two very different manifestations of our attention. While caring is an act of love, where our focus is on the other's needs, caretaking is an act of dependence driven by a motivation to make sure our needs are met. Caring is about being there for others as our whole self gently holds space, leans in with empathy and expresses kindness towards a person in need of support or love. Caretaking is more about needing to be necessary to another, as our entire self is invested in being a martyr or saviour and in rescuing someone because we believe they are helpless—not because they actually are. Caretaking erodes the other person's self-confidence and self-esteem. Caring affirms to the other that they belong and are inherently lovable. In caring, we affirm a loved one's independence; in caretaking, we confirm their dependence on us in a dance of give and take, reward and punishment.

It's early in the year, a beautiful time to take an inventory of our love life and friendships, to be honest about how we love and relate, and perhaps check our egos for people we're really caretaking when we believe we are caring.

❀ January 11

I tried a social experiment yesterday. I stood next to someone much taller than me and quietly took notice of what I started to think—and then feel in my body. For most of us, standing next to a really tall individual stirs up thoughts of being little or tiny, and it can make us feel inferior, insecure, even scared. If we stand next to this person long enough and close enough—say, facing each other—we may start to feel as though we're in physical jeopardy and that we need to get ready to defend ourselves or run away suddenly. In the group I was in, there was a really tall person who was working with a partner standing on a chair. "That's incredible," she said out loud. "This is the first time I've ever felt threatened by someone else. Is this what people feel when they stand next to me?"

Next, the experiment suggests that we stand beside a person who is obviously shorter than us. It takes a few moments for the earlier feelings of vulnerability to ebb, and then something really interesting begins to happen: we may start to feel superior, larger, physically more powerful. Slowly and steadily, thoughts that we're smarter, more capable, that we "tower" over this person start to creep into our minds.

I've seen people at this point in the experiment behave as if the shorter person is a child and they a parent, speaking to them or putting their arm around them in false benevolence.

The point of this fascinating self-research is to have us question, in a gentle way, who we really are and how our minds fabricate stories. Are we powerful giants, lording our physical size and greater capacity over others? Or are we small and vulnerable and less capable? What are we to believe if both experiences feel real? And if our thoughts and feelings and even our behaviour can be affected so dramatically, what does this mean about who we are—or better still, who we have told ourselves we are?

For many, this is how the story of themselves begins to unravel. The truths that they have always assumed were concrete facts about their character and personality, capacity and nature begin to weaken and crumble. It is a curious, challenging journey we are all on. Have patience and faith: a new person is about to emerge.

🌸 January 12

Take a moment to remember a person who listened to you without interruption. Remember what that felt like and what that meant to you. If you have not had the experience of being heard, tap into that longing.

What if all that we search for, all that we pursue, we can find in listening?

Listening is a sacred experience available to each of us—and it is a skill we have not yet learned. That's because we have a built-in resistance to listening to another. Move beyond that resistance today. Find a teacher, a text, a source to teach you empathetic listening. Take a step into learning. We all need support and instruction to overcome cultural norms and listen this way. As Brenda Ueland writes in *Strength to Your Sword Arm*:

When we listen to people there is an alternating current, and this recharges us so that we never get tired of each other. We are constantly being recreated. There is this little creative fountain inside us that begins to spring and cast up new thoughts and unexpected laughter and wisdom. If you are very tired, strained, have no solitude, run too many errands, talk to too many people, drink too many cocktails, this little fountain is muddied over and covered with a lot of debris. The result is you stop living from the center, the creative fountain, and you live from the periphery, from externals. That is why, when someone has listened to you, you go home rested and lighthearted. It is when people really listen to us, with quiet fascinated attention, that the little fountain begins to work again, to accelerate in the most surprising way.

Listening will change your life.

❀ January 13

Dive deep into more taste. Close your eyes and imagine biting into a fresh, crisp, ripe apple. The sweetness and tartness fill your mouth as you crunch down and through the fruit, closing your mouth, ready to move the piece to your molars to chew and release the flavours even further. It's delicious, right? One bite communicates so much.

Could you eat the whole apple with this much awareness, biting and chewing and swallowing with your full attention focused on the experience? Now let's back up a couple of steps and imagine if you had selected the apple with as much care as you took with that first bite. Where would you buy that apple? How do the various types of apples compare, and which taste profile best reflects your preferences? What kind of apple would you buy, and what does it look like? What does it feel like?

Diving deep into more taste leads us to focus our attention on giving our experiences more and more depth and fullness. That makes us more knowledgeable about what we like and what brings us joy. The pursuit becomes a passion, helping us to create an intimate relationship between our minds and bodies and the thing we are pursuing. It's true: we become intimate with ourselves simply by being more conscious of something we really enjoy.

Years ago a very dear friend of mine was dying of prostate cancer, and it was his wish to be moved from hospital to a hospice for his final days of life. When I arrived at the hospice to visit him, I was amazed at how beautiful the space was and the attention that had been paid to every detail and experience. My first thought was "This is a place full of life, where people could really heal themselves." And then the irony set in.

Plugged into the wall next to my friend's bed was his 1960s La Pavoni espresso machine and two small cups and saucers. "It's not a luxury," he said. "I've enjoyed coffee from this machine for most of my adult life, and I want to make sure I can enjoy an espresso and have that taste on my lips on my last day." And three days later I watched as his son, with great care and love, pulled the last shot of espresso that my friend would ever taste from that machine.

To savour, in the classic French definition of the word, means to taste, breathe in, appreciate and care for; it is a personal relationship formed between the taster and the world they take in. To be savourers means to appreciate and prioritize quality over quantity. We place greater value on the depth and meaning of an experience than the quantity or volume. We crave experiences that fuel our passions and deliver greater intimacy with ourselves. It means we dive deep into carefully selecting that one apple we absolutely must bite into.

✳ January 14

I know someone who is so afraid, you can hear it in the way they breathe. The short, staccato, wheezing inhalations squeezed in between words and sentences make it sound as though this person is experiencing a heavy, taxing physical strain every single moment of their life. When I hear them speak, I find myself distracted by the sheer effort of their breathing. Likewise, much of the content or message they communicate is about being on guard, worried, concerned and hurt as ways of being. In their mind, there is always someone who will take advantage of them, rip them off, treat them unfairly, judge or betray them. To be in this person's company is so overwhelming at times that I often find myself feeling afraid for no reason, as if their anxiety is contagious.

It is so clear to me that this person's view of the world and their physical experience of being alive are connected in a tightly constructed continuous loop. Nothing separates the way they see the outside and how they feel on the inside. This person is overengaged in what happens around them, and the effect of their intense focus is the physical pain of hypervigilance.

Maybe you know people like this, or maybe you are this way yourself.

In his book *Emotional Survival for Law Enforcement*, the American behavioural scientist Dr. Kenneth Gilmartin describes hypervigilance as a loop in which intense alertness over long periods of time leads to exhaustion and apathy, emotional mood swings and the physical symptoms of extreme stress. Dr. Gilmartin is describing police officers and first responders, not the rest of us. So why are so many people feeling this way as well? Why are we living with such high levels of stress, followed by periods of extreme exhaustion and burnout?

It's because we're too widely focused in our lives. It's time to pull our energy back from being involved with people and places we can have no effect on and narrow our focus to those closest to us and those who make our lives richer and deeper.

The person who cuts you off on the expressway is a stranger, so while their actions may be careless, even reckless, they are not indulging in a personal attack. Let's not pursue "likes," hearts and retweets with more intensity than we devote to making sure our friends and family are growing in fulfillment. And let's not live our lives as if we are constantly under threat. The most powerful lesson we can learn from those who have lived through and triumphed over severe traumas is that despite the chaos around us, we can choose to be at peace.

❋ January 15

The other day I overheard someone say, "When I text someone and they don't reply right away, I find that so disrespectful. After all, texting is supposed to be immediate."

I wondered why that should be. Sure, as a form of communication, a text message can be sent and received very quickly, but who decided that the speed of delivery determines how promptly we should respond? Then I noticed something that hadn't occurred to me before: when a text message is sent, we all see that it has been delivered, and in some cases read, and then we see the icon telling us the recipient may be writing a reply. It is so subtle, yet the effect is profound. The design of the software so closely mimics a physical conversation that we find ourselves as deeply engaged as if we are actually in a deep, in-person moment.

And now it is possible to have an almost unlimited number of these conversations simultaneously. Which many of us do. And along the way, some of us have become overreactive and less responsive. We're saying less, but doing it more quickly, and we need someone to answer.

There are people who are more interested in being seen than heard. They talk excessively, urgently; they're driven to fill every moment in a conversation because silence or pauses make them feel deeply uncomfortable. When texting or emailing, these people flag every note as urgent and count the seconds it takes for us to send a reply. We may feel overwhelmed and respond by distancing ourselves, taking a while to answer or not replying at all. Sensing that we've pulled away often makes these people more demanding of our time, if they don't simply seek out someone else to fill their need.

The joy of an intimate in-person conversation lies in both the exchange of thoughts and words and the sharing of emotions and senses in the moment. Nothing can replace this experience. It is immediate, dynamic, connective and equitable. The whole of your physical being is listening to the other, and you respond based on what you hear, see and feel.

Pauses or extended silence in an intimate conversation are very powerful moments. They can deepen a feeling or thought, create closeness or distance, or communicate what is unspoken. We don't feel overwhelmed in an intimate conversation. We feel closer to the other person, more connected to ourselves, and although we may feel powerful emotions, our souls feel lighter.

❋ January 16

The song "The Real Work" by the Canadian band Great Lake Swimmers is an ode to the acceptance of what is. Part of the lyrics go like this:

And the real work is to be it, believe it
With each new set of eyes and the visions they provide
Be the taste, the warmth, the measure and the glow
By embracing it all, and then letting it all go
The real work is never done, and has no clear beginning
And shows no result, no losing, no winning.

So many of us see our lives in terms of beginnings and endings, starts and stops, that we can lose sight of the fact that our whole existence is part of a continuous, cyclical truth. There is no real beginning or ending, only transitions. There is movement everywhere, all the time. Most of us will experience setbacks in our lives when events or people trigger tremendous difficulty, pain and suffering. We will believe that we have been dealt a serious blow, that our lives have been blown off course or that we have found ourselves in a constant or repetitive state of being stuck. At these times, we want to rebel against or deny our pain, or we live frozen in fear. We may even choose to end our journey so that our pain ends, not realizing that it will transition and continue for someone close to us.

M. Scott Peck chose to open his book *The Road Less Travelled* with this passage:

> Life is difficult. This is a great truth, one of the greatest truths. It is a great truth because once we truly see this truth, we transcend it. Once we truly know that life is difficult—once we truly understand and accept it—then life is no longer difficult. Because once it is accepted, the fact that life is difficult no longer matters.

We marvel at the resilience and strength of wild animals when we see them in nature or in a documentary where the narrator remarks on how tough a teacher nature truly is. We also have this strength. We have this resilience. We can—and we have—come through tough times.

Come back to the one big truth. We are part of a cycle. Your life is a cycle of cycles. There is movement all the time, and what is happening now will change. You are fluid, you are constantly moving—sometimes fast, sometimes slowly, but always in motion. Experiences in your life become stories you tell; hardships become lessons you share. Feelings ebb and flow and you can move lightly through transitions.

✿ January 17

"You can't teach an old dog new tricks."

A friend recently offered this adage to explain why she wouldn't mend a rift with a work colleague, a rift that was stressful, causing her to be anxious and frustrated and making her restless at night.

"So you're saying you're set in your ways and your ways are right, even though you don't feel great?" I asked.

"They're right for me," she said, clearly drawing the conversation to a quick close.

It does seem to be true that as we age, we become more rigid in our beliefs and more firmly rooted in our identities. The openness and flexibility of youth diminishes and hardens as we experience the complex nature of people and our world. We replace exploring the world around us with protecting the world as we prefer it.

Later in the day, still feeling unsettled, I spoke to my friend and offered, "I've always known you to be a caring, strong person. Have you changed?"

"No, I haven't changed," she said. "With this person at work, I just need to be right."

And there it was: the bottom line. My friend had chosen to sacrifice her way of being to be right.

Rigidity is not a natural way of being for us. We are designed to always be searching and exploring, learning from new experiences, increasing our awareness of ourselves and the world around us. Being rigid or closed requires much more energy. It's like having one foot firmly on the brake while the other foot is pressing down on the accelerator, holding you in a frustrated state of suspension. Being so set in our ways is a powerful act of rebellion against the natural flow of the universe. "I will not change!" it screams out to the world. Yet so many of us take this position because, deep down, we feel hurt. And when our hurt is not healed, it becomes the fuel for our hardening.

Our goal is to restore our openness and be lighter. Express your hurt to someone who will listen, witness and empathize, and then let it go. Release yourself from attachments, such as needing to be right, when you feel yourself becoming more rigid or closed. We can greet each day with a mission to discover new sparks of life and find new mobility in our bodies and nimbleness in our minds by stretching our perspective. We can replace rightness with lightness.

🌸 January 18

Shinrin-yoku, or forest bathing, is a nature therapy practice first developed in Japan during the 1980s. To take a forest bath means to spend a conscious amount of time under the canopy of a living forest, walking in a relaxed manner. The Japanese have researched and demonstrated that forest bathing offers numerous health benefits, including boosting our immune system, reducing our blood pressure, reducing stress, lifting our mood, increasing our focus, improving our sleep and increasing our energy levels. There are more than sixty forest therapy camps across the country.

Giving ourselves a forest bath is a balm for our souls and our senses. The environment around us is alive, growing and bursting with energy. There are scents for us to breathe in. Sounds and rhythms to hear. We can feel the cool, rich lightness of the air on our skin. There are vibrant colours to absorb. And, if you desire, there is an abundance of tastes to forage. A forest is a community of communities, each with its own distinct patterns and cycles that merge in layers of synchronicity and mutual benefit. A forest is a living, breathing history book where we can observe the past, see and embrace the present, and witness the birth of the future.

Deep inside a forest, we are also deeper inside ourselves. Our rhythms reset themselves to the inhaling and exhaling of the trees and plants, and we explore our own importance while walking among giants and being gigantic. I am cleansed and lightened by the rich oxygen all around me. My concerns and burdens are released to the forest floor while my emotions dissipate, clear and evaporate to the tops of the trees, elevating my mood. My mind empties, slows and, searching, finds my heart. Now, with head and heart joined, I am connected and at peace.

❀ January 19

Do you love your work? Perhaps the more revealing question would be: Do you love who you are when you are working?

The search for work that is fulfilling or meaningful or just plain enjoyable becomes important for many of us at critical points in our lives. When the thrill of a new job or career path wears off, it is our intrinsic motivation, or motivation from within, that keeps us getting out of bed every morning. Our drive from inside is deeply connected to how we feel about ourselves when we're engaged in our work. Do we like ourselves? Do we feel challenged? Is our work rewarding for us? Is it helping us grow? Do we feel heavy or light when we are engaged in our work? These are all key questions that we can ask, regardless of the nature or type of work we do.

How we relate to our work, how we see ourselves relative to our work, begins with us. We—and what we really know about ourselves—create the patterns of the what, how and why of the work we do. Here are some more questions about work you can ask yourself: What part of your work brings you the most contentment? What's the deepest lesson your work has taught you about yourself? Is your reputation at work aligned with how you want to be seen? What part of your work brings you so much fulfillment that you lose track of time?

We all work at something, but only a few challenge themselves to make their work reflective of their hearts and souls.

🌸 January 20

The other night, I ate at a real nice family restaurant.
Every table had an argument going. —George Carlin

Family members can be some of the most difficult people we encounter in our lives. Family comes with strong emotional ties and pulls, some of which we are aware of, while others lie deep in our unconscious, steering our behaviour in ways that confuse and frustrate us. Family members have expectations of each other—"shoulds"—that are communicated out loud or loudly in silence. Like in a well-scripted play, we can behave with our families as if we are actors in predictable and repeated scenes. Your family may be dramatic, while you're a comic; or your family may be silent and distant, while you are the rebel or perhaps the diplomat.

Navigating family relationships with lightness begins with understanding, to the best of your awareness, who you really are and how you behave. Seek to understand what role you play in your family and which parts of that role may be fulfilling your ego rather than filling your cup of contentment. Know your family's dance—the rhythms and tones that underscore what happens when your family comes together—and what part you play in the dance. Then, with as much awareness as you can gather, look to change the patterns and relationships that leave you feeling heavy or stuck.

In the beginning, it may be that you have to set boundaries with a sibling or shed light on the language a parent uses when talking about you or to you. Be gentle with yourself and with them, even though you may be desperate. Families are systems that do not like to change, and any movement can require hard work and occur at a glacial pace. Remember that you are doing this work for you. Growth can be uncomfortable, sometimes even painful. We know that as we grow taller, we may experience growing pains as our bones lengthen and our muscles expand and stretch; the same is true about becoming emotionally mature. Our views change, our beliefs are challenged and our roles in our families evolve as we shed the trappings of our character that no longer make us feel good about ourselves.

The strength of a family is based on its openness and willingness to expand and grow to embrace and celebrate all the differences of its members. Weak families promote "sameness," melting everyone into a common, safe and rigid identity; a strong family raises the people in it to become their highest, most evolved selves because they understand that love is expansive and inclusive.

❋ January 21

I love my partner's laugh. It can make me cry tears of joy and even trigger full-body convulsions in which I'm fighting for air. Sometimes it's just a snicker or a chortle; other times I find myself looking into wide eyes that plead, "Is there anything more crazy and ridiculously funny in this moment?"

Deep, gasping laughter is one of my life's greatest pleasures. Any troubles or burdens I may be carrying, any dwelling on the past or worrying about the future, disappear when I laugh. I love laughing so much that I surround myself with people who have the gift of making others laugh. My partner and I laugh at ourselves, especially in those moments when we've become way too intense. It's a pact we have, an unspoken agreement to keep each other light. We know each other so well that we can each use laughter to nudge the other out of the closets of behaviour and thoughts that can become safe places to hide. Laughter is one of the ways in which we each come back to the other after an argument, as if to say, "The issue was important, but we were ridiculous."

Laughter is powerful medicine. A good, hearty laugh delivers the short-term benefits of bringing more oxygen into our bodies, invigorating our hearts, lungs and muscles, and triggering the brain to release higher levels of endorphins, all of which soothe tension and stress and aid muscle relaxation, bringing us an immediate, good, relaxed feeling. Over time, laughter increases the release of neuropeptides that help fight stress and boost our immune system. Laughter triggers the body to release its own natural painkillers and creates a boost in mood that can linger, helping with depression. Most important, laughter empties us, allowing us to feel lighter and full of joy.

Look for laughter in your day. It won't be hard to find, and if we train our minds to seek it out, we will find it almost everywhere. I see humour in a child playing an imagination game or blowing bubbles in a glass of milk. I find it in the way our cat lies on my arms while I'm trying to type, or when I see a pair of fuzzy dice tied to a car's rear-view mirror. I laugh at strange sounds, bad smells and horrible tastes. I laugh at my grey hairs and my feet that are still growing. Laughter is one of my pathways to lightness.

🌸 January 22

Hope has strange messengers. I once met a man named Hasim, who shared a remarkable story with me. Hasim is in his mid-thirties, and when he was a few years younger, he had a stroke. In the beginning, he couldn't figure out what was happening to him; he just felt weird and different. One moment he was sitting on the edge of his bed, trying to put on his socks, and then suddenly everything slowed down: he remembers being outside his body, watching himself be carried down the stairs of his home by paramedics and transported to the hospital, and then darkness. When he woke up, Hasim found himself in a hospital bed, unable to move his legs. A different kind of darkness crept into him, crippling his self-confidence and sucking out his hope. What kind of life was he going to live now that he could not walk? Hasim lay like this for several days, his despair and self-loathing growing deeper and deeper.

Before the end of Hasim's first week in the hospital, a man came into his room and stopped by the foot of his bed. "Is today it?" the stranger asked. "Will today be the day you will walk again?"

Hasim looked at him in shock. He couldn't believe what he was saying. He was so deeply offended. Did this man not know who he was, what had happened to him? Hasim scowled at the stranger and told him to move on and leave him alone.

The next day at exactly the same time, the stranger reappeared. "Is today the day you walk again?" Again, Hasim dismissed the stranger, becoming more bitter and angry and convinced that his life was over.

For six weeks, every day and always at the same time, the stranger visited Hasim at the foot of his bed and asked his question. Hasim's reactions to the stranger evolved from anger and denial to distance (trying to pretend the stranger didn't exist), then curiosity (Who was this person? Was he crazy?), and finally a kind of acceptance. He began to look forward to the stranger's visits and the question he asked. A reassuring, familiar feeling was beginning to stir inside of Hasim.

"Is today it? Is today the day you will walk again?" asked the stranger one morning. But something was different today. Hasim had felt it when his eyes opened. "Yes," Hasim answered. "Today is it. Today is the day I will walk again."

"Then I will help you get out of bed and place your feet on the floor," said the stranger. "I will help you take your first step again."

At this point in his story, Hasim looked at me and cried. "That man saved me," he said. "I was lost."

Hope is everywhere. And when we can't find hope inside ourselves, we may see it in the eyes of another—even a stranger.

Today Hasim is a stranger who visits patients in the stroke recovery ward of the same hospital, and he stands at the foot of their beds and asks, "Is today it? Is today the day you will walk again?"

✿ January 23

Do not feel lonely, the entire universe is inside you.
Stop acting so small. You are the universe in ecstatic motion.
Set your life on fire. Seek those who fan your flames.
—Rumi

Can you be fire? Can you summon energy from all parts of your body and focus all that force into a single kinetic moment? Can you imagine being that initial spark, igniting from nothing and bursting with light? Would you race and rage through all you encounter, consuming and annihilating everything and everyone in your path? Or would you silently creep and climb, licking the kindling to reach higher and higher as you breathe in more air? Does your fire radiate from your hands as you hurl flaming balls of power, or does it shine like a blinding light from your eyes? Is your fire destructive, out of control, roaring and screaming with abandon, an intense, orange cry for help and release? Is your fire inviting and glowing, whispering to all around, "Come closer"?

Today you can be fire—any kind you wish. You can shift all that restlessness and tension from the farthest reaches of your body and feel it bubble from your fingertips and toes, rising inward and upward from your hips to your heart to your head. Imagine your fire gathering in intensity like a swirling mass inside you. Feel the heat and warmth you generate; feel it rising in temperature, feel its pulsing rhythm. How long can you hold this fiery energetic tension—minutes, or forever? Are you a fireball or an enduring volcano?

When you are ready, when you no longer want to hold your fire inside, focus your mind on releasing it out to the world. Imagine letting go of all the burning force—let it leave your mind, blasting through the top of your head or from your eyes and mouth with its fullest force. Let it run down your body and out through your hands and feet, pushing it farther out with powerful exhales. Let your fire go until all that remains is a smouldering, steaming you. Be in the stillness of the aftermath, with your body trembling and your mind lightened and empty. Hold this moment with reverence. Notice how cleansed you feel and how light you are. Hold the moment longer and longer. You are air, water and earth—and, when you choose to be, you are fire.

🌸 January 24

Friendships can be our most rewarding connections because our friends are people we choose to have in our lives. Whereas a family is a system of relationships we are born into, friendships form a web of our own creation. Friends bring safety and inclusion; they can lighten us up when we feel melancholy and deepen our souls with understanding and empathy.

Friendships are formed in countless ways, but there are three essential ingredients for them to steep and blossom. We must like, trust and respect our friends, and they us. While liking takes the form of a magnetic pull between people, trust and respect are earned as you and your friend become more and more familiar with each other's behaviour. You learn to trust that your friend is mostly consistent in being early or late, that they will regularly call or text at a certain time of day. We respect our friends for being individuals, for working hard, for being passionate, giving, kind, loyal and truthful.

Some of us have friends who expect too much of us and our friendship. These people put conditions on the relationship and test our connection to them. Drama is frequent, and you find yourself running to their rescue or engaging in a pattern of breaking up and making up. Our relationship with a friend like this is part of a pattern of wounded intimacy that they carry in their lives. They're not familiar with healthy intimacy, so they unconsciously run their life through a series of codependent relationships that satiate but never fulfill them. These people feel like work, while true friends are easeful.

I have a "rule of hand" for friendships. A rule of hand means that I have as many close, intimate friends as I have fingers on one hand. This lets me focus my efforts on building and growing these five friendships, which for me represents the upper limit of energy I am able to expend and still feel content. I have many people in my life; most of them are warm acquaintances, or even friends because we share one thing in common. I am careful not to overcommit with them, and I'm honest with them that I have close, intimate people in my life already, so I cannot bring them in closer and still be a good friend to all. Trust me, this is a difficult and awkward conversation to have with someone, but for me it is important. I place such a high personal value on friendship because to be a good friend and have good friends is one of the ways I keep my life light.

✿ January 25

A friend who places conditions on your friendship is very different from a friend who has expectations of your friendship. Conditions are based on preferences; they are "can'ts" and "mustn'ts" and "never dos," and they are always meant for the self-interest and self-protection of the person who sets them. Friends who set conditions believe and act as though they are more powerful and important than the other person. They say, "To be my friend, you can't talk to that person." Or "You must not act this way." Or "You must do what I do or like what I like." Or "You must always have my back, even when I'm wrong." A friendship based on conditions puts us on edge and makes us feel unsure and heavy. We can never be ourselves because we're afraid that the friendship will be threatened or will end.

A friendship based on expectations is founded on such principles as honesty, kindness, respect and trust and is always designed to enable both friends to grow and mature. Expectations are mutual invitations to work at some aspect of the relationship and to be our better selves with each other. They say, "We're not perfect, and we will challenge each other, but we are expected to be honest and kind."

Take a moment to reflect on your friendships through the lenses of conditions and expectations. How many friendships do you have in which you feel restricted and believe you really can't be yourself but have to fit into some kind of mould of acceptability? Alternatively, do you have a friendship in which being together feels light and open, and you feel like you can breathe fully and be yourself? Does your friend support you—your growth, with all the bumps and bruises of your learning—or do they want you to be a mirror of them and judge you harshly when you step outside the lines they have drawn for you?

It is our choice to form a friendship—to be willingly and openly intimate and close with another person. Choose friendships with expectations rather than conditions, and you will be on the path to lightness.

✿ January 26

The other day on Facebook, a friend of mine shared a comment that attracted quite a long stream of comments: "The news is so negative, I can't bear to listen or watch it anymore. I feel so hopeless for the world!"

Her words really connected with the people who responded. I was amazed how many people shared that they felt similarly stressed about the level and depth of tragedy and deceit in our world, and as I read more and more of their words, I noticed that I too was starting to feel more and more weighed down and empty. As I absorbed *their* words, they were having a stressful effect on me that kept intensifying. I was also believing their responses were the truth—not just *a* truth, but the *only* truth.

This is what author Eli Pariser, in his book *The Filter Bubble*, describes as the echo chamber effect or echo effect. Pariser says the effect is much more widespread than we know.

> It's not just Google and Facebook either. This is some-thing that's sweeping the Web. There are a whole host of companies that are doing this kind of personalization. Yahoo News, the biggest news site on the Internet, is now personalized—different people get different things. *Huffington Post*, the *Washington Post*, the *New York Times*—all flirting with personalization in various ways. And this moves us very quickly toward a world in which the Internet is showing us what it thinks we want to see, but not necessarily what we need to see.

With more searching I discovered that this information bubble Pariser describes is not a new phenomenon. In fact, it is human nature to be attracted to and seek to bond with others we think are like us. This strong inner drive to belong to a group we can identify with helps to reinforce and strengthen our own identity, giving us a sense of direction and purpose in our lives. We feel more secure when we're among others who are like us. We become rooted in our group and its views, and we become more convinced that our group is the right one to belong to. The sophisticated learning algorithms used by social media sites like Facebook are merely responding to our habituated human behaviour. They're tailoring news and content to give us more of what we choose to read and like.

Achieving lightness when we find ourselves in the online echo chamber requires that we seek information to counterbalance our preferences. It means breaking out of what you may reflexively choose to read and like, and searching instead for content that challenges your deep beliefs. In the beginning, it will seem odd, but be patient—let those algorithms catch up to your choices and see if your view, and then your mood, changes.

🌸 January 27

I've been exploring the world of ASMR, or autonomous sensory meridian response—also commonly known as "attention-induced head orgasm," or AIHO. The purpose of ASMR is to draw people into a relaxed state of being by having them watch, listen to and experience someone gently whispering, moving their hands in a relaxed manner, smacking their lips, creating brushing sounds, making scratching sounds or tapping their nails on hard surfaces. Its devotees report that they feel a tingling at the back of the head or along the spine—some even describe it as "the chills." Millions of people subscribe to YouTube channels with such names as Gentle Whispering or Ephemeral Rift. What I truly love about this experience, and what I believe is valuable for all of us, is the ability of ASMR to bypass the hyperactivity of the cognitive mind.

Call it our ego or our "inner narrative"—it is the stream of thoughts and questions and beliefs inside our heads. I don't remember when I first became aware of it, but I can honestly say there isn't a moment when I am truly free of it. There are times when it rules my thought processes and behaviour—when I am the dog being wagged by the tail—and thankfully, there is a growing number of moments when I can turn down its volume to just a murmur so that I can think and behave with more awareness and purpose. I've never really been great at meditating (the quiet seems to ignite my ego), and exercise creates only a brief interlude in the chatter. ASMR, however, is more of an immersion therapy for my mind, giving my brain something to focus my attention on, while at the same time drawing me deeper and deeper into the experience.

Prior to discovering ASMR, I would make a point of walking along the beach where I live or staring into the crackling orange glow of our fireplace. But these two strategies required me to be close to water or home. ASMR videos are something I can watch any time I need to, on my phone or my tablet, and the calming, euphoric effect is immediate and lasting. I know many people are prone to "busy head," or chronically overthinking their lives—if you're one of them, ASMR may be something that works for you. Try it. Your peace of mind is worth every moment.

🌸 January 28

I offer you an intention for today: be kind.

From this moment forward, choose to be kind to every person you encounter throughout your day. Beginning with the most important person—*you*. Treat yourself with kindness. Let every thought, every action begin with kindness. What you wear, what and how you eat, how you greet people, how you work or play with others, how you consider and care for your home, your neighbourhood or the planet— let all of this be steeped in kindness. Listen with your full attention, consider a new point of view or see an old belief through a new lens. Pick up a piece of litter that yesterday you might have walked past. Genuinely smile at someone, for today you are consciously choosing to be kind.

His Holiness the Dalai Lama says that his religion is kindness. I ask you to hold his vision, just for today. Craft your consideration, compassion, empathy, generosity, thoughtfulness, patience, acknowledgement and concern from the infinite supply of kindness within you. To your last moment of wakefulness, and as you set your intention to sleep, be kind and know that today you cared for yourself, you considered others, you made the world a safer, more content place to be, and your life mattered.

🌸 January 29

I've been learning how to become the leader of our small herd of horses, following Carolyn Resnick's twenty-one-day Chair Challenge.

Carolyn Resnick is renowned for her understanding of the behaviour of wild horses and for teaching humans to use methods developed with wild horses in mind to relate more effectively to domesticated horses. Horses have powerful lessons for us about leadership.

For a little while each day, I sit with the horses, neither moving nor speaking, but focusing on reaching a neutral state of my own. Being with the horses, without petting them, talking to them or looking at them. Being there without being acknowledged by them and without sending mental messages to them. For the first nine days of sharing territory, not one of our horses approached me.

On the tenth day I realized I was secretly still hoping for the horses to respond to me, and by doing so, I was sending an unintended communication of neediness that was keeping the horses away. I returned on day eleven determined to focus only on my own state, to be there only for my own self-interest and enjoyment. That is the day one of the horses approached me—*chose* to be with me.

By being in a state of peace for my own sake, I made myself safe and inviting.

The more peaceful we are, the safer we are to be with, and the higher up the hierarchy we rise.

The most peaceful one is chosen to be the leader.

❀ January 30

Gratitude. There is so much to say about this state of being and its influence over our lives. I remember being taught to say "thank you" as a social grace before I was old enough to really understand what it meant to be thankful. Now, with a few more years of living behind me, I can see that being grateful is one of the keys to living a fuller life; gratitude and kindness are the true mentors of contentment.

My own definition of gratitude is "the state of being appreciative." With this in mind, I can provide and receive all sorts of gifts to the world around me. I can easily offer a heartfelt "thank you" to the person who pours and serves my coffee. I can hold a door for someone who is struggling. I can feel excited to be given a taste of someone's lunch. I can feel warmed by the sun and I can appreciate the beauty of a well-crafted song.

Positive psychologist Roger Emmons has written much about gratitude. In 2003 he coauthored a study in which participants began a daily practice of being thankful. After ten weeks, the participants reported significantly higher levels of optimism, specifically in the areas of health and well-being. Being grateful lightens us, as it shifts our perspective from our stresses to what is easeful and good in our lives. Appreciating how we benefit from the generosity and kindness of others, especially when it is unexpected, has the power to dissolve our aloneness and connect us not only to a community but to a force greater than ourselves. Gratitude is the state of thinking, "Yes, I see chaos, pain and suffering, but I also see flow, beauty and peace. I can see and feel balance inside and all around me. Everyone and everything that is alive benefits from life."

Life is our benefactor; we are its beneficiaries. There is no reciprocity with life. Our only task is to deeply appreciate and be thankful for the unexpected spark that is in us and all around us.

❁ January 31

Our son asked me the other day, "What makes you happy?"

I answered without hesitating, and very much in the moment, "These socks make me happy. I love them." After staring at me in disbelief, he said, "Socks can't make you happy," then walked away, shaking his head.

But they can. Socks *can* make me happy. Or, more truthfully, I feel content when I wear these socks. I deeply appreciate having warm, dry, comfortable feet, especially on days when it is freezing cold and wet on our farm. Warm feet, warm heart. It's a saying I repeat to myself often and unconsciously, not really knowing where I first heard it.

But this isn't about socks. It's about how we chase after happiness, that ever-elusive butterfly, rather than grounding ourselves in experiences that make us feel content. The Danes have a word for this—it's an old word that has resurfaced recently: "hygge" (pronounced HOO-gah). Author Louisa Thomsen Brits, in *The Book of Hygge: The Danish Art of Contentment, Comfort and Connection*, describes hygge as:

> a quality of presence and an experience of belonging and togetherness. It is a feeling of being warm, safe, comforted and sheltered. Hygge is an experience of selfhood and communion with people and places that anchors and affirms us, gives us courage and consolation. To hygge is to invite intimacy and connection. It's a feeling of engagement and relatedness, of belonging to the moment and to each other. Hygge is a sense of abundance and contentment. Hygge is about being, not having.

What I love about her definition is that it is clear that hygge is a deliberate and conscious way of being in the world, one that gives purpose to what—and how—I choose to say and do and provides a focal point for building relationships with the people I wish to have in my life. Comfort and contentment—it is so simple to imagine how many ways I could achieve both. Here, Thomsen Brits suggests a few questions to ask ourselves: Where do you feel most at home? What activities and customs anchor you? Who makes you feel at ease? What contributes most to your sense of well-being? What do you do to unwind? What do you reach for to create comfort?

What the Danish appreciate is that these questions are not answered, and hygge is not achieved, by surrounding ourselves with more things and more opportunities for distraction. Rather, hygge is about simplifying and deepening our presence within ourselves. In

North America we would say, "These socks are so comfortable, I will buy ten pairs of them." By comparison, the Danish might say, "I feel so comfortable in these socks, I want to wear them as often as I can."

Never underestimate the joy that can come from warm, dry, cozy feet.

February

✳ February 1

I am the one who decides that I belong.

All along, I've thought it was others who had this power.

How wonderfully freeing to get to choose! I feel grounded in my new-found ability, and a great peace, because I know that what and whom I choose will receive all of my heart.

And my choices, bundled together, help me understand who I truly am.

Belonging is a larger state of being that includes all of me—my love, my kindness, my commitment, my hard work, my best. It's a slogan on a T-shirt I would proudly wear; a name or a title I would be honoured to take. It includes the places I identify as home because they echo parts of me that are true.

This is an exciting lens to look through today and ask myself, "Do I choose to belong with you, or do I simply find myself here for now?" How lucky are those I will choose!

✳ February 2

Our dance with being alone and being with others is one of our greatest challenges, especially in the technology-rich twenty-first century. Since the days of the earliest philosophers, we have understood that solitude is not only beneficial but necessary if we are to truly see and experience ourselves. Solitude brings all that is inside of us to the forefront: both the enemy and the friend within sit beside us and demand that we engage them. As rich a learning experience as solitude can be, intimacy too requires awareness from us as we seek to belong with others as fully and deeply as we can. But in our modern world it appears that we are much too distracted to live fully in either experience.

Walking around with our minds inside our headphones or our VR goggles, we design walls and places for ourselves that keep the reality of the outside world out but never allow us to enter into ourselves. And social media sites where we can easily engage with large networks of friends and acquaintances give us the illusion of intimacy while we sit by ourselves, tapping on keyboards. We snack on synthetic intimacy and solitude every day without ever feeling full.

As an introvert, I enjoy my aloneness. Each moment that I am by myself fills me up and helps me to feel grounded. I like the peace, the quiet and the way that I can seemingly slow down time and my mind to savour the world through my senses (as I type this, I am watching the water evaporate off the sunny windowsill in rising waves of steam and mist).

As an introvert with an extroverted personality, I also embrace being with people—to a limit. I love deep dialogue and laughter, and I treasure my loved ones for the way I feel when I am with them.

Intimacy and solitude are ways of being that each of us must experience daily. Our journeys come with moments of togetherness, community, belonging and safety, as well as times when we walk alone, hearing only our own echoes.

Aloneness and togetherness feed each other, rely on each other, flow into each other. When I allow myself to move to the rhythm of the dance, I become richer, more aware and more content.

February 3

Children have a gift for seeing themselves in all the living creatures around them. As a child, I remember believing I could run like a cheetah or wishing I could soar like a seagull, even pretending in my play that I was a ferocious bear. When we're young we feel empowered by our imagined animal traits, transcending what may have been a scary dinosaur and our fears of being vulnerable.

When our son was seven, he had the opportunity to run the 100-metre dash in our city finals. Up to this point, he had competed easily, running with abandon and great speed to decisive qualifying wins. Now, with the city finals approaching, he was unsure—he didn't know if he would be fast enough. At first we tried logic, letting him know that his speed and skill had brought him to this incredible point. Then, appreciation: we told him we were proud of him and that regardless of the results, he was talented in our eyes.

None of this worked, which will come as no surprise to those of you who are parents. Then, one day, he asked me about my tattoo, the bear paw in the centre of my back—what did it mean? After I shared its symbolism and connection to me, he went away, reflective. A few hours later he came back with a felt-tip marker and asked me if I could draw a "fire rabbit" on his arm. He had been mulling over the idea of an animal while playing with his friends, when suddenly the image of a rabbit made entirely of blazing flames came into his mind. The image sent shivers down his spine and into his stomach, and he knew he had found his inspiration for speed.

I drew my best fire rabbit on his arm and he breathed a sigh of relief. The next day, just prior to the race, he rolled up his T-shirt sleeve to reveal his fire rabbit, touched the image and entered the starting blocks. It was a tremendous race; he gave it all he had and came in third out of eight tough competitors. At the finish line, he was ecstatic, and the look in his eyes was priceless.

Sit somewhere and, with a quiet mind, let your thoughts wander. Which animal comes to you? Which of its traits or instincts enliven and empower you? Welcome your new animal as you would an old friend.

❋ February 4

I confess that one of my guilty pleasures is reading the obituaries. I've learned over the years that this is not a passion that many people embrace or share with me. Most find it a morbid pastime, as though reading the announcements and summaries of other people's lives inevitably draws death closer to us. I don't share this superstition—death will come to all of us in its own time and manner.

What I love about reading the obituaries is the effect they have on me. Rather than feeling heavy and tense, I feel lighter and actually relieved as I take in the stories of the lives others have lived. It can be a cathartic experience; when we read a good story, our brains release oxytocin, the bonding hormone, into our bloodstreams, which enables us to feel empathy and helps us to relate.

I also think it goes beyond relating for me. Taking the time to read about the lives of so many different people, their accomplishments and sometimes their struggles, takes some of the mystery out of life and the fear out of death. People who never connected while they were alive find themselves companions in the obit columns.

Reading obituaries inspires me. I read about the nurse with the affectionate nickname who worked for forty years in the same ward; the grandmother whose family legacy comprises three long paragraphs of names; the teenager with cystic fibrosis who refused to let his disease define his life; the jazz bassist who quietly and unassumingly jammed with many of the giants of the genre. These were rich lives, and yet I wonder if the people felt this way. Did they see their lives as inspirational, or, like those of us still above the grass, did they struggle to see them as meaningful? What if they knew that one day someone like me would be reading about their lives and relating to them—would that knowledge make them change how they lived?

Do you see the irony here?

February 5

I used to chew on blades of grass and purple clover on summer days. Today I picked a purple clover and, as I sat with it for a minute in the sun, memories washed over me from those summer days as a child.

The smell of its sweetness, distantly mimicked by human perfume
God, I love that smell
Sweet, moist purple, unlike any cut flower
Purple clover flower on a long, slender stem,
Wearing three branched leaves that carry smaller purple kin
Sophisticated, gorgeous, fabulous clover
Cool like a jazz singer
So much woman

February 6

As the result of a rare surgical complication, part of my small intestine was brought through an opening in my stomach called a stoma, and covered by a bag to catch waste. I have always been critical of my stomach, so this took my self-consciousness to a whole new level.

One day, I started talking to my stomach because it was gurgling—making the cutest noises. When I looked down, I realized that these sounds, which I used to think were the rumblings of hunger, were actually being made by my stoma as it squeezed liquids and nutrients out of the food I had eaten, digesting it. I was in awe of how hard this little organ was working. I became curious about how it functioned, what made it be still, what foods made it talk. Then I worked up the courage to touch it, and after that I started thanking it for doing such a great job. The little stoma and I had become friends.

Leaning into my discomfort about my stomach and the ugliness and crisis surrounding the stoma led to a moment of curiosity, one that forever transformed my relationship with my body.

These days, my stomach sags with mid-life and butter tarts. A reversal surgery tucked the little stoma back inside my body, and my belly button is now an interesting line of puckering scars running down my belly. When I look in the mirror and the judgments start, I always remember the joy and good nature of what is happening inside my body, and it is hard to stay mad or find fault. My body works too hard and is too good a friend. It deserves better. So I wear a bathing suit without shame, I try to remember to touch my stomach with gratitude, and I smile when I hear it gurgle.

Our bodies delight in our kindness.

🌸 February 7

Have you noticed how you feel when you touch an animal, real or even stuffed?

I get very quiet and my senses activate through my hands. It is a direct connection to my heart. When I hug a stuffed animal, I experience the same depth of heart response.

Touching an animal puts us in the flow of pure love.

🌸 February 8

I saw this sign at a country fair:

> A craft project; it allows you to hold something concrete in your hands even when everything around you is swirling out of control. It allows you to take tiny risks and solve tiny problems and achieve tiny victories. It reminds you that there are calm and good parts of your brain where you can retreat when the rest of it feels like a war zone, and that you can, in some small, brief way, save yourself. Also, you may get a lifetime supply of hand-knit socks or scarves.

So much of our world these days seems unresolvable, incomplete and beyond our influence. Every day, new problems surface and seem so complex that they linger, adding to the tension all around us.

Where do we even begin?

We begin with us—you and I. We turn our attention and will-power towards accepting what we can influence and change—where one person can make a difference. Look closely around you and inside of yourself: Where are you needed most? Buy a hungry person a meal. Give a cold person a sweater or a pair of socks. Pick up a piece of litter when you see it. Through these seemingly tiny acts, each of us can become a force of change as powerful as any global movement.

And let's, please, learn a craft. Choose something to pour our heart into, something that makes us use our hands and engage our mind. Imagine knitting needles and crochet hooks calling out; a scrapbook waiting for us to come home and add to it; a guitar silent until our touch awakens it.

I needed to hear this today, and I hope you did too.

February 9

In the universes of DC and Marvel comics, "metahumans" rule the world. A metahuman is a fairly average-looking person with extra-normal powers and abilities. Sometimes these powers lie dormant in a "metagene" in their bodies, and then, when the person experiences extreme stress or intense psychological distress, the gene is triggered and their powers are unleashed. These powers are far-ranging and can be cosmic, mutant, scientific or technological in nature, or they may imbue the metahuman with skill in a mystic dark art.

In July 2018 the Harvard Medical School initiated a special program based on a radical approach to cancer treatment. Until now, protocols to treat cancer and most diseases have been based on medical averages—what works for most of us, most of the time. Harvard's new program seeks to study and understand the experiences of special medical anomalies called "enigmatic exceptional responders." These are people who have beaten the odds, outliers whose bodies and minds leave doctors and research scientists scratching their heads. Harvard's aim is to create the first national registry of these real-life metahumans, people who mysteriously and miraculously respond well to treatment protocols that have failed to help others.

Dr. Zak Kohane, co-founder of the new program and chair of the Harvard Medical School's Department of Biomedical Informatics, says, "If it's ten years out from your breast cancer diagnosis and you're doing fine, thank God, you're not that unusual. If you're ten years out from metastatic lung cancer and you're alive, you are a miracle."

Maybe we're all metahumans. I trust that at some point in your life you have beaten the odds and defied being average, and your experience may enlighten and heal someone else. Or perhaps your powers have not been triggered as yet—the pressure you are now experiencing in your life is part of a process that will one day intensify and explode or implode, releasing your super gift.

We don't know who we truly are until we are tested. The stress in your life is a necessary and crucial force for rebirth, as you come out of the fire, emerging as a superhuman.

✸ February 10

You've had an argument with your partner or someone who matters deeply to you. It was painful, and now you're trying to figure out how—or perhaps whether—you can make it back to each other. Words have been said, and they are still bouncing and floating around you both, unable to find an escape from the room. Saying you're sorry won't help you find your way back to each other—at least, not yet—so remorse remains locked inside both of you—or, worse, spills out in empty capitulation.

How well do you understand the other person's point of view? Do you know what is really upsetting them—and why so deeply? What about your viewpoint—why is it so important to you, and what are you truly defending?

The fastest, most effective way through any conflict with a loved one is to first be courageous and then be honest with yourself about what you understand. Offer what is true for you—simply, clearly and at the deepest level of truth you have been able to uncover. For example: "I'm angry, but really I'm afraid. I feel like I'm losing control, and I can't live in chaos."

Own what is ground zero for you, and then hold a space for your loved one—invite them with your silence to do the same. They may or may not; it's not important whether they do. You have spoken from your heart, and in that respect you can stand in confidence without needing to be validated. Let the other person take time with their feelings and thoughts, and with your words. This is a sign of respect—it says, "I know you're hurt and I respect your need to be with your pain right now." They will come forward with their true heart in their own time.

Imagine that your argument, perhaps even your relationship, is a battlefield, each statement and action a campaign to be fought and won. This is how many of us live our love with others, and it is at the centre of our relationship conflicts. I'm not saying that relationships should be free of pain and conflict—quite the opposite: to have a deep connection with another person, you have to break through every wall that would sabotage your love. Contentment is found only by those who know their bond is strong because they have tested it time and time again with fire. They have a trusted way to steer into and through the eye of the storm because they hold dear the experience of being together—it is their precious reality.

February 11

Wallace Nichols writes about water's wonderful impact on our well-being and creativity—on our flow, if you'll pardon the pun—in his book *Blue Mind*. He describes "blue mind" as a mildly meditative state that activates when we are near water—oceans, lakes and rivers, of course, but also fountains, bathtubs and showers. These are called "blue spaces." Isn't that a lovely term, blue spaces?

The magic of water lies in its negative ions—oxygen atoms that come with an extra electron. Negative ions come from the natural environment—from sunlight, air and water. Negative ions in our bloodstream are believed to produce biochemical reactions that increase levels of the mood-regulating chemical serotonin.

I often notice water throughout my day because it makes me feel so good. A hot shower, a cold plunge in the lake, a glass of lemon-infused water, soaking my feet, dew on the grass, spraying our kids or our animals with a hose in the summer heat. If I tune in, I can feel water cleansing me as it touches my skin or enters my body. Has that ever happened to you?

Water literally turns on our flow.

February 12

Certain songs lodge themselves in our minds. For me, "Take It Easy" is one of those musical residents. It's the song I sing out loud in the shower or hum to myself as I drive my ancient Chevy pickup along our two-lane country roads. Once, on a trip through Arizona and New Mexico, I had the chance to stop in Winslow, Arizona, and yes, I stood on a corner. Jackson Browne and Glenn Frey wrote this ode to lightening up and being laid back (despite living in a world filled with heartache) when they were neighbours in Los Angeles in the '70s, and the Eagles' hit version from 1972 is on the Rock and Roll Hall of Fame's list of "Five Hundred Songs That Shaped Rock and Roll."

The message of the song sticks with me because sometimes I can feel myself overthinking my life—as though I'm a car in a perpetual tailspin. Overthinking is worrying gone mad. Fuelled by uncertainty, we grind our minds into an endless spiral of scary "what if" scenarios.

Maybe today you have the chance to break free of whatever has got you agitated. We all have this power, but we seldom recognize it. Overthinking is like a friend who talks at us endlessly. We forget that we can tell them to be quiet, or we calculate that a confrontation would be too much of a hassle, so we avoid it.

One of life's greatest ironies is that a light mind is a disciplined mind. Becoming a disciple of peacefulness means regulating our minds' activity, reining in the chaos and wildness.

A long time ago I pictured my mind as a hitchhiker I had picked up while driving. I got so lulled by this passenger's familiar voice filling in all the quiet spaces that although I was still behind the wheel, my mind became the navigator. One day, for a reason I can't remember, I wanted to turn left, but my mind insisted that I stay on the course we were on. I resisted, questioned and then observed how my mind tried to convince me that its route was the better choice. My way was going to be full of uncertainty and fear, so it had to be a bad choice. I couldn't be trusted to keep myself safe. My mind knew what was best for me.

In that moment, I said, "No!" And then I turned left and set a new course for my life. The hitchhiker is still in the car with me, but now my mind knows its place, understands that *I* am the driver and this is my ride. And I roll down the windows, turn on the radio and sing "Take It Easy" out loud.

🌸 February 13

"I don't see it. Show me again."

I connected the twinkling dots for our daughter once again and showed her the pattern. "There," I said. "See? It's a large pan. That's the Big Dipper."

"I think it looks like a spoon," she said. "And if you bring that one in and then that other one and that one down there, it looks like a turtle."

"Yes, I see it too. That is a turtle," I said.

And after a moment of silence, she whispered, "I think we can see anything we want to."

"Yes, we can. That's true," I whispered back. "Sometimes all we need to do is step back and let our minds wander."

🌸 February 14

According to Dr. Gary Chapman, there are five universal languages through which we can give, receive and understand love. From among these five, we choose a dominant language, and it's often the one we grew up receiving and find most familiar. My invitation to you today is to decode all of the different ways you communicate love to those you care about and claim your dominant language. Is it words of affirmation? Quality time? Receiving gifts? Acts of service? Or physical touch? Likely, you may feel that all of these speak to you, but look deeper to discover your preferred avenue of love.

Once you think you know it, take a look back over your life and through all of your relationships and see if your answer holds true. If it does, and you are certain of your love language (you may feel a physical "aha" moment when this happens), claim it for yourself: "I love quality time with someone" or "I know I'm loved when someone offers me a reassuring touch or reaches out to hold my hand."

This is your truth about how you express and experience love, and it is a powerful channel to your soul. Share your love language with your loved ones—let them know about this direct path to your heart. And, with the curiosity of a child rising inside you and a fully open heart, ask them, "What is *your* love language? How can I communicate so that you feel loved?"

✸ February 15

Everyone is born with the ability to sing, even if some of us prefer not to do it. Singing is our birthright. To open ourselves up, letting air rush in and then pushing it back out of our bodies through our throats, thus releasing "our" sound, is innate. Sometimes words, other times random sounds, moans, roars or whispers—all of these form our unique song. When we are children we freely express our thoughts and feelings in song, letting the world around us know who we are and what we feel. Then, as many of us age, our songs become lost inside of us behind doors of judgment, self-criticism and shame. Our sound evolves from the lightness of childhood to an adult's murmur and mumble as we barely move our lips and starve our voice of oxygen. But this is not our natural way.

During the 1950s, Hungarian musicologist and composer Zoltán Kodály developed an original approach to musical education now called the Kodály method or Kodály concept. At the heart of his method was the experience of singing, giving children direct access to the world of music without the technical or financial issues involved with the use of an instrument.

When children sing and participate in Kodály-oriented musical activities, there is a noticeable increase in their powers of concentration, a rise in their levels of achievement and an increase in their social harmony in and out of the classroom. One of the profound outcomes of a Kodály education is the development of the child's inner hearing ability—literally, their ability to imagine sound. Kodály also discovered that it was best to concentrate first on "mother tongue" songs—in other words, the child's native music or the folk songs of their place of origin.

I offer this to you today because there is music inside of you. In fact, there are likely many songs within you. I want to remind you that you have songs of joy, of struggle, of celebration and of deep meaning. Songs to be sung in your mother tongue, songs that express your separate self and songs that connect you to the whole. Songs that begin as sounds rising from deep within you. Songs that, at one time, you chose not to sing—which I now encourage you to release from your soul.

🌸 February 16

Imagine running a mile every day, in all types of weather and with all your friends, and the entire time, you're having fun—so much so that you look forward to running this mile. Now imagine that you are as young as five or six, and all the way up to your early teens.

This was the vision British educator Elaine Wyllie imagined. Her students were sedentary, distracted, unhealthy and disconnected from the natural world. She was aware of research showing that her students' current reality was the beginning of a downward trend that would result in record levels of obesity and poor academic performance by the time they had completed elementary school.

Wyllie founded a program called the Daily Mile, which begins in nursery and primary schools, whereby students engage in fifteen minutes a day of running or jogging. It is non-competitive, inclusive and social. To date, the Daily Mile has had such a transformational impact on children's health and well-being that it has been embraced by over five hundred schools around the world. Wyllie believes that the key to the Daily Mile's success is its simplicity for children and teachers alike: it is free and fun and everyone is outside in the fresh air. It requires no set-up, no special equipment, no cleanup and absolutely no training.

Elaine Wyllie recognized a truth about children: they are designed to be active. Is that not true of all of us? Fifteen minutes of activity every day with our friends, where we are all having fun. It sounds amazing to me! Imagine what we could unleash, shed and enjoy in just fifteen minutes.

By the way, Wyllie says there is a side benefit: children and adults are fit within four weeks, and the program raises academic engagement and performance.

🌸 February 17

Email is now a reality of life for many of us. I look back on those early commercials for AOL, with its computerized voice announcing, "You've got mail," and I laugh when I imagine how often we would hear that today. Many of us are overwhelmed by the sheer volume of email we receive each day—some get upwards of five hundred separate messages! It is physically impossible to read all of these effectively, and therein lies the conundrum for many people: we get so much email that we can never feel good about how we comprehend and respond to it. Researchers have discovered a new physiological impact of email called "email apnea," in which people will respond to emails the same way they respond to fearful events—either with rapid, shallow inhales or by literally bringing their breathing, briefly, to a full stop.

I try to be aware of how I behave in my relationship with email. I know that I sometimes rely on it to distract me from other priorities, and at other times I interact with it on a very selective, need-to-know basis. Part of my personality entails being a sorter, so I tend to go through the critical mass of messages I receive and file them into categories and boxes based on their senders, their subjects and even their importance. I am also working on my self-discipline by blocking out two or three breaks in a day when I deliberately sit and answer those notes that are timely or time-sensitive. In short, I have repositioned the task of dealing with email as something I do during a break from more important tasks or projects, rather than the other way around.

What is crucial with email is that I find ways to preserve my sense of completion and fulfillment, so that I resist behaving in ways that add stress to the experience. I pay attention to my level of stress as I answer email, and if it is rising, I walk away from my computer. I am also very conscious of my breathing, and when I notice I am taking short, rapid breaths or holding my breath, I also push myself back from my keyboard, stretch, deepen my breathing and only return to the inbox when I'm more at ease. This way, I stay focused and am able to gain fulfillment from making progress on what I deem important.

🌸 February 18

Ronald Reagan did it.

So did John F. Kennedy.

In fact, twenty-six of forty-four American presidents did it. They all doodled!

Reagan drew cowboys and football players, Kennedy drew dominoes and Theodore Roosevelt sketched children and animals. Years ago when I was working for a large entertainment corporation, at our weekly update and marketing meetings there was one individual who would arrive with a blank pad of graph paper and fill page after page with elaborate and detailed doodles. At first I couldn't understand how this person could concentrate on the meeting and the conversations taking place and still produce these elaborate sketches. Then I realized that the doodling was a focusing strategy in itself.

Pablo Picasso said that to draw, "we must close our eyes and sing." And it seems that doodling delivers on both accounts. In 2009 researcher Jackie Andrade demonstrated that doodling improves our ability to retain information we have heard (especially if that information is monotonous or boring), and helps us to rest our minds when we need a break from intense focus and concentration. Doodling is a form of fidgeting whereby mind and body work in sync to create spontaneous drawings. Random sketching has also been shown to aid with psychological stress because it puts our mind at ease and helps us make sense of our experiences and our lives.

I draw triangles and three-dimensional rectangular boxes. I also sketch simple cabins and roads with telephone poles that drift off into the horizon. For years, I have created the same large nose and lips, always in left profile; sometimes I use criss-crossing layers of diagonal lines to suggest shading, and draw downward spirals that can fill the page with mini-tornadoes. I enjoy my doodling for the way it puts me at ease and adds some humour and whimsy to my day.

My hope for you today is that you tap into your mind's inner creative force and, using your pencil or pen as a divining rod, cover a page or two—or ten—with a flood of doodles. Doodle your mood, sketch a cartoon, make a line into as many shapes as you can or transform the holes in a loose-leaf page into dramatic, far-seeing eyes.

A little squiggle has the power to keep us light.

✳ February 19

I feel you may need this today. Take a few moments to learn the "box breath." This deliberate way of inhaling and exhaling leaves our bodies deeply calm and our minds alert and focused. Try to find a moment in the morning, or perhaps while you are standing in line or on an elevator, or sitting in traffic. It helps me if I first imagine a square in front of me, tracing each side as practice, but as long as it is relatively quiet where you are, you will find your own way to begin.

First, empty your lungs of all their air—deflating your chest by gently forcing the air out. Now be empty for a steady, rhythmic four seconds—one . . . two . . . three . . . four.

Now breathe in. Let the air rush in through your nostrils, and feel your chest inflate to its fullest point as you again count—one . . . two . . . three . . . four. Hold this breath, resisting the temptation to squeeze your chest or throat; rather, let your chest stay expanded. Hold for one ... two ... three ... four.

Now exhale, letting the air flow freely and steadily from your mouth for a count of one ... two ... three ... four.

Fantastic! You have just completed one full square.

The first time you try the box breathing technique, repeat it for two minutes, then resume your normal breathing. Lean on this breathing technique whenever you feel your shoulders tighten or your neck becoming stiff—or even when you first notice that your breathing is rapid and shallow. Allow this practice to open you up and reaffirm your commitment to being light.

🌸 February 20

It rained here last night. Coming in waves and driven by the wind, the rain pounded our house, then washed over our roof and onto the ground, creating foamy rivers down our driveway. It rained so hard, I woke up just from the sound of the drops hitting our windows. It felt like the rain wanted in, as if it was determined to wash our house away, reducing it to its base elements so that they would dilute in the water and return to the land. At the downpour's most intense moments, the wind and water pressured their way into tiny fissures in our home and came down as persistent and insistent drops, filling every bucket and pot we could place on the floor.

The wind roared around our structure, pried into our house's siding and ripped pieces back, flinging them deep into the trees and scattering them across our fields. The trees were under siege to the wind as their branches whipped and their trunks bent at impossible angles, snapping back during the gale's brief pauses.

In a storm like this, there comes a moment when the thought "I'm in danger" presents itself forcefully in your mind. All you can think about is safety—for yourself and for those you love. You start to think about grabbing the necessities and the most sentimental items you own and getting away. Your whole life boils down to who or what you can carry, and time flattens—there is only the present, felt by the second.

We weathered the storm as it continued throughout the night. Early this morning I looked out the window, and as the sun rose above the tree line, I could see all the pieces of our lives scattered across our farm. Movement high in the trees and in between the debris caught my eye—a remarkable sight: thick, heavy waves of mist rising from everywhere in the sun's heat. All that wet destruction now being liberated by a more powerful force.

And I thought, "This is life."

February 21

Imagine that every secret you are now keeping has a physical weight. There are light secrets—truths that would be embarrassing if shared—and big, heavy secrets that could be harmful if they were ever known. There are also secrets we are holding for others, and these weigh us down and become obstacles we must navigate in our relationships.

I grew up in a secretive family, so I learned at an early age the code governing how to keep others' secrets. I carried many, many secrets for others without ever understanding their cost or their impact on me. I think I was in my forties when I realized that the telling and holding of secrets was responsible for the emotional distance and loneliness I felt with my closest friends and family. Being a vault of secrets meant I couldn't be truthful with others, and I came to trust that everyone was holding their real truth from me and that I was expected to do the same. We were all skating on the thin ice of niceness rather than braving the unsteady water of honesty.

Two bold acts released me from the chains of secrets I was dragging behind me. The first was a series of phone calls with my family in which I said, "I just want you to know that I'm going to assume that anything you say to me is something you're comfortable with me sharing." Hesitantly, they all agreed—"Sure . . . okay . . ." was what they said—but the immediate effect was a change in their behaviour: they simply stopped sharing their judgments or gossip about one another with me.

The second act was harder, with more at stake. I have a dear friend who, at this same time, asked me to lie for him, to cover for an indiscretion. "I would go through a brick wall for you," he said. "That's what true friendship is—we're loyal to each other." Taking a deep breath, I replied, "I would go through a brick wall for you too, and my loyalty is never in question, but I won't lie for you . . . and I expect the same from you." This was a line I drew in the sand and an invitation for a new paradigm for friendship.

These were both tough changes to make, and there was an uncomfortable period of adjustment in my relationships with my family and with my friend. Many other people were critical of my choices as well, but I had achieved my goal: my vault was empty and I was well on my way to living my life honestly and deeply without the extra weight of secrets.

February 22

Leadership—I never use this word, do you?

When my friend put up posters in her community telling predators they would be stopped and the local children would be protected by all the neighbours, I didn't say, "You're an awesome leader." With tears in my eyes, I said I wished she lived in my community and that she had safeguarded the lives of all the children.

At work, we are asked to lead teams, projects, even change. I often become lost and uncomfortable, up in my head, trying to "lead." When I step up about an issue or try to help a community member, I come across as angry and judgmental or I am ignored. Does this happen to you? Yet I don't often put up with being ignored in my personal life. Why is that?

In my personal life I use my intuition, my feelings and my heart as my guides. Because I am passionate, I feel big feelings. I stumble over my words, I cry and yell in my journal, I call my friends and talk with my partner about how to encourage my dad to face his fear of medical treatment without offending him. I hold my tongue and use restraint while my family is crumbling after a recent passing. I send messages on Facebook about our children, as a bridge we can all relate to, while we live in the midst of grief.

I wish I were this passionate and messy and opinionated about the world and my place in it: the atrocities and injustices happening every single day, the non-stop bombardment with news stories that I cannot keep from entering my dreams.

I feel safe in my personal life—safe enough to speak up and try things. I admire people who have the courage to act the same way in their public lives as they do in their personal lives. To me, *that* is true leadership.

In my last corporate job, I would bring a box of beautiful little cupcakes to every customer meeting. I took some heat for it, but my company made room for me to continue my cupcake tradition for five years. I saw how much it meant to people, how they valued having a tasty treat to share with their teams. I was doing the job my way.

If I could bring public issues that matter to me into *my* world, I would bring heart and caring as well as brainpower. I would show the same love that I give my friends and family. The world would get my unique best, and I would feel satisfied and proud and happy. I would be free to contribute as a work team member, and I might have the courage to invite a foster child or a refugee family into my world, or to campaign to protect a nearby lake. I would feel fulfilled.

🌸 February 23

Where is home for you? How many familiar places and experiences can make you feel at home? These are the questions I'm thinking about today as I write. I've just come back to our home after a couple of days away, and what I noticed on the journey was a building nervousness inside me. It wasn't a worry about something going wrong; it was more of a worry about being too far away. Friends had offered to meet me to catch up, but I told them I wanted to get on the road sooner rather than later to avoid traffic. Which is partially true—but the deeper reason was that I didn't want any further delays in coming home.

Sure, I live in a beautiful wild setting surrounded by animals and fresh air, but it's more than a craving for the pastoral that I feel. I'm truly most content when I'm home. My well-being jug begins to fill up once I'm within an hour of our house—as soon as I begin to see the blue of the freshwater lakes around us, the pinkish gold of the rock cliffs and the soaring pine trees. I can feel myself relaxing as the highway narrows from six lanes to four, and then, after a while, to just two. As Ilse Crawford writes:

> We still carry within us, in a small warm spot, the idea of home. Home as a safe place, a loving place and a creative place. A place of comfort and privacy. A place where we can explore our inner life.

Home is much more than a physical space; it is a mental and emotional construct where we can be genuine, content, comfortable and connected. Home represents a reciprocal looping relationship as we bring pieces of our inner selves out into the world and we bring nature into our living spaces—on the one hand, a cozy blanket to a park or our favourite mug to the office; on the other, a bowl of freshly picked pine cones on a table or a blazing ochre maple leaf on a windowsill.

Where is home for you?

❋ February 24

Sometimes, taking a few moments to write down what I observe is very soothing; it opens a magical door to a place that, I am comforted to know, is there for me any time I want.

I didn't see the bird, only its shadow against the leaves as it flew by
Steam coming off the dew, as light touches—exciting
Leaves falling down in circles
I could stay here forever
I am well when I am here
I am in the healing
The most amazing insect floating sideways,
The way an air jellyfish lands on a leaf
The birds are shadows on my eyes
I like to walk sometimes too
To warm the back of me in the sun
Movement creates movement
Stillness creates stillness
Woodpecker stripping bark with its beak as it taps
We are in agreement to move
I don't mind being last, to walk in the sun
We all know we are going together
And they wait for me; they invite me to come too
One by one, they pass me by
I smell my grandmother is here
I am at peace

February 25

Today I'm going to try faith. Faith in myself, faith in things working out, faith that everything will be okay. Having faith leaves very little for me to do.

What if I'm already in the flow? That would leave me feeling grateful, I guess, for having everything I've ever wanted. I'd say "thank you" sincerely, then take a breath and realize I could use some rest—and a big glass of water.

It has taken me several months to work up the courage to let today be about faith. I'm seeing that stepping back shows me how the dots connect. Choices present themselves. If there is anything for me to do, it is to hold the faith and choose what appears.

I'm holding the intention that things are working out for me. I'm eating a snack and enjoying my cats lying in the sun spot on the couch.

It's been an hour. So far, so good.

I'm holding the intention that it's all working out for you too.

February 26

When you look outside right now, what do you see? Are the clouds dancing, or is the sun smiling? Do you see the wind playing with a balloon, or are the moon and stars hiding behind a thick fog? Is a storm threatening, or do you see the sky crying?

There is a literary term for descriptions like these: pathetic fallacy. It's a way of attaching human characteristics to the appearance or behaviour of things in the natural world that are not human. When writers use natural phenomena to underscore their characters' moods or experiences, or a revelation in the plot, they're using pathetic fallacy. Filmmakers make similar use of this device—by, for example, showing us scenes in which the weather seems to reflect or influence the way we feel about the characters and the action.

Maybe you're not sure what you feel today, and you are trying to find words to describe your mood; or maybe your emotions are clear and powerful and you need a way to own them and release them. My invitation to you is to begin with a fresh, blank sheet of paper, sit where you can look outside and write down the words that describe what you see—the weather, the type of light or darkness you observe, the comings and goings of the living creatures that catch your eye and all the sounds you hear.

Our feelings and moods are meant to flow in and out of us freely and fully. Sometimes we know what we feel, yet we can't find a healthy way to let our feelings out; they are often vague and uncertain, and we need to do the work of searching for them and connecting them to give voice to our experience. Throughout our history as a species, we humans have seen our emotional selves in the natural world and imbued nature with our feelings to help us understand and express what we experience.

To describe your outside world as you see it is a way of giving voice to the world within you. Are you a blustery wind, a lonely cloud, a triumphant sun or a chipmunk scurrying away from shadows?

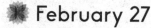 February 27

Minimalism is a tool that can assist you in finding freedom. Freedom from fear. Freedom from worry. Freedom from overwhelm. Freedom from guilt. Freedom from depression. Freedom from the trappings of the consumer culture we've built our lives around. Real freedom.
—Joshua Fields Millburn and Ryan Nicodemus

Less is truly more.

That's the underlying principle behind Josh Fields Millburn and Ryan Nicodemus's approach to minimalism. Their bestselling books, website, podcast and documentary revolve around the liberating effect on our lives of loosening the unconscious emotional bonds we have to our things; this in turn lets us choose what is meaningful in our lives, showing us how we can have less and become lighter, more aware and free.

Both Millburn and Ryan began their lives in families without a lot of wealth and went on to make money, only to struggle to find meaning in their work and lives. Their brand of minimalism is based on a discipline of conscious choice rather than simple deprivation. Both men would argue that the latter approach only increases our hunger for a given thing. Conscious choice, on the other hand, means we ask ourselves what is really important, and whether having an item helps us achieve what is important. We also need to question whether the cost of having that thing forces us to sacrifice or compromise in other parts of our lives that matter more.

Years ago I forced myself into an experiment that helped me look at my relationship to stuff. It began as a challenge: put $140 in an envelope to represent a week's worth of spending (not discretionary spending—total spending!). I gave myself twenty dollars per day, and if I didn't spend the full amount, I would carry what was left over to the next day—but I couldn't take from the next day if I had spent my day's allotment. The challenge was to repeat this weekly for six weeks and see what changes took place.

Briefly, here's what changed:

- I shopped more frugally, ate healthier food and spent more time preparing meals with my family.
- I spent less time driving and more time taking transit and walking, which gave me more time to read.
- I hosted people more often instead of going out, and our get-togethers were more fun.
- I made coffee at home and brought it with me, and it was far better tasting than what I was buying before.

My average spending per day was just under seven dollars, and not once did I feel stressed about money or think that I had less!

Initially, my ego had screamed at me about how crazy I was, insisting that I maintain my spending and accumulating behaviours. But I learned that much of my consumption was done out of boredom or convenience, comparison or distraction. I soon became aware that my contentment really did come from the simplest pleasures.

Today I invite you to check out Millburn and Nicodemus's site, theminimalists.com, and discover for yourself which attachments may have the greatest cost to your lightness and well-being.

 ## February 28

I am thinking about balance today . . .
Yin and yang
How everything is in a state of balance and imbalance
Comfort and discomfort
Empty and full
Slow and fast
These are moments in time, states of their own beingness

When I look at my day this way, I want to walk more gently, to honour the act of balancing so many things, big and small, that make up my day and my life. Focusing on the feeling of balance and imbalance explains so much; it's reassuring to me. States of balance are states of grace. I am in a state of grace.

I breathe in and out
I spend and I receive
I give and I take
I ask and I answer

I work and I rest
I laugh and I cry

We are all balanced in some way. Whenever one side may be more weighty, small movements can tip the scale in the other direction.

Or I can let the imbalance be
It is up to me
Balance always roams free

Can you feel the balance happening in yourself and your life? May this thought bring you comfort today. May you feel your states of grace.

February 29

Are you present in this moment? How about this one? No? Are you present in this moment? Is your awareness somewhere other than this moment right now? Are you reading this hoping for a distraction or a treat? Or are you reading this to become attuned to this moment right now?

We cannot choose or decide how long we live—our life expectancy is a piece of string we carry with us, never knowing its length. We may have a hand in how we die, or our end might come unexpectedly—but it *will* come. In John Irving's novel *A Prayer for Owen Meany*, the main character, a young boy named Owen, sees two dates on a tombstone during a school play: the date of his birth and the date of his death. The rest of the novel weaves a tale of fate in which Owen understands and lives out his life's purpose and, yes, dies on the date foretold on the stage prop.

You and I don't have the luxury of that knowledge. Yet I imagine you have a number in your mind—the age you believe you will live to, or hope to live to. Does that number give you comfort? Does it give you time to sit and relax in life? Is it giving you the space to be preoccupied with feeding your ego, or are you looking at that number and narrowing your choices down to what is essential for you to live your fullest life?

I'm not perfect. I waste my time as if I have an unlimited supply of it. I waver between being present in the moment and being lost, drifting between the past and the present. No one told me how much work it takes to be present and aware—no one impressed upon me how necessary this work is to living.

Today, the twenty-ninth of February, typically comes once every four years in our calendar—if you are reading this on that day, then I'd like to gently remind you—urge you—to understand that your time is not yours, but that the way you live in these moments is 100 percent your choice.

Are you present in this moment?

March

✳ March 1

Let's take stock of our regrets today. We all have a running list of "should haves," "could haves" and "would haves" when we look back on our lives and judge our own behaviour or the way someone else behaved. Sometimes we believe, in hindsight, that we were capable of much more at the time—that being better or doing better was within our grasp. We had a chance, or the other person had a chance, and it didn't go right. Our regrets become those weighty moments we drag around, holding us back from accepting and deeply loving others and ourselves.

One of the unique opportunities I've been fortunate to have is the ability to speak with so many people who live with a terminal illness or have had a near-death experience. What is common among them is their choice to shed all the baggage that hinders their enjoyment of living. In every conversation I have had, there was a moment when they looked me in the eye and said, "I realized my biggest regrets were no longer important—I had to let them go and move on." These people forced themselves to change their relationships with their regrets, making a conscious choice to understand them, learn from them, address them and then move on from them.

Can we do the same today? Can we take a more critical look at our regrets—opening up that symbolic storage locker with the intention of emptying it out? I hope your answer is yes!

I believe there are two actions that help us let go of our regrets. The first is to ask ourselves, "Is there anything I can do, anything that will melt this regret away?" If the answer is yes, then our second action is to do what it takes, regardless of any discomfort. If the answer is "No, there's nothing I can do to absolve this regret," then let it go. We are empowered to address a regret either by taking action or by letting it go.

A regret on its own adds no value to the quality of our living. But if we learn from it, act to heal it and move on from it, we grow as people and our daily lives are enriched and lighter.

🌸 March 2

In his 2012 book *Seven Thousand Ways to Listen*, Mark Nepo frames listening as much more than just hearing. For him, listening is an act of understanding and appreciation, of connection and communion. How would you let this perspective shape your behaviour, with yourself and with others? If I invite you to listen to understand, listen to appreciate, listen to connect and listen to commune, how do you behave differently?

Mark Nepo offers this:

> I didn't know when I began this book on listening that my hearing was already breaking down. It's been disorienting and yet freeing. I only know that my need to listen more deeply has been answered with an undoing that has made me listen with my eyes, my skin. Now I wonder softly: Does a plant listen by breaking ground? Does sand listen by accepting the waves it can never escape? And how do stubborn souls like us listen? I feel like a painter who, after mastering certain brushes over the years, has come to the end of brushes; who in an effort to get closer to the light has thrown his brushes into the fire, to ignite more light. I am left finally to paint with my hands.

This is my invitation to both of us today: to listen as though we are both learning to listen for the first time.

March 3

We have all lied. That's a truth.

A popular meme that recently circulated on my social media feeds pleads, "A single lie discovered is enough to create doubt in every truth expressed." And while I believe the meme's creator was referring to those lies we spread around or that are told to us by others, what strikes me is the power of the words when you think about the connection between lies and the way we feel about *ourselves*.

Having listened to people share their lives with me for thousands of hours, I am acutely aware of the way that lying erodes a person's self-confidence and self-esteem. It seems the more truth we withhold, dress up or simply fabricate, the more damage we do to the bricks and mortar of our sense of self. Our egos grab our lies and use them as evidence against us, digging a big pit of self-doubt in our souls.

The hardest part of being a counsellor to someone who believes in lying and lives with so much self-doubt is helping them re-establish a bond with the truth. It is like building a foundation of toothpicks you hope will support the weight of a house.

I know that my way of lying is to withhold—I hang on to information or views and opinions until I have worked them through a process: at first, caretaking the other person and their feelings, before eventually coming around to speaking my truth and placing my integrity and theirs above all else. I also self-withhold, starving myself of acknowledgement and encouragement in those moments when I need it most. I'm more aware of this pattern now, and I work hard to share all the truth I know with kindness, regardless of how much discomfort it causes in the moment.

How—and why—do you lie? This is what I ask you to reflect on today. Let's be aware of our lies as we walk towards the truth.

❈ March 4

Have you read that neuroscience is exploring the gut as our second brain?

This is an incredible new doorway, beyond which may lie an explanation of what drives the rampant attacks on our well-being that so many of us experience and what we might be able to do to regain control of our moods, our weight, our energy and our well-being.

Our gut has its own nervous system, called the enteric nervous system or the "little brain," which is made up of more than a hundred million nerve cells lining our gastrointestinal tract in two thin layers. The big brain (in our heads) and the little brain are connected, using the same neural networks and endocrine and immune pathways.

More than 95 percent of our serotonin (the neurotransmitter that regulates our mood) is produced and stored in our gut. Dr. Emeran Mayer, a gastroenterologist and neuroscientist who has written a book called *The Mind-Gut Connection*, wrote in *Psychology Today* that there is evidence that a healthy gut can curb inflammation and cortisol levels, lower our reaction to stress, improve memory and even reduce neuroticism and social anxiety. Researchers at Johns Hopkins University are investigating how activity in the digestive system might affect cognition—that is, thinking skills and memory. And evidence shows that healthy and diverse gut microbes reduce anxiety and depression.

Information about how to improve our gut health and build up our stock of microbial buddies—the gut microbiota—is widely available. I was surprised to learn about diets that emphasize foods our stomachs and small intestines don't absorb easily—foods that instead pass through to the colon and large intestine, where they feed the beneficial bacteria that live there. By personalizing our digestive systems and imagining the microbiota as wonderful friends we are hosting and feeding, how much better and empowered we will feel!

✺ March 5

The 2018 Planning & Progress Study, an annual research project commissioned by the Northwestern Mutual insurance company, explores Americans' attitudes and behaviours regarding various financial issues. An overwhelming 87 percent of those surveyed agreed that nothing made them feel happier or more confident than having their finances in order.

Money was the number one source of stress (mentioned by 44 percent of respondents), putting it well ahead of personal relationships (25 percent) and work (18 percent). And the top three causes of financial pressure, all of which are beyond a person's control, were

- the rising cost of health care (mentioned by 59 percent);
- unplanned financial emergencies (55 percent); and
- unplanned health emergencies (53 percent).

Happiness that my finances are in order reminds me of the expression "putting my house in order." My house is in order when I remove clutter and the place is neat and tidy. As someone who likes feeling inspired, positive and energized, what's most important to me is that my house feels in order when I tap into my senses—with a lovely fragrance in my atomizer, visuals like fresh eggs in a basket on the counter, music playing in the background, or a blanket or my cat on my lap. My senses are activated by these cues, and I relate to them with a feeling that all is well.

Can money form a connection with our senses?

Our eleven-year-old daughter told me recently how distraught she was when I asked to borrow her fifty-dollar bill to pay someone. She said it was the first fifty-dollar bill she'd had in her whole life, and she recounted how she had received it years earlier, unexpectedly, as a reward for her generosity—from the mother of a friend to whom she had given her dollhouse. Our daughter was emotionally attached to that particular physical bill, not to its monetary value.

When I was little, my dad used to take me for breakfast every Saturday morning. We would always start with a trip to the bank machine, and I remember the bills rolling out of the machine and him putting the stack in his wallet, then taking my hand to walk into the mall. It is a comforting memory.

The hardware store we went to had a machine next to the cash register that would send the customer's change down a winding slide and into a cup, where the customer would scoop it out. It was a treat to be allowed to collect the change, and the coins made a wonderful metallic clinking sound as they travelled towards my hand. I have a kinesthetic correlation between the sound of money and fun. I feel delight and I smile every time I find a coin on the ground... every time!

Think of pleasant money memories or dreams you have. What feelings do they evoke? Which senses come alive?

If you're among the nine out of ten people who say nothing makes them happier than feeling like their finances are in order, I invite you to describe that feeling in more detail. I bet those feelings are connected to pleasant, valuable memories and experiences and senses we can recreate for ourselves as adults.

A *Business Insider* article called "5 Things You Can Start Doing Today to Attract Wealth" says:

> The rich see money as a special friend that can help them in ways no other friend can, and these positive feelings lead them to build a stronger relationship every day. . . . Rich people have more fun than anyone I know because

> they have the means to do anything they want. What
> may look like work to most people is actually a person
> living life to the fullest with every available resource at
> his fingertips. Take time to enjoy the road to wealth. Don't
> wait to have fun. Have fun now!

The article, published in December 2016, is written by self-made multimillionaire Steve Siebold.

Perhaps we can do more than put our finances "in order." We can relate to money emotionally, and in so doing, have fun and relax about our finances—and maybe, through positive money memories, dreams and stories, we can actually attract money to us.

✹ March 6

Today, let's reflect on boundaries—our boundaries.

A boundary is a line we draw for others to delineate the ways we want to be treated, respected and loved, and to set these apart from behaviours we will not tolerate. For some of us, boundaries also involve our relationship "must-haves," or non-negotiable elements, such as honesty, trust, kindness and support. Our personal boundaries are things we discover over time, through repeated experiences in relating to others. Some of us have strong boundaries—the consequence of pain inflicted by others. Many of us have thin boundaries that are difficult to maintain when our sense of being loved or belonging is threatened.

The boundary I'm most curious about today is the one you've set for yourself. I learned many years ago that I was in a pattern of high-risk behaviour that would always result in me hurting myself. I treated my body and my mind as if they were both inanimate machines that were there to serve me. I was hard on them, took advantage of them and took them for granted. My body is a map of scars that detail this history, and I have stories that are now legendary of how I abused my mind.

One day I was home after a twelve-hour group therapy workshop at which I had a full-body rage release, writhing across a carpet and smashing my arms and legs on the floor. I was tired, physically spent and emotionally exhausted, and all I wanted was a hot shower. Stepping into the steaming spray, I was expecting relief. Instead, a wave of searing pain, like jolts of electricity, screamed from everywhere on my body and overwhelmed my mind. I yelled out loud, hoping to force myself through the pain with rage, but each second under the water brought new rounds of pulsing pain.

Then, from deep in my belly, came a whisper: "Stop hurting me." My mind registered the plea, but ignored it. Again the whisper rose: "Please . . . stop hurting me." My body was speaking to me and telling me it had had enough. I chose love for myself in that moment, and I have worked hard ever since to maintain a boundary about treating my body and my mind like dear friends.

I wish that for you today—to find a way back to your body and your mind so that they become dear and treasured to you.

🌸 March 7

Some days I am acutely aware that I am the one on this journey. I am distinct and separate and unique, as are you. Some days I really need comfort and love and reassurance that everything is okay—that I'm okay.

Motivational author Louise Hay is a hero of mine. She developed a twenty-one-day program involving mirror work and affirmations designed to help build self-confidence and self-esteem. Looking at myself in the mirror is an incredible way to give myself actual love, hope, kindness, care, support and understanding in ways that satiate my need like no other person ever can.

Something magical happens when I look into my own eyes in the mirror and say what I've been longing to hear about myself, *for* myself: "I love you." I take a deep breath, staying with my eyes. "I believe in you." Still staying with my eyes. "I see compassion. I see love. I see understanding." That moment is so powerfully comforting and healing. I trust those eyes. I believe the messages. My cup fills.

❋ March 8

There is comfort when I look at the wall calendar in our kitchen and see the full days that have passed. The calendar is dedicated to seeing the non-work parts of my life—home, projects, family and friends—come together.

It is deeply satisfying to get off the screen for a while and see a portion of life posted on a wall, decorated with colours and hearts, scratches and checkmarks, doodles and birthdays. Cats doing yoga, beautiful scenic places, dreamy beaches, yummy food themes—all are mascots for our "trip around the sun," as country singer Kenny Chesney calls his year-long tours.

A calendar reflects the intentions we have for our year—the things we want more of and the things that deserve our attention. If it makes us smile and laugh out loud too, that's awesome!

Look at your weekly or monthly calendar page. Notice the amount of open space, the level of clutter and busyness. How does breath come when you look at the calendar—in sharp, shallow motions or deep inhales and exhales?

What names appear for gatherings and outings and birthdays? Is anyone missing? Is enough time set aside for the people you want to see? Does the calendar seem balanced to you, or is it tipped a little too far towards an activity, a person or a time period?

Sales of paper planners are on the rise, according to a study by the NPD Group in 2016. They encourage us to colour-code, add creative themes and track our progress and moods. There is still something precious about making entries in planners and calendars by hand; in addition to tracking the things we want to focus on, it allows us to enjoy the beauty of imagery, lines, colours, graphs and dots.

Today, let the calendar be a personal reflection of your life—your time dedicated and your creativity expressed.

March 9

Research has shown that most of us wear about 10 percent of all the clothes in our closets, drawers and wardrobes. Which means that, collectively, there's about eight billion dollars' worth of clothing every year that, once purchased, rarely or never sees the light of day. I don't know about you, but I have a few drawers that could use a shakedown. Come to think of it, I'm reminded that when I was a child, I had one pair of shoes, and now, when I look around our house, it seems I have shoes for every conceivable function and mood. Perhaps the same is true of all of my clothing—and yours as well.

Back to trimming down our excess and lightening up.

Let's be honest with ourselves: we may own much more clothing than we actually can or will wear, so outside of our emotional attachment to certain pieces in our wardrobe, we could easily shed a third of it. With that goal in mind, let's go into our closet—or today, a drawer—and spend about ten to fifteen minutes whittling down what we wear.

Some choices will be obvious because a piece will be worn out, faded or beyond mending. Other decisions will be tougher, and you may feel like you want to linger and think these through—but do not pause! Keep your mind focused on the time limit and your goal. Place all of the items you are culling into dark garbage bags (so you won't be tempted by what you see in the bags) and, when your time limit is up, stop, tie the bags and take them out of the room.

We donate our clothes locally; you may choose to do the same, or give them to an organization that sends them overseas. Regardless, be sure to complete the task by getting the bag(s) out of your home.

This is a simple exercise in letting go, and it forces us to be honest with ourselves, to examine and evaluate our true emotional connection with something we own, and then make a conscious choice to let that item go. Lightening up is all about being aware of the choices we make to be emotionally involved or attached to people, places, events and things. So many of us are hanging on to things, like clothing, not because they make us feel good, but because we don't want to feel sad in letting them go.

🌸 March 10

The other day I was having a conversation with a group of people at a party. The topic was retirement, and the overwhelming majority of the folks I was listening to couldn't wait to be finished with work so that they could begin living their lives.

Later that same day I bought a slice of pizza in a shop near where I live. The owner, a man in his fifties, was working alongside his father, a man in his late seventies. With the conversation about retirement still fresh in my mind, I asked the older man, "Have you ever thought about retiring?"

"No," he said. "Never crossed my mind. This shop is my life."

I looked right at him as he said these last words, and there was a smile in his eyes. He was telling the truth.

Given that work is such a necessary aspect of our modern world, why is it that so many of us work to live rather than live to work? How many of us choose our work based on what it pays us rather than how it fulfills us? How much of our daily stress and exhaustion are rooted in the dislike or hatred of our jobs? People who find "their work" don't complain about hating their jobs—they may still be tired and stressed, but these feelings are counterbalanced by an inner love for what they do.

Inside of each of us is a set of important values and beliefs that form our inner or intrinsic motivation to work. We hope that each job we hold ticks off many if not all of the boxes, but sadly, most of the time we find ourselves settling or bargaining with ourselves, sacrificing what is really important to us. It's this settling, bargaining and sacrificing that lead us to tolerate our work rather than enjoy it. And after a while, tolerance leads to resentment.

But it doesn't need to be this way. Your life isn't about having *the* dream job—just finding *your* dream job, whatever that may be.

🌸 March 11

In the ebb and flow of life, our wishes, dreams and ideas are in a constant state of flux and growth. Some rise up like a tall oak tree, solidly taking its place in the world—so solidly that we might have forgotten our role in planting it. Some dreams are like proud little plants with roots that run deep, but that need care and nurturing. Some are newly planted and some might still be seeds in a jar on the project table, waiting for spare minutes to be put in their place in the earth.

Take a step back today to reflect on the state of your wishes, dreams and ideas. Which have come to life and are already flourishing? Which are in need of care?

Look at the jar of seeds that are waiting . . . the ideas, wishes and dreams that might have been tucked away for a while. Open the jar and look at the inventory you have. List each seed (in your mind, or even better, on paper) and notice which ones capture your attention the most. Make the list as complete as possible—dreams have a way of connecting as they settle into our fuller awareness at some point down the road.

Jack Canfield, author of the *Chicken Soup for the Soul* books and a leader in what he calls peak performance strategies, is one of many experts teaching people how to make their dreams come true. He says this about visualization techniques: "[They] have been used by successful people to visualize their desired outcomes for ages. The practice has even given some high achievers what seems like super-powers, helping them create their dream lives by accomplishing one goal or task at a time with hyper focus and complete confidence."

Today, pick the seed from your list that has your attention. Visualize yourself and your life *after* this dream has been realized.

Now bring this dream into today. Add as much detail as possible in your spare moments. Picture exactly how you feel in your life with this dream come true—see the details, the colours, the people around you, what you are doing, what you are wearing, where you are, all crystal clear. Personal time might be scarce. Use time in the bathroom or shower, on the subway or train, while waiting in line or watching a show. Add more and more detail until you can really feel as though it's happened, in all dimensions, as real as this book.

Are you reading this with belief, or with disbelief? Either is okay—and helpful, because it simply shows where you are *today*, in relation to dreaming the perfect life for you. And tomorrow might be different.

Today, give yourself the gift of dreaming.

March 12

There is something that fuels you and lives inside you that no one can ever take away or diminish. This part of you rises up when your back is against the wall, when you are on the verge of being emotionally crushed or physically challenged, when your hope that others will save you disappears, or even when hope itself breathes its last breath. This part of you is resilient, grounded, empathetic, timeless, even innocent. This is your soul, and it places no demands on you; rather, it invites you to connect with and nourish it so that you may live a more meaningful life.

You may be asking, "What is my soul?" or "How do I know I'm

connected to my soul?" Gary Zukav, in his bestselling book *The Seat of the Soul*, reveals, "You experience your soul each time you sense yourself as more than a mind and body, your life as meaningful, or you feel that you have gifts to give and you long to give them."

For many of us, our souls will speak to us as an instinct or a gut feeling we are invited to consider or experience in order to shed light on the truth of who we are. Our souls see our existence through the lens of relationship—letting us understand how we are connected to the people around us, the other living beings on earth, the earth itself and the universe. Our souls will speak to us in the language of connection—a chord of music played on a guitar interacting with the newly rising hairs on your arms, or the lump forming in your throat.

Your soul is light, and it expands the more you nurture your bond with it. Today I invite you to find some of the doorways to your soul. Extend your hand inward to your soul and invite it to come out and play.

🌸 March 13

Saying "thank you" is what I invite you to step into today. On the surface it may seem that these words are intended as a way for us to show our appreciation for something another person has said to us or done on our behalf. And that is true. Saying "thank you" is a beautiful way to acknowledge another's presence in your life and appreciate their generous nature and behaviour. To say it in a heartfelt way causes us to be aware of what is happening in the present moment and to feel the person's impact on our life.

But these words can work much more deeply. To experience gratitude fully, we must also see ourselves as others see us—we must recognize that we are worthy of receiving generosity and appreciation, and thus worthy of being loved. Feeling that we are lovable, and loved by others, begins to move us into a deeper connection with ourselves.

I've seen the power of this insight first-hand while speaking to people about the most important moments in their lives. They stop mid-sentence in reflection when they realize that the generosity of another person had a more profound meaning—that they were seen and appreciated and loved. Their dignity returns and their self-love blossoms. And after a brief pause, a warmth enters them and a smile appears on their faces—some even well up with tears and get a lump in their throats as they tell me, "I just really want to say 'thank you' and let them know what they mean to me."

This is my invitation to you today: say "thank you" as fully and with as much meaning as you can.

March 14

We are living in what the *New York Times* referred to in August 2016 as post-truth times. Opinions, estimates, interpretations and lies are used, more than facts, by governments, businesses, schools and churches. Margins, approximates, retractions and corrections are core to weather forecasts, money markets, the real estate industry and politics. Infractions, untruths and violations abound. In some parts of the world, this has been a fact of everyday life for centuries; in other regions, there has been a more gradual shift of awareness.

My attachment to truth has caused me to give away my power. I rely on people I have never met to educate me, protect me, safeguard my finances and keep safe from harm the earth I call home. I have put my physical safety, my financial well-being, my health and that of my children, my partner and my family into the hands of people I cannot trust to tell the truth. There. I said it. Exhale. Big inhale and exhale.

Have you already come to this realization?

I can trust that people around me are not always true to their word. I can trust that there is no one truth.

Without a single truth, there are as many truths as humans on the planet. This idea makes me curious about the others. What is true for them? It causes me to ask clarifying questions, to find common ground with them. It makes me rely upon myself to choose what feels right. I must pay attention to my surroundings, use my instincts, access my senses.

It also means I can drop others' definitions of me, and expectations and judgments, because they are not true. Only *I* know if I am beautiful, if I am a good person, if I am talented, qualified, funny, successful or healthy.

We will decide for ourselves whether another's "truth" resonates.

This is actually a much more empowered way to live.

I put myself in control of my life, my thoughts, my actions, my beliefs. I feel free to live by my own compass and truth. I feel lighter without needing to blame or justify, defend or deny. I feel excited that I can live in relationships with friends, family, groups and communities, each with our own truths.

Where have I made trade-offs or sacrificed my truth? Where am I hiding my truth? What *is* my truth? Ruminating on these questions will help me see my power.

March 15

Take a moment and imagine a sound, perhaps even the sound that brings you the most comfort. Do you have it in your mind? Can you bring it fully into your awareness? For some people, it is the babbling of running water, the low drone of a fan gently whirring, or maybe the constant, rhythmic ups and downs of people talking close by. For me, the whispering of the wind through pine trees immediately places me in a soothing, contented place.

Can you hear your sound—the one that calms all parts of you? Where does it come from? Is it a natural sound, a familiar one or perhaps both?

Science confirms our experiences: researchers have found that sounds from artificial sources tend to trigger patterns of inward-focused attention in our brains, putting us in a state akin to worrying or anxiety, while sounds from nature prompt patterns of external-focused attention, helping us to commune with our surroundings.

Familiar sounds can also have a similar calming, almost hypnotic effect on our minds. Listening to the radio this morning, I heard an announcer relate a story of how the play-by-play commentary of a hockey game—a sound she would often hear in her home as a young girl—had the power to lull her to sleep.

What if we could be more deliberate about enjoying this relationship with our favourite natural or familiar sounds? Let's imagine you are about to create your own personal soothing-sound spa. Which aural experiences will become your sanctuary, and where will you listen to them? Can you see yourself in that place right now? What do you hear?

March 16

Thoughts are the most powerful tools we have to create health and happiness for ourselves.

I read in an article from the National Science Foundation that the average person has between twelve thousand and sixty thousand thoughts a day. Are you as stunned as I was to consider that fact?

Neuroscience has proven that our thoughts activate responses of either fear or love in our body. Fear or love—that's the bottom line. Dr. Athena Staik explains this process on her blog *Neuroscience & Relationships*:

> Fear puts our body into a state of protection, generates cortisol and shuts off learning.
>   Love puts the body into a state of safety, generates

serotonin and oxytocin and opens learning, reflective thinking and connection.

Love is the only state where change is possible. I cannot change when I am in a fear state. Love is the only state where connection is possible. I cannot connect with another when I am in fear.

I can have everything I want by putting myself into a state of love. I can trick my brain into a state of love. I can make a smile or a laugh. I can look at a screen saver or wall calendar with cute animals on it. I can water my plants. And there are many tools out there, such as meditation and mindfulness, to help me stay in a state of love as a way of living.

When I slip into fear today, I will tell myself it is okay because my brain will generate new cells, so I will have more chances to train my neurons to wire themselves for love. I am going to comfort myself with a thought about love.

Today I intend to be in an open state of love. I am focusing my thoughts on gratitude, love and happiness. I am thinking about puppies, doughnuts, winning, people I really love and things that make me laugh. I am looking for situations and conversations that provide opportunities to feed my love state. In doing so, I am creating a lovely day for me and for people I connect with, and I am creating momentum for my wellness tomorrow.

I am focusing all of my thoughts on love.

✳ March 17

One of the more difficult parts of loving someone is knowing when I've cared too much. That may sound odd to some of you, but let me be clear: I'm not talking about the nurturing type of caring; I mean the overinvolved and overattached type of caring that has us in a kind of 24/7 state of alert in an attempt to insulate our loved ones from all the danger in the world, or that makes us need to be a part of every moment of their lives. The name for this type of caring is called "codependence," and it has many faces in our relationships.

If you "live for your children," you are likely codependent.

If you have a relationship where your partner's problems are a drama you can only react to, you are likely codependent.

If you give of yourself to everyone around you to a point where there's nothing left for yourself, you are likely codependent.

If many of your relationships have been with so-called "lost puppies" or "birds with broken wings," you are likely codependent.

If you "hide who you really are" from friends and family, preferring to play a role rather than be yourself, you are likely codependent.

If you believe that those around you are incapable of taking care of themselves and they need you to rescue or protect them, you are likely codependent.

If your self-worth is built up or eroded by what someone else says or does, you are likely codependent.

Codependence is not caring, and yet those who are codependent deeply believe this is what they are offering. Codependency is a type of relationship addiction where we form a dysfunctional helping partnership with someone we see or perceive as weak, sick or broken. A codependent only feels worthy or lovable when they have someone they can mend, heal or protect. Codependents feel heavy, stressed, anxious, angry and lonely.

If this describes how you feel much of the time, you are likely a codependent.

This is your wake-up call. Take a moment—take the whole day, if you need to—and try to come to terms with this without judging yourself. Your life is now on a new course.

March 18

Hello, my friend,

Thank you for being with me yesterday. I love being with you, listening to you and watching you explore the world and who you are with a renewed curiosity and an open heart.

You inspire me and I live to commune with you every day.

Until tomorrow,
With love,
Me

 ## March 19

Have you tried making a family tree or taking a DNA test? Our growing fascination with roots and lineage has permeated our culture. We can now go on DNA-inspired vacations, and in March 2018 *National Geographic* reported that the largest digital family tree yet created had just topped thirteen million people.

By connecting myself to more names and more geographies, tracing my family line to historical events and social settings, a tapestry appears, offering me the chance to see my place within a much greater whole. I am surrounded by people and stories, should I choose to delve into them.

Invented by Murray Bowen, a genogram is a graphic that takes the idea of a family tree a bit further, displaying not only a person's family relationships but details about each person's medical history, occupation, age and cause of death, marital status, health concerns—including mental well-being—and major life changes and traumas. When I did my family genogram, even though my parents are sketchy on many of the details of my grandparents' and great-grandparents' lives, new familial patterns surfaced. On both sides of my family, people made pivotal choices to leave the countryside and move to the city, where they suffered poverty and familial separation. I learned that depression and mental illness occurred in every branch, on both sides, in every generation. So did asthma and arthritis.

When I related my genogram to my own life, I recognized that my lifelong yearning to live in nature might be rooted in a greater familial calling to return to the country. The amazing similarities—and even relationships—between the geographies of my genogram validated my deep sense of comfort when I'm in pine forests.

The genogram can also reveal clues about current-day challenges and traumas we are experiencing. Belief systems and biases from generations ago may still affect us today. Patterns may emerge about such issues as money, power, equality, community, God, abuse, addiction, freedom and empowerment. We can find connections to societal traumas that include epidemics, displacement, immigration, war, oppression and enslavement, the results of which are still playing out in our lives.

So many of us are searching for a sense of belonging and purpose. Thanks to science and spirit, familial discovery and ancestral healing is available to us all.

Think about your ancestors, those who walked the path before and who are well in spirit. Imagine the support and wisdom they may have for you.

March 20

These are strange times. I look around and I see our world in so much chaos and flux that all I want to do some mornings is stay in bed. Do you ever have mornings like that?

I had one just yesterday. The feeling came on the second I opened my eyes and it intensified throughout the entire day. Tasks were harder or more complicated than usual, and problems entangled me like a network of cobwebs. My energy was flat, I was tired and irritable, and I had a strong urge to get away from everything and everyone. By dinnertime I was in a state of full resistance to life.

It was a really crappy day.

But it passed.

And no matter how bad I was feeling, I had a sense deep down that the way I was feeling wasn't the whole picture—my mood was emotional cloud cover or a brewing storm that would pass. When I was younger and these storms would occur, I'd let my mood fester and I'd ruminate over painful, hopeless thoughts until the darkness enveloped me. I have to confess that I sometimes enjoyed these gloomy pits because they gave me an identity I could feel.

As a young adult I shifted my approach and would try a variety of positive tactics to skirt what I had labelled as negative feelings. This was always a lot of work, though, and I ended up feeling tired and superficial.

Somewhere in my later years I just got tired of trying so hard to avoid these stormy moods and I began to hold them as intense, temporary disruptions that blow in and out of me. Some days I know what sets them off, and other days I just wake up that way. Regardless, I now trust that they will pass in their own time—when they are ready. I've learned to ride them out and live with them, rather than avoiding or disguising them altogether. I've discovered that, as I am more patient with my storms and myself, I also become more resilient and mentally strong. And when I am more accepting of my dark moods, I also have more openness and empathy for the emotional storms affecting other people.

As you read this, you may be having one of those days. Try to be with your mood today as fully as you can. This is your reality for today. You still have to take care of your basic needs and the needs of your loved ones, and it's important that you provide yourself with security, comfort and nurturing. Resist the temptations to out-think your mood or rain your darkness on others.

This is your storm.

It will pass.

March 21

Let's do something nice for ourselves today.
I am deserving
Of wanderlust, magic and soulful meanderings.
Today, let the flow of life be gentle.
I am allowing myself to feel good, to matter, to be filled.
I am blessed.

March 22

The true secret of happiness lies in taking a genuine interest in all the details of life.
—William Morris

It isn't easy in our complicated world to enjoy the pleasures of ordinary living—children, family, neighbourhood, nature, walking, gathering, eating together. I imagine life not as an ambitious quest, but as an anti-quest, a search for the ordinary and a cultivation of the unexceptional.
—Thomas Moore

The simple things we do every day can have the greatest potential to bring us contentment and ease. Making a delicious cup of coffee or tea, peeling an orange, our morning routine, sitting with our favourite people for lunch, lighting a candle at dinner—these small actions, which bring us comfort, are the rituals that transform everyday experience into something that is both practical and soulful.

Rituals are different from habits—which are unconsciously repeated behaviours—in that they require us to deeply attend and be present to every moment, thereby deepening our contentment. When we make the bed out of habit, we do so to get it done. When we make the bed as a ritual, we prepare it as a sanctuary, imagining the comfort we will experience as we lie down to sleep.

In the mass-production style of psychology that arose in the late nineteenth century and continues to be rampant today, these everyday rituals are repositioned as tedious, inconvenient work. We need machines or hired help to rid us of the dirtiness and drudgery of these tasks so we can be free to play and relax. Every new innovation showcased at world expositions and trade shows is designed to make all work disappear so that we can lead lives of leisure and convenience. A leisurely life is a meaningful life. Once upon a time, we were all going to live like the Jetsons.

It's not that hard to see that this quest denies an obvious truth about being human and alive: work, especially our approach to work, can be more rewarding in and of itself. And never is this more obvious than when it comes to the essential place of rituals in our lives.

As Louisa Thomsen Brits puts it, "We can move more happily through our busy lives by being aware of the value of routine chores, enjoying some of them as small instances strung through our day where we find ourselves comforted and our sense of purpose restored."

Rituals are the mile markers of purpose and caring in our daily lives. They lay out the path ahead of us and help us reflect on the quality of the moments we have already experienced. We can find contentment if we return to thinking of chores and everyday tasks as rituals full of purpose and meaning. If we make that first cup of coffee in the morning delicious, if we prepare our child's lunch with care, if we sweep our floors as an act of self-love, if we wash our clothes knowing that we will feel good when we wear them, and if we make our bed imagining it as a cozy invitation waiting for us at the end of the day.

✹ March 23

Have you written your will? I am writing mine in letter form, using a "spiritual will" format I discovered on Rabbi Rachel Barenblat's award-winning blog, *Velveteen Rabbi*. I hope to have many years to come, yet writing my will feels empowering, as though I am taking charge of my time here with a little more clarity, gratitude and ease. I hope you find writing your will to be rewarding and heartwarming.

A spiritual will is a document that outlines what I hope to leave to those I leave behind, not just in the tangible sense of possessions and money, but in an emotional, intellectual and spiritual way. I am sharing with you a part of the will I wrote for my daughter. I hope it inspires you to share who you are and the gifts you leave.

Dear beautiful daughter,

I am writing this first draft to you at the age of fifty. I tried to write this letter when you were born, and again several times since, but I haven't been ready. Today I am writing because it is so important to me that I tell you what is in my heart, even though you already know.

You have been my biggest gift in life because of who you are. Your light is so very bright, and today, when you are eleven, it shines so brightly. You come from heaven, you awake singing in the mornings (and in the shower), animals are your best friends and you understand people and see deep inside them.

My hope for you is that feeling deeply leads you to a rich life filled with loving people and colourful experiences. I want you to know that life is hard at times, really hard, and can lead to disappointment and loneliness. In those times, I hope you feel comforted by people and animals and plants you love, and that when those difficult times pass (and they always will), you will see that life is better because of how deeply you feel. I want you to be happy, healthy and safe.

I appreciate your creativity as an artist, a baker and a maker. You create independently, being confident and willing to try. I hear you singing and feel you at peace when you sit crocheting or painting. Please keep that always.

I love watching you run! Your body straightens from your core and you become still and so very focused, while your legs gracefully stretch forward. So lovely. Please keep running in your life.

I am completely myself when I am with you. Here are the gifts I leave with you.

My appreciation of nature and giving every being and thing a name.

Laughter—taking over our bodies, silent steam-whistle laughter, being ticklish around my neck, carefree and looking silly, dropping everything to wrestle on the grass to make each other laugh.

Belief in possibility—I want you to focus on what you want, in as much detail as you can, and it will happen. The universe will send you even better gifts than you imagined.

Gift of tears—crying whenever I am touched, moved and inspired. I can't help myself!

Travel—I see as many parts of the world as possible. I want you to see pandas and Japan and everywhere else that calls to your heart. I love Africa, and travelling to a place you already love is very rewarding.

Spices—rich, flavourful curries; ginger, nutmeg and cinnamon; cardamom and garam masala—cook with them. Be friends with people from those places, like Auntie Michelle. Ever since you were little, your favourite restaurant to celebrate your birthday has been a Pakistani place in Toronto. I love that. Be spicy, girl!

God, spirit and angels exist. Ask for their help. Pray and trust as often as you need.

Live a life you love now. Don't wait for someday. And choose with your heart. We moved to the farm from the city because nature was calling us, and we listened. Even though it was a risk and a big change, we have never regretted that decision and it has made us very happy.

Money is unlimited, and the more you have, the more you can create and share. Money is a good thing.

Do your best—I am still learning to do my best, and it is very satisfying.

Saying I am sorry—we apologize when we speak in anger or fear and when we are wrong. We always accept apologies and are willing to start fresh. How many handshakes we have shared since you were a toddler, to restart the day and be connected!

Singing "Hush, Little Baby," lying together as you tell me about your day and what is in your heart, then singing your lullaby while I scratch your back or play with your hair before completing our day with promises to meet you on the mushroom top in our dreams.

You have a family that spans Bavaria, Saskatchewan, Quebec, Newfoundland and England. You have your awesome brother, and I wish for you two to stay close to each other and take care of each other for the rest of your lives. You have cousins, aunts and uncles, and quasi-aunts and -uncles. You have special people who care about you, like Nancy the librarian; Margaret, who owns the ice cream shop; Coach Lynn from curling; neighbour Morgan, who babysits you; and many more amazing women who know you are special and want to be with you. Let good people help you. Learn from them and know that you are a gift for them in return.

Molly, thank you for being you. I love you always and I will be with you always.

March 24

Do you know who your harshest critic is? The person who judges your performance at work or your skills and abilities as a parent? The individual who says you're unattractive, unsuccessful or unhappy? Who is the person in your life who told you that your greatest idea was crazy or that you didn't possess the courage to pursue big dreams? Who ridicules your body and gives you lots of reasons why you don't have any real friends?

It's you.

One of our greatest fears is that others will judge us painfully and relentlessly, but in truth, we are our own worst judges. No one will lay blame and criticism at your feet more often and more quickly than your own ego. It is your personal critic, trial judge and executioner, and it's working 24/7.

But why? Why does our ego seemingly seek to destroy us and the life we wish to live?

It wants to protect us.

Strange, right? Our ego's primary purpose is to help us understand the people and the world around us. It works on a pain bias, which means that it knows that we humans are pleasure-seeking and pain-avoiding creatures. So the best way to keep us safe is to create a world for us that is ruled by fear and disappointment. Our ego's rationale is that less risk equates to our being more accepted, a greater sense of belonging and, ultimately, higher contentment. The ego loves to rejoice in our self-pity, which it takes as a sign of a job well done.

"Stay small," it says. "Don't be a tall poppy! Don't try. Listen to me—I'm here to help you."

If your ego has an Achilles heel, it's that it is very young and naive. For most of us, the ego acts and sounds like a young child or an adolescent. It sees the world as a big, dangerous playground or the daunting hallways of your high school. Some of us have an ego that sounds like a parent or caregiver who scolds us into compliance, using the same tone and phrases we heard years ago.

Don't. Fall. For. It.

Today, put your ego in its place at the back of your mind. Notice its tone and vocabulary and be aware of the messages it sends you. Be conscious of its purpose and choose for yourself how you wish to live your life.

Heed D.H. Lawrence's words in "Self Pity":

I never saw a wild thing
sorry for itself.
A small bird will drop frozen dead from a bough
without ever having felt sorry for itself.

March 25

"Always" and "never" are extremes and absolutes I am training myself to remove from my vocabulary. I hadn't realized that these two words have given me years of shortcuts and surface-level living that have become deeply unsatisfying.

I used to think they made it simpler to decide, to let go, to move on. Then someone I was dating kissed another. I believed in absolutes at that time—"I would *never* love someone who would do that—*never*." But I *did* love them. They kissed another and I still loved them. I had to come to terms with the grey areas within that reality. I chose to be uncomfortable and forgiving because I wanted the relationship more. That was a turning point in my life that gave me way more options and more of what I wanted.

"Never" and "always" give us a false sense of security. Yet these absolutes exist only in our own minds. When we stay rigid, the world will crush us in order to make us move. Critical illness, death, divorce, scandal and job loss are the life events that usually force us to our knees. I would rather learn to bend.

Consider letting go of your rigidity. We all have it—it's embedded in our human design—and words like "never" and "always" show us where.

🌸 March 26

Living lightly is a paradox—"a seemingly absurd or self-contradictory proposition that, when investigated or explained, may prove to be well founded or true" (thank you, Google Dictionary, for that definition). Living lightly often requires us to go deep, slow down, have intentionality and practise patience. How ironic.

In my childhood, we leased our cars, rented our houses, moved every few years and made new friends. I learned to adapt, to be flexible, quick-minded and quick-witted. I made friends quickly. I didn't learn a lot about commitment, long-term planning, deepening relationships, tradition or honing a craft, and yet these were the things I wanted most in my life.

By learning to live with paradoxes, we become effective at dealing with the world's complexity and wholeness. Courses in leadership and organizational design use paradoxes to encourage people to stretch out and think more inclusively and creatively. Think of the concept of yin and yang—the opposing yet complementary forces that, according to Chinese philosophy, form a dynamic whole.

To live lightly, become *more* attached to people and places. Rely upon traditions and routines, care about what happens next time, next year or in a hundred years. This will bring us great satisfaction and peace.

✳ March 27

In Afrikaans, a language spoken by some in South Africa, a common response to "thank you" is "pleasure," pronounced "pleh-zhah." I found it delightful. Pleasure is one of the six best customer-service words, according to CBS MoneyWatch, and employee training at Chick-fil-A includes saying "My pleasure," a bit of elevated language that is part of the company's culture.

Whenever I hear or read the word, I remember the time I spent visiting South Africa, and I feel light and tingly in my heart. Do you have a word that does that for you?

Researchers at the University of Vermont and the University of Adelaide asked people to rate words for their happiness quotient. The top ten were these:

> laughter
> happiness
> love
> happy
> laughed
> laugh
> laughing
> excellent
> laughs
> joy

The next ten were these:

> successful
> win
> rainbow
> smile
> won

pleasure
smiled
rainbows
winning
celebration

Take time today to consider the impact of words, and choose happy words to feel a boost.

March 28

I believe that the deeper our roots, the more freely we can live.

For some of us, roots mean the house we grew up in, a person who helped raise us or a particular place. Roots help us feel safe and grounded, and they lay the foundation upon which our entire life is based.

In Hindu tradition, there are seven main energy centres in the body called "chakras," which are located between the base of the spine and the top of the head. Each has unique characteristics and is associated with its own colour. The first of these is the root chakra, located at the base of the spine and linked with the colour red. The root chakra represents our sense of feeling grounded and safe, as well as our relationships to tribe, belonging and money.

A weak root chakra—the most common point of weakness for most of us—makes it difficult to commit. Strengthening the root chakra is seen as a way to deal successfully with issues concerning money, security, family and belonging, and to delve deeper into personal growth and healing. And the good news is that we can accomplish this with small steps taken in a single day.

Everyone can strengthen their roots and balance their first chakra by connecting to Mother Earth. Deborah King, Deepak Chopra and Seane Corn are just a few of the many master teachers of chakra healing.

Walking in nature—especially barefoot, if possible—is a perfect way to clear the first chakra. Playing with the colour red—wearing red clothing, eating red foods, having red flowers and red jewellery, to name a few—sets a deliberate intention to strengthen the root chakra. Thinking, saying and writing a first-chakra affirmation, such as "I am safe" or "I am grounded," further strengthen the rebalancing.

The more rooted we feel, the easier it becomes to commit. Putting down roots might entail opening a business in our hometown, giving people a lot of time to come around after an argument, or sponsoring a local team or a community award. It might mean making our family name visible in the community with a plaque in the library or by running for civic office. It might mean renting out our home while we travel or live somewhere else, and then returning to it.

Tapping into the power of roots and being a visible part of a community is where building a legacy starts. And legacy is very powerful—for us, for future generations and for the community. Living our dream lives and being our best selves can start with the colour red today.

✸ March 29

I'd like to make you aware of something that is in short supply in our day-to-day lives: kindness. As with all other expressions of genuine care and compassion, kindness begins with the way we see ourselves. And in judging ourselves, there are two fundamental questions we can ask: "Are we kind?" and "Are we worthy of kindness?"

Chances are you'll answer the second question more easily than the first, believing that you are worthy of other peoples' nurturing and consideration—that you are generally a good person and deserving of kindness. And I imagine that, for most of us, this is true. The first question is harder to answer and be honest about. Are you kind? To be kind means much more than doing things for others, and it has nothing to do with popular multilevel-marketing slogans such as "givers get."

To be kind is both a state of mind and a deliberate course of action. A kind mind is an open mind. It is clear and present and is attuned to ourselves *and* to others. With a kind mind I can work to surface and challenge my unconscious biases and prejudices. I can tame my hubris to coax and heal all of my thoughts of rescuing, superiority and inferiority, and indifference. A kind mind melts our narcissism, causing us to pivot from needing to be seen and acknowledged for our kindness, to embracing the impact we can have on another person's life with our actions. A kind mind is collaborative, not protective. A kind mind lets us see ourselves in the faces of all others.

If only we were all willing to think kindly about ourselves and everyone else, I believe that our world would change fundamentally. Changing our mindset is really that powerful. But thinking kindly on its own would not make our world a kinder place to live. Actions—specifically, kind actions—are necessary to build on our change in thinking and turn our world into a kinder reality. Actions are our intentions put into motion. In my view, the most impactful actions are those we offer every day—and they are simple and lightly kind. Smiling; saying "thank you" and "hello"; listening; doing small, unasked-for favours—these are all light and easy actions that move and grow the energy of kindness forward.

Today, all I invite you to do is one kind action.

March 30

A few years ago, Google conducted a two-year study called Project Aristotle, in the hopes of cracking the code for what makes workplace teams collaborative and highly effective. The finding that interested me most, as reported in the *Harvard Business Review* in August 2017, was this: "Highest-performing teams have one thing in common: psychological safety, the belief that you won't be punished when you make a mistake." It occurred to me that psychological safety must be present in all of our group relationships, including those with our families and friends, if we are to feel like we belong.

How do we recognize psychological safety? By evaluating how threatening or rewarding it is to take interpersonal risks in a relationship or a group environment. Are new ideas welcome and built upon, or are they picked apart and ridiculed? Are others supportive, or do they embarrass or punish us for offering a different point of view or for admitting we don't understand something?

In groups with high levels of psychological safety, members are willing to share information and ideas. They thrive on learning, discuss mistakes openly, and ask for and receive feedback. And they experiment.

Does this describe your family or your circle of friends? Are you someone who craves belonging to a group that feels and behaves this way? How much of our daily stress is due to having few, if any, places or communities where we truly feel like we can grow and take risks? How much of our heaviness is caused by fear of being embarrassed— or worse, shamed—by others?

I wish someone had suggested to me when I was younger that the way my friends made me feel was an indicator of whether I was psychologically safe, and that this was the best litmus test in choosing friends. Or that as a parent, if I wanted to know whether the family I had a hand in creating was psychologically safe, all I had had to do was look around to see whether all its members felt as though they could make—and talk about—mistakes, share new ideas, learn and grow. I wish someone had shared with me that, in addition to attraction, intimacy would be guaranteed with any romantic partner with whom I felt psychologically safe.

I really wish someone had told me all of this.

I really wish someone had told me.

✳ March 31

Today is the last day of this month. Pause for a moment to reflect on the last thirty-one days of your life. How did they go? Was the month a blur? Did you feel like these last thirty-one days got away from you, or were you able to wrangle them in day by day, week by week, ensuring that they aligned more closely with the intention you had set at the beginning of the month?

What was easy for you this month? Where were you challenged? Can you recall the flow of energy—*your* energy—this month? Were there days and weeks when you felt tight and heavy? Were there moments when you felt light? Was there anything you felt too emotionally invested in this month, something you would like to create more space for in the coming month? And what was drawing you closer to yourself over the last thirty-one days?

Reflect with honesty.

Learn with compassion.

Listen with curiosity.

Steep in all of this today and tonight, and before you lay your head down, speak your intention for the next thirty days.

April

April 1

Let's begin with a fresh sheet of paper. Write down, in a simple sentence, your intention for this month (the one you spoke out loud last night). Try beginning with an "I" statement and use active language, as in "I discover new ways to be in nature every week this month" or "I enjoy a close, deep conversation with my best friend once this month."

Set your intention—only one—and then focus your mind on being in delight and curiosity and ask for its help in achieving your intention.

You are alive with a deliberate, heartfelt intention for the next thirty days.

April 2

If you are looking for new inspiration or want to spark your creativity, try switching hands to write.

Our non-dominant hand lets us access the "inner child" living inside each of us. Bestselling author John Bradshaw coined the term "inner child," and today it's a core modality in therapy that we learn to be a good parent to our own inner child so that we balance its creativity, exuberance and energy with the boundaries, love and care that come with being a healthy adult.

We all know when we or someone else is being run by the inner child. Temper tantrums, out-of-control behaviours, lack of boundaries or limits, and emotional outbursts are just a few indications that the inner child is in charge!

When our inner child is nurtured and protected and encouraged through acts of self-love and self-care, we are dialed into our most authentic self—connected to great wisdom, our purpose and our joy. Our "little" is safe.

On a sheet of paper, write a greeting and a question that you would like more insight into, then switch to your non-dominant hand to answer it. Ignore the clumsiness and the extra effort it takes to write, and you will start to see answers flow. The language and length will be at a toddler level, yet the depth and quality of the messages will surprise you. Remember to thank "little" and even write "I love you" if you can.

While you ride the excitement of a new source of inspiration, wisdom and creativity inside of you, you will start to care about your inner child, and that is where the incredible journey really starts—the journey to becoming your own good parent. Whether this is a new concept or familiar to you, a positive relationship with "little" leads to peaceful, balanced and empowered living.

❇ April 3

Being on this journey of living lightly brings us into an awareness of two different perspectives that work in tandem. I call them the "short game" and the "long game." Our short game is measured in moments, and it invites us to bring ourselves fully, with all our presence and awareness, to what is right in front of us, around us and within us. Our short game is about our feelings, our senses and our actions.

Our short game is won by immersing ourselves experientially. It teaches us immediate lessons about who we are because it surfaces reactions, mostly unconscious, that we can hold up or step out of, thinking about them and changing or adapting to what supports us and shedding whatever holds us back. In our short game we are facing forward, our bodies in motion—also forward—and our hearts open and ready to feel.

Our long game is measured in months, even years, and it invites us to engage our far-sightedness while looking both ahead and behind. Our long game is about our ability to see patterns, transitions, objectives, celebrations and challenges.

Our long game is won through our objectivity and honesty as we take in not only the times of forward momentum but the periods of stalling and stuckness. Our long game is about developing our gifts of compassion and acceptance as we see ourselves as part of a whole—all of us travelling. In our long game, we are paused, standing where we can see all the way to the horizon, or from the bottom of a deep valley or from atop the highest peak. Our eyes are narrowed, our mind is active, our heart is open and we breathe deeply.

Today I invite you to observe, experience and become aware of the intertwined dance of your short and long games.

✳ April 4

Today I invite you to find a comfortable place to sit—one where you can place your feet firmly on the ground. Tilt your pelvis slightly forward and gently straighten your spine, imagining that your spine and back are growing upwards. In a relaxed way, bring your shoulders back, expanding your chest and rib cage, and start to take a deep breath in through your nose.

At the peak of your inhalation, start to breathe out through your mouth steadily and evenly until your lungs feel completely empty. Now take in another breath through your nose, and when your lungs feel almost at their capacity, roll your breath out through your mouth.

Repeat this cycle of slow, easy, deep, rounded breathing for five more breaths. Let your shoulders sink, relax the muscles around your eyes, open your mouth and softly move your lower jaw as wide as it will open.

Imagine that you are sinking, sinking, sinking into the chair and that your feet are becoming one with the ground. Your sit bones and your tailbone are moving downward into the chair. Now, in a rolling, clockwise motion, press your feet into the ground so that all parts of your feet make contact. You are disappearing into the chair every time you inhale and sinking lower towards the ground every time you exhale.

Now bring your focus into your mind. Imagine your mind is a house with many rooms. Starting with the room farthest away, and being slow yet deliberate, close the door to each room until you have arrived at the front door of your mind's house. Breathe steadily and evenly, inhaling and exhaling gently, noticing how much lighter you feel as each door closes and you arrive at the front door.

Pause here, just for a moment. Five more breaths.

Now open the front door and take in the fresh air—the day that you see in front of you. Use all of your awareness to feel this day—the sounds, the smells, the temperature on your skin. Pause here for a moment longer. Four more breaths.

Gently turn your attention to the front door. Pull the door closed, leaving everything that was in your mind behind you as you stand on the front step, looking outward. Pause here for three more breaths.

Gently and lightly stand up from your chair and greet your day.

❀ April 5

How well are you sleeping? Sleep has a huge impact on our everyday performance and our long-term health. Our body is naturally designed for sleep, so if we can manage the ways in which our lifestyle tries to interfere with it, we can help ourselves get back to our natural rhythms.

I like these questions posed by Dr. Frank Lipman on the *MindBodyGreen* blog, because they clearly remind me that the quality of my sleep is important to my overall health. My stomach churns when I read them because of their potential impact.

- Do you wake up feeling tired rather than energized?
- Do you need coffee or some other form of caffeine to wake up?
- Do you find that you don't have enough energy to get through the day comfortably without the use of sugar, caffeine or other stimulants?

When we sleep well, we wake up feeling clear and centred, both emotionally and physically, in a fresh neutral or open state. I want to wake up feeling that way every day, don't you?

Our bodies rely on two sleep systems to make sure we get a proper night's rest. The first, the circadian rhythm, is our body's biological clock, the tool it uses to sync our body functions with environmental cues such as light and sounds. The second, the homeostatic drive, is what makes us feel sleepy at night and wakeful in the morning by releasing cortisol and melatonin into the bloodstream. We have four stages of sleep, each lasting about ninety minutes and all necessary.

When we don't sleep well, our moods, judgments, decision making, focus, patience and even hand-eye coordination are not working fully. Not getting enough sleep could be linked to the buildup of certain proteins in the brain that are linked to such problems as Alzheimer's disease and other neurological issues. A recent report by the Centers for Disease Control and Prevention found that one in three American adults does not get the recommended minimum of seven hours of sleep. (Seven to nine hours each night is ideal, according to the National Sleep Foundation.) Between fifty and seventy million people have trouble sleeping, and most of us know someone who is taking a sleep aid, whether prescribed or over the counter (the number of prescriptions is on the rise).

Our bodies need sleep to reset our brains. Sleep flushes out waste products called metabolites that build up in our brains during the day.

There are many wonderful resources we can tap for help. For starters, here are some tips I've learned from Dr. Lipman.

I am turning off sources of "blue light" (from fluorescent and

LED bulbs to computer and cellphone screens) an hour before bed, because this sort of light sends the same signals to the brain as sunlight, blocking production of melatonin, the hormone that tells the brain to go to sleep. I'm also dimming the lights in the evening because this helps produce melatonin—one of my new best friends.

I am aiming for a room temperature between 60 and 68 degrees Fahrenheit, which is ideal for sleeping. Dr. Lipman also suggests a warm bath—when you get out of the tub, your body temperature drops, which promotes sleep. I don't always have time for a bath, but I can dial down the thermostat.

I read a few pages as part of my bedtime ritual; it helps me wind down. And I go to bed and wake up at around the same time each day, setting a pattern so that my body expects to go to sleep at a certain time.

Whenever possible, I take a short afternoon nap (ideally for twenty minutes between 1 and 3 p.m.), not as a sleep replacement, but as an afternoon reviver. Our performance naturally declines through the day, and a nap can reset us.

It makes me hopeful to know that our bodies want to sleep well and are *designed* to sleep well. It also feels gentle for me to pay attention to my sleep ritual to help my mood, energy and overall well-being.

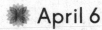 April 6

According to a poll conducted in 2007 by CBS News, 30 percent of us have stopped speaking to a sibling for a time. Could you be one of these people? If so, is this just a temporary break from your brother or sister, or have you been separated for quite a long time? How do you really feel about being distant from your sibling? Whichever one of you is right or wrong is not important; I'm asking how you feel about the time that has passed without that person in your life. And what reason lies at ground zero to prevent you or your sibling(s) from reaching across that divide to mend the fence?

The saying "We don't choose our family" is almost a cliché, but it supports the notion that we are born into family bonds, and these are often painful and restrictive to our individual development. We are typecast in a role within our family structure and its drama, and despite our efforts to grow beyond the limits of that role, our family either triggers the old behaviours in us or refuses to see us as different from our traditional role.

So you either fight for your independence, conform or live in some type of limbo, being your true self outside of the family and reluctantly stepping back into your role at every family gathering.

Every family has at least one truth teller. Often scorned and ridiculed, even labelled as the "problem child," the truth teller sees the reality and insanity of the family. Maybe you are your family's truth teller and you're sitting on the outside now because everyone else is complacent and complicit in keeping the family drama thriving. Or perhaps you are the brother or sister whose sibling is telling you that the family is sick and needs healing—that being in the family is painful and limiting—and you're the one who doesn't want this to change.

I find it hard to believe that 30 percent of us think a familial relationship is beyond healing. The path towards getting back together may be a difficult one, and what you hear and experience may rock your world, but we don't truly heal without the fire of honesty.

Today I invite you to think of a fiery, honest, loving truth you would be willing to share with your sibling. A truth so powerful, it is undeniable and inarguable. It is your truth, and its intent is to build a bridge across the divide.

April 7

Sometimes the best way to learn something is to teach it to someone else. I observed this the other day when I picked up a copy of *Harry Potter and the Chamber of Secrets*. Our daughter had started to read the novel and was inspired to start writing and imagining her own fantastical plots and creatures. I noticed I was struggling in our conversations to drop into the dreaming and imagining world she could so easily see—I was lodged firmly in the practical day-to-day of being a parent and an adult.

At her invitation, I embarked with her on a project in which each of us took turns writing scenes for a book. While her ideas were dreamlike and her creatures whimsical, mine were quite logical and obvious. Yet she was looking to me to guide her and help build momentum for our project. And sometimes she would get stuck and ask me to help her with her writing.

That's when I decided I needed to learn how to write in a different style, and for me that meant immersing myself in J.K. Rowling's writing. I realized that in order to show my daughter she could write in a style like Rowling's, I needed to also write in that style. I needed to share with her not only that it *could* be done, but *how* it could be accomplished.

I imagined that each of us was climbing a mountain of our own, and from my mountain I could see what was ahead of her on her climb. I am now able to teach her because, on the one hand, I can see the challenges she is facing, while on the other, I have my own experience of overcoming similar challenges.

Teaching others what we ourselves are learning deepens our understanding and felt sense of that knowledge. Teaching is more than passing on tips or strategies; it is about using skills and ideas to build new connections and thoughts to pass on to someone else in ways that suit their hunger to learn.

What are you in the midst of learning right now? What is it that you truly wish to learn but are anxious about beginning?

If you hunger to learn, then teach. I promise that you will learn much more deeply.

April 8

Walking barefoot on earth is good for the soul.

Walking barefoot on earth—on natural surfaces such as soil, grass or sand—is called "earthing," and Dr. Isaac Eliaz has written that it has become "a scientifically researched practice [that] restores the natural relationship between our body and the electrons in the earth."

Do you walk barefoot on earth?

It feels good to stretch beyond norms of acceptable barefoot practices, beyond temperature, weather, workdays and other people's reactions, to experience this gift more often.

I love the feeling of soft pine needles on my bare feet. I love stepping lightly on damp, green, spongy moss. Standing barefoot on rock, especially if warmed by the sun, is soothing. Fresh grass feels amazing, and I have taken my shoes off in the city to enjoy a patch of green for a moment. Bare feet and hot sand is a decadent combo. Sometimes I walk barefoot in dirt or mud, and I revel in the pleasure of allowing my feet to get dirty. The more I walk barefoot, the more aware I am of my feet inside my shoes, wanting to be rid of the barrier keeping them from the earth. Feet are one of the most nerve-rich parts of our body.

How amazing that we can recharge ourselves by absorbing earth energy through our feet whenever we want. Today I invite you to walk barefoot on the earth (regardless of temperature!).

April 9

Hello sadness, anger, disappointment and fear, my old friends.

Does that sound odd to your ear? That I would hold these feelings as so familiar that I welcome them? Did you read the words and automatically fold them into the melody of the 1964 Simon and Garfunkel song "The Sound of Silence"?

Maybe try reading the opening line again with that melody in mind. Do the notes and metre change the meaning of the words for you in any way? Does it make them more acceptable?

As pleasure-seeking, pain-avoiding beings, we spend a great deal of our lives contending with many forms of painful, negative feelings, yet so few of us truly accept these feelings—or understand the importance of embracing them for our well-being. The generally held belief is that we need to avoid any and all pain, and move away from it as far as we can, lest it return.

New research reveals, however, that those of us who work through and accept our painful feelings live more lightly, with greater mental resilience and stronger psychological health. In a series of experiments conducted by researchers at the University of Toronto, participants who were able to talk freely about their sadness, fear, anger or disappointment were also more likely to report that they felt their mental health was strong and enduring.

"Maybe if you have an accepting attitude toward negative emotions, you're not giving them as much attention," speculates Dr. Iris Mauss, an associate professor of psychology at the University of California, Berkeley, and a senior author of the study. "And perhaps, if you're constantly judging your emotions, the negativity can pile up."

So it's now clear that where our painful feelings are concerned, we no longer need to "just suck it up," "swallow it down," "run it off," "work it out," "sleep it off" or "drown it out"; we only need to say it, own it and feel it, and accept it.

Say it: *"I am feeling so sad right now."*
Own it: *"I am full of sadness in this moment."*
Feel it: *Crying, sobbing, wailing and moaning.*
Accept it: *"I have so much sadness inside of me that I am moving through."*

Did you notice that in the list above, the first letters of each line combine to spell the acronym SOFA? I've done that so you'll remember that your painful feelings are always a comfortable, nurturing, safe place for you to come to and experience.

✹ April 10

Often when my partner speaks, I react defensively. I do this even though our love is deep and we've been together for a long time. I react before I think. I get super-emotional. I take what is said personally. It is exhausting for both of us.

I do this because I feel safe with my partner. Time and again, I have been listened to, endured and forgiven. If I cross the line, my partner will come back around to tell me I've breached the boundaries. But I am rarely interrupted, never judged and always forgiven. My partner is living one of the four agreements contained in Don Miguel Ruiz's famous book of the same name. And that agreement is: "Don't take anything personally."

I am well behaved with friends, at work and even with total strangers. It is with those closest to me that my true self—along with all I hold in and hide—comes out. With some people, like family members, I reinforce their stories of me when I act out, although they may not realize the stories they hold about me or that their love can be conditional. Unconditional love, empathy and kindness come when my partner sees *through* my behaviour and my feelings, sees this is *not* who I am and sees they can provide me with comfort. That is unconditional love, and I am so grateful for the relief it gives me. I feel safe and protected and accepted as I shed complex feelings of shame.

Receiving unconditional love is teaching me how to offer the same. I am practising allowing the people I love to be frustrated and impatient, angry and sad, and to turn their words towards me while I hear them, uninterrupted. It is hard for me to do this because my defences are still so automatic, but my love is strong and I am safe, and I have this gift to offer.

Here's what Dr. Abigail Brenner had to say in an article for *Psychology Today* in 2014: "Some say a good visual is to imagine yourself in the middle of a meadow with a white picket fence surrounding it. That's your space. No one is permitted within it unless you allow them to enter into it."

As I practise holding space, people come closer to me, rewarding me with their lightness, their closeness, their willingness to share their innermost thoughts and feelings with me. What a gift—to give and receive unconditional love. We both feel lightness of being.

The people closest to us fight with us because they feel safe with us. (I'm not talking about strangers or abusers or people in higher authority.) Holding space for another is one of the most beautiful gifts we have to offer.

I invite you to pick a person or an animal from whom you receive unconditional love. Notice how they listen to you, how their love for you is unwavering as you let all of yourself show. Give them unconditional love today and let it be a beginning for you.

🌸 April 11

Can we talk about overwhelm today? It seems so many of us feel this way, as if it's just a fact of our modern life. We face all kinds of pressures from our families, our jobs, our friends, our partners, bill collectors, marketers—the list goes on and on.

And sometimes our reaction to all these competing pressures is to get angry, run away from them or procrastinate, hoping they will disappear. Did you notice the words I chose in that last sentence—"angry," "run," "procrastinate"? What do they make you think of? How about fight, flight and freeze—the three primary reactions we have to fear?

So many self-help books and blogs tiptoe around this fundamental reality—that our first reactions to stress are the same as our reactions to fear—offering "simple tips" to deal with the things that are causing us stress without helping us deal with our fear. If we can find healthy ways to process our fear and move through it, I think many of our life's stresses would lighten and in many cases cease to be stressful. By becoming better at feeling our fear, I believe we develop more capacity to handle stress, thus keeping ourselves from feeling overwhelmed.

The best strategies for managing fear all involve three basic elements: breathing, rational assessment and action. When we are afraid, the feeling centres of our brains—the limbic region—send signals to our lungs and chest muscles, which create rapid, shallow breaths. We need this style of breathing for running and fighting. It is also much easier to hold short breaths when we need to freeze and disappear. Taking deep, long breaths when we're afraid floods our bodies with oxygen, naturally creating relaxation.

Rational assessment means we use our ability to examine our reality and compare it to the level of fear we are feeling. If, for instance, you are feeling a great deal of stress-based fear, a red-alert level, because you have a work project to finalize or you have people coming over for dinner, you may want to breathe, then assess. Ask yourself: Is this situation really life-threatening, or am I in impending personal danger? It may feel as though the latter is true, but you have to be fully rational and ask yourself whether it really *is* true. If the answer is no, then it's important that you start talking yourself down. Talking ourselves down is an example of taking an action. Actions are critical because they reinforce our deep, unconscious belief that we can and will take care of ourselves. Overwhelm is a feature of all our lives, and when we see that our fear is the force that makes overwhelm a painful experience, we take the first step towards letting the wind out of overwhelm's sails.

❋ April 12

"You think too much."

That's what my best friend in high school told me one day. Her words hit my mind like a blinding light. Upon hearing them, I couldn't think of anything else. I was shocked, for sure, yet what she said rang true: I *did* think too much.

Looking back, I saw that the thinking I was predominantly overdoing was the circular, repetitive, mental rumination that comes with worry and anxiety.

There are many ways we can think, of which worrying is only one. I realized I was putting too much energy into this type of thinking and little or no effort into thinking reflectively or critically, or even visioning. All forms of thought have the effect of producing both feelings and more thinking. Worrying creates stress and fear; critical thought creates contentment and purpose; reflection creates openness and lightness.

So you see, thinking "too much" is really not the issue. It is when we tip the balance of our thinking towards only *one* form of thought that we experience an issue. Cognition is one of our many great gifts as human beings, and it is part of our purpose in life to work the many different muscles of our thinking to become well-rounded, balanced and light beings.

✹ April 13

According to the University of Calgary's Energy Education website, resistance and friction are forces that cause energy to be lost. This is a powerful analogy for our personal lives.

Today I was resisting my partner—unfortunately, a common occurrence. We were talking about something fairly mundane, and I noticed that I was questioning, suggesting and advising . . . then arguing and defending. I suddenly felt very tired of this same pattern. I stopped talking in mid-sentence because I was unclear about why I had such a strong opinion. I wondered, "Why am I exerting so much of my precious energy on this topic?" I noticed that my emotions were out of proportion to the topic.

I took a deep breath and said, "I am going to stop talking now. I care about something, but it isn't actually what we are talking about. When I am clear, I'd like to come back and talk to you about it. For now, I trust what you are doing and I don't need to be involved."

Wow. I felt so powerful in that moment! I let go and I felt space inside that hadn't been there the moment before.

I had become used to resisting as a way to keep myself safe from change and taking risks. I do it subtly, and I come across as a perfectionist, controlling and overinvolved. Lately my resistance has been expanding to keep those I love from change and taking risks too. Not as subtle.

Resistance can be sneaky and unconscious. It isn't always as obvious as "no." Sometimes it is covered up by behaviours like mine— criticizing my partner. It can also take the form of procrastination, sudden food cravings or fatigue.

I may resist people who want to talk, especially seniors and children, when I am pressed for time or distracted. When I find myself in a battle, trying to escape or being distracted while someone is talking to me, my breathing is shallow and I am impatient. I am in resistance. Resistance doesn't feel good. And as the famed psychiatrist Carl Jung said, "What you resist not only persists, but will grow in size."

It takes so much of our energy to resist, and yet, as Elisha Goldstein wrote on the website Mindful.org in September 2014, resistance is our default setting. We don't always know we are resisting, and it is always linked to fear. But resistance also offers an opportunity to get clear about what truly matters to us. Yes, I am resisting. Yes, I must be afraid of something. What is it I care about and want to protect in this moment? Answer that question and it will become crystal clear what you value most, always honourable and sacred and deserving.

The instant I stopped and questioned my resistance in the conversation with my partner, I felt relief and space. I was pleasantly surprised to discover that what I wanted was not only reasonable, but honourable and loving, and most of all it wasn't in conflict with my partner at all.

Our resistance wants to be heard, and once it is, it lets us go. Find your resistance today. Observe yourself resisting the people you care most about and pause. Stop talking, take a breath, look at them and give them the moment. You don't need to know why—you'll figure that out later—and you don't need to tell the person what you are doing. A moment of release will give you a deep sense of power and peace that will carry through your day.

🌸 April 14

How are you at receiving care and nurturing? We all need to love and be loved, and most of us work hard to put other people's needs ahead of our own to make sure they feel loved. But how open are you when someone tries to love you back? How willing are you to be loved, cared for and nurtured?

I've met people who believe that love is in short supply or that it will hurt them in some way, so they receive love gingerly or reluctantly, anticipating the moment when love will cause them pain or be taken away suddenly and forever. I've met men and women who hoard love, taking every single morsel of attention and affection that comes their way because they have learned that love isn't always available. I've also met people who keep a love ledger in their minds, tracking how much care and nurturing they have received from people in their lives and giving the same amount of love in return—these are people who have learned that love must be reciprocal and equal.

Who showed you how to receive love? Are you more like your mother? Your father? A sibling or caregiver? Do you prefer relationships where the love is freely flowing, or do you feel more familiar and comfortable in relationships where you receive more love than you offer, or where you love more openly than your partner? Which way do you prefer the love balance to be tipped?

We can love and be loved openly. We can nurture and be nurtured with ease. We are able to care and be cared for with comfort and gratitude. We are all born ready to receive and needing to receive love and to connect—our very survival depends on this. In those first few moments of life, love has no rules or guidelines for us. But gradually the people around us teach us about love—their rules and ways and preferences—and we learn that love has conditions.

And one day, perhaps today, we begin to question those conditions, and we start to unravel the rules we have been taught and have simply accepted as truth. We begin to recognize our needs, and we are compelled to find ways to receive and give love the way we really feel love.

We are on a journey back to our own innocence.

April 15

In order to engage in the world in a direct and practical way, it is essential that we stay healthy and grounded.
—Ariel Kusby, *Garden Collage* magazine, March 2017

In the moments when I am most balanced, peaceful and productive, I also feel grounded. "Grounded" is a popular term. For me, it means my awareness is in my centre, literally in my core, and lower—my root and my legs feel activated. I can picture and am aware of my feet— how they feel inside my shoes and the texture of the ground. Being grounded in my body is so important to my feeling happy and being physically and emotionally safe, because it means I am also self-aware and spatially balanced vis-à-vis other people and things. I have forward momentum and am conscious of my own emotional energy and what belongs to others. Pretty key to having a good day!

It is easy for me not to be grounded or to be "in my head." I am wired that way. I know when I am in my head because the top of my head and sometimes my face tingles. I can feel light-headed—unclear, foggy, even dizzy. I am off balance, both emotionally and physically. Sometimes too much caffeine puts me in this state, as well as too much email or screen time.

You know what it's like to talk with someone who is in their head . . . their eyes are vacant or far away, they aren't really listening and they're easily distracted. There's not a lot of them available for you to connect with, and it can be very unfulfilling to try. When someone is ungrounded, they ignore or can be slow to respond to a distraction, and it really throws them off to try to return to their task. By contrast, people who are grounded may be intensely focused on something, to the point that they may not hear us approach, but they will immediately snap out of it to respond to us.

I can be really grounded or really ungrounded while watching a movie. If I'm grounded, I am in my body, likely sitting up, alert, aware of my surroundings and the people I am with, as well as the movie. When I'm ungrounded, I am staring, I'm thinking about other things and I'm likely lying down. My energy is lower.

When I want to get grounded, I eat things like nuts, carrots or meat—foods I have to chew down hard on. I stomp my feet on the ground. A trick that works well for me is to place one hand on top of my head and the other on my tummy while I am walking or stomping. It kind of "caps" the energy I want to contain within myself. Getting exercise is another great way to get grounded.

Being grounded is an optimal state for all of us to be in, and it helps explain why some interactions are unproductive or unsatisfying if one or both people are in an ungrounded state. There is little point in my trying to get their attention, because they will not really be there. Best to come back when they are fully with me.

Choose to be grounded today, and choose grounded people to be with whenever possible. You will have better interactions with people and the world, and especially with yourself.

✸ April 16

The news can be particularly bleak some days. When there simply seems to be too much chaos and upset in the world, how do you take it all in? My partner and I have very different strategies. I am selective, choosing to follow only certain stories and events as they develop. I like to be deep in a news story, appreciating all of the nuances and connections, and I do this while disregarding many other events that happen in the world. I'll follow a protest over oil drilling rights on a First Nations territory but ignore a refugee migration or a famine. I'm aware that these events happen in the world, but I know I can't possibly be fully engaged with everything, and that to try to do so would leave me overwhelmed and stunned. My way leaves me feeling slightly incomplete and, honestly, a bit ashamed that I can't absorb more.

My partner also feels overwhelmed by current events and chose a few years ago to not watch the news at all, preferring to engage instead with friends and family and hear what they are following—what's important to them—to learn what is happening in the world.

I think we have both come to a place where we feel as though our sense of hope for the world would be lost if we somehow had to take in more news than we can handle. Have you felt this way? Does hope seem elusive or scarce to you in the face of what you see and read? What approach seems to work best for you?

What I know to be true is that hope, like love, is infinite. There is hope everywhere, from the deeply personal moments we have within us to what we experience and observe in the world around us. I also feel the truth of balance, which means I know that pain, desperation and suffering live alongside joy, inspiration and hope. But sometimes I forget these truths. Sometimes, unconsciously, I find myself heading into a labyrinth of bad news and I forget that hope is the thread I hold, helping me find my way out of the darkness.

To grasp the thread is to accept that pain lives with joy, people can behave in both good and bad ways, and love and hope are infinite.

Acknowledging and accepting these truths rather than expecting that life must only be one way can lead me to change my behaviour in regards to the news. I can find a more balanced approach to taking in the information.

We can make sure we seek out stories and events that are difficult to absorb, as well as those that make us feel light and full of hope.

We can see the world as full of bad and good.

🌸 April 17

Countless studies have shown that human beings are healthier and less stressed when they are in close proximity to a plant: houseplants, science shows, increase general well-being and happiness. Succulents, philodendron and aloe are easy keeping, air purifying plants. All plants improve indoor air quality, some even remove heavy metals and toxins. Being near the soil is also helpful and healing, thanks to microbes in the soil called "out-doorphins," that boost mood and reduce stress.
—Ariel Kusby, *Garden Collage* magazine, March 3, 2017

Do you have a plant at home or in your office?

I used to think of plants as one more thing I didn't have time for. I saw that they were alive or dead, I knew they were releasing oxygen, but I didn't value them or connect with them.

I think plants intimidate me. If I look deeper, the act of caring for a plant reflects where I am with my own self-care. I remember that the people who had plants at work usually also decorated their cubicles to feel more at home. Schools invite students to read to their plants, which melts my heart.

My years of indifference towards plants makes sense, given my low self-esteem and poor self-care habits at the time. I still struggle to make a priority of caring for myself, and though I have plants, they are outdoors. I am evolving and my heart is opening as I age. I was recently given a small glass jar of earth and moss and grass that sits on my night table. I am going to mist the plant today and give it a name, in honour of all of us and our journeys towards self-care.

❀ April 18

**Firemaking is part of the Scandinavian concept of hygge—a sort of cosiness. "For us," says Danish-born, London-based Peter Agertoft, "fire is an integral part of life." Indeed, so passionate is Agertoft, he speaks of fire-building almost as an artform.
—Jemima Sissons, *Financial Times*, December 2016**

I feel blessed to have been taught the basics of how to make a fire, and I have much more to learn. About gathering the wood—kindling and logs, split, carried and stacked. That starter wicks made of twisted paper are invitations, not guarantees. Understanding how air and fire dance together. The patience of trusting an ember. That the colours of the flames reveal where you are in their cycle of wanting more.

Making a fire is a craft, a ritual and an art that brings people together and is deeply satisfying. There are layers and layers of insights and observations, practices and perspectives when it comes to building a fire. Every time I walk through our wood room, I feel protected by moss-covered guardians; the energy is palpable and I remember how rewarding it was to carry and stack the logs.

"Carefully crafted fires give a sense of calm, and as you gather around the flames, there is a code printed deep inside every human that the place is safe," Jemima Sissons writes.

Build a fire soon. Learn or teach, expand your knowledge into an expression, get into wood selection, stacking and chopping techniques.

Teach children how they can safely build a fire. You will feel proud to be connected to the miracle of fire.

✸ April 19

"What is your next step?"

This is the question I asked my client as she was finishing her story about the traumatic and conflict-ridden divorce she had just gone through. She had come to me for counselling, referred by a close friend of hers who was also a client of mine. "She tells her story to everyone," her friend shared with me. "It's always the same story, and she just tells it over and over again. Please help her."

I listened to her unfold her story, and I could hear the moments she had shared many times with others. They had a familiar tone and rhythm to them, sounding like slogans designed to reinforce her beliefs and pain. I listened to her story without interrupting, commenting or giving advice until the pauses in her speech began to appear—the places where the familiar words were running out and her feelings and reflections were settling in. I listened until the pauses became longer and longer, and finally we just looked at each other in acknowledgement—we had both experienced similar pain.

"No one lets me finish my story," she said. "You're the first person who has let me get it all out."

"You deserve to be heard," I offered. "I can hear how painful this experience was for you, and I imagine you didn't want to hold on to that pain for a moment longer."

After a long silence, she said, "I have nothing more to say."

And then I asked her, "What is your next step?"

My question invited her to look at her story and her life in that moment from the highest possible viewpoint—thirty thousand feet above, as if she could see herself and witness her life in the third person. My question was both practical and pragmatic, as well as open-ended and esoteric. I was asking her if she could see a path forward for her life, and whether she could understand what this event—the end of her marriage—meant in her life and how had it shaped her.

After reflecting, she said, "I see my life can go in any direction I want it to. I was married, I am divorced, and now I'm free to make my own life."

"What do you see right in front of you?" I asked.

"Opportunity," she said. "Opportunity and hope."

Today I invite you to take another look at this moment of challenge you may be in. Rise as high as you can so that your view of yourself and your life is as wide as it can possibly be. What perspective do you take in from this vantage point, thirty thousand feet above? What does this challenge mean to you in relation to your view of your whole life?

Ask yourself, "What is my next step?"

❀ April 20

When we cease to view shopping for and eating food as tiresome chores, we rid ourselves of an unhealthy mindset toward our daily bread. By reevaluating how we're shopping and being intentional with what we buy, food will become less of a constant battle and more of a joie de vivre.
—Gabriella Patti, *Verily*, July 14, 2017

I've become more intentional with food and grocery shopping over the last few years. While I don't love the supermarket experience and prefer farmers' markets, being intentional has added quite a bit of joy.

A wonderful article I read points to the French as being great role models for food shopping. The story lists (and elaborates on) five perspectives the French bring to food:

- Shop daily and mindfully.
- Choose quality over quantity.
- Fresh is best.
- View meals as creative rituals.
- Shopping goes hand in hand with walking.

Before spending four days at a wonderful family cottage—tiny and accessible only by boat—we would each plan two meals and add our favourite fruits and vegetables, desserts, snacks and wine. I remember feeling a surge of joy and satisfaction as we put away the groceries we had brought, knowing exactly what I would make with each ingredient. We cooked, and then used leftovers as ingredients for the next meal, and I took great joy in watching the supplies get used. Fruits and vegetables needed to go on the counter, and I enjoyed watching the tomatoes ripen over the few days and the sight of the produce displayed in the same bowl. I focused more on ingredients we loved, trusting that meals would emerge.

A dish of nuts was always out. There would be vanilla ice cream, with the toppings changing from day to day. A wire basket of eggs sat on a red checkered cloth. All so heartwarming, harking back to my grandmother and my dear friend from Trinidad, both of whom also favoured shopping daily and locally.

At the end of the four days, we packed up. Very little food was left over to be brought back in our cooler, and that made me feel smart and creative.

That cottage experience stayed with me, and we now shop similarly at home. I have staples at the house—flour, sugar, oats, cheeses, crackers, rice, dry pasta, granolas, different kinds of beans. When I shop, I focus entirely on choosing a meat or a sauce or a taste profile. It makes everything so simple to decide. Simplifying and separating shopping trips for staples and fresh ingredients allows me to focus on high-quality items, shop faster and get joy out of what I create. I am connected to what is in our pantry and fridge. I use my time purposefully and try to prepare one large homemade meal and one large homemade dessert to carry through our lunches for most of the week. I feel so good knowing that we are eating foods made with love.

The popularity of lovely salad jars is a great example of our growing awareness that fresh, beautiful food feeds our bodies and our souls. A January 2018 article on MyRecipes.com about the resurgence of the Mason jar refers to its "self-expressive possibilities." Each jar is "a relatively inexpensive blank canvas for customization and personalization—that [has] made it ubiquitous in millennial homes."

And don't you love the term "joie de vivre"? My food choices aren't always perfect, but I am grateful for the days when I put love and intention into them. If your relationship with food is difficult, today you can think about drinking water. Create a love affair with your water and display that love in your home. That is also joie de vivre.

🌸 April 21

I love music. I really enjoy music of all genres, and I love to discover new artists and styles as often as I can.

What interests me most about music is its ability to mirror or shift my mood and fully engage my mind. Music evokes feelings, and researchers have studied for some time how effective it is at bringing people together in a harmonized state of emotion, whether the emotion is excitement or melancholy, agitation or relaxation. We also know that music speaks powerfully to both the cognitive and emotional parts of our brains; for instance, helping those with degenerative brain diseases recover memories, or creating bridges of non-verbal, common communication for those who live with autism.

For me, music is a deliberate tool I use to help me set the tone for my day. I enjoy creating playlists of songs that help me stay in a certain state of mind or that act as a backdrop for a specific activity. I'm conscious, however, not to use music as a way to tune out of my world; rather, I look to it to help me attune or commune with whoever and whatever is around me. I prefer my music to help me become a more keen observer, rather than dulling my senses and causing me to disengage or unplug.

Sometimes the music I listen to can encourage deep reflection—the *Trouble Man* soundtrack by Marvin Gaye, or songs like "Trouble" by Ray LaMontagne or "Midnight Train to Georgia" by Gladys Knight and the Pips, can evoke closeness and connection for me.

I invite you, as an act of self-love today, to create a playlist of music that evokes lightness in you. Choose songs that put a smile on your face, make you move, deepen your breathing, stimulate your powers of observation, or even elevate your mind into daydreaming.

How many songs you include in your playlist is entirely up to you, although I would invite you to come up with at least five, or about fifteen minutes of music. Have fun with this today—you deserve this loving gesture from you to you.

April 22

Isn't it magical to consider that there is a whole web of coincidences and beauty and awarenesses right in our daily routines, just waiting to be discovered? A book on the shelf that calls to us, a name we keep seeing, a spiderweb freshly woven . . .

One way to become attuned to life is through mindfulness. There are many amazing resources to help. The five steps below, taken from a July 2017 article in *Mindful* magazine, are just one example:

- Be aware of your body.
- For a few minutes, expand your attention to sounds.
- Shift your awareness to your sense of smell.
- Now move to vision.
- Keep this open awareness of everything around you.

Advance through these five steps intuitively, and refresh through the day as you find yourself distracted. Start with a big breath in, and then exhale. Bring this expanded awareness into your meetings, conversations, writing, reading and dinners, and notice the newness flowing in. Remember: lots of breathing in between. You may want to take notes throughout the day. No need to make sense of them just yet; trust that the process is already happening inside.

Practise mindful travel between destinations, wherever and however you travel. If you are a driver or a pedestrian, look the other person in the eye to acknowledge them, even with a vehicle between you. See and be seen today, without words. Do your best to "single-task."

With strong intentions in our day, mindfulness offers us a new level of listening and awareness that fuels us as we reach towards our goals. What am I aware of, in this moment, that helps me in my intention to connect, understand, generate, create, help, comfort or appreciate? The things we notice may not be obvious or linear. In fact, important awarenesses can seem at first to be random or insignificant. These are the ones you especially need to write down!

Be open to the day and be curious about what it offers you. Mindfulness brings us to the magic in our every day.

✽ April 23

I've listened to literally thousands of people, and I can tell you honestly that you and I have many more things in common than things that set us apart.

I have to confess that, until a few years ago, I was someone who tended to notice the things that made me different from others rather than the ways we were all united. I had my own history of pain, challenges and life-defining moments, and others had theirs. I was attached—too attached—to the specifics of my life, and I would hear people share their stories through a filter of who had it worse: them or me. As a result, I found it difficult to relate to other people because no one I met had led a life exactly like mine—I was attached to the belief that relating meant finding my mirror in another. I know now that that mirror will never exist.

Relating, I have learned, is about appreciating what is universal among us. This too is a filter—one through which we see strong connections between ourselves and others based on our shared emotions. To relate means to find that place inside our own self where we have felt the same emotion as others, even if we haven't necessarily experienced the same event.

I have felt joy and elation—but have never won a lottery jackpot.
I have felt separation and loss—but have never been a refugee.
I have felt despair and grief—but do not have a terminal illness.
I have felt curiosity and wonder—but I am no longer a child.

The universal truth is that our feelings bond us. And when we hear the details of another person's life journey, it helps us to develop a deeper appreciation for them as a person rather than giving us markers for how they are different from us. We can hold them in higher esteem for what they have experienced and relate to them more profoundly for how our two journeys feel aligned.

By shifting our filter on the world from one of seeing difference to one in which we notice similarity, we also unintentionally give ourselves a deep gift of belonging. We see the truth as it has always been and always will be: we are not alone.

🌸 April 24

Have you noticed faith, spirituality and religion coming up in your conversations? Are you reflecting on faith for yourself?

My friends cite certain practices, like singing and gathering at church, as things they miss since they left their religion. I began thinking about faith as another path towards feeling peaceful and fulfilled.

Beyond my closest relationships, I still feel a longing for a connection with what I would describe as the holy part of myself. That longing has put me on a new path of spiritual reflection, and I am just getting started.

An article that ran in the British newspaper *The Guardian* in 2018 suggests I'm not unusual:

> Faith is on the rise and 84 percent of the global population identifies with a religious group. The numbers paint a current picture of faith around the world.
>
> Christians form the biggest religious group, with 2.3 billion adherents, or 31.2 percent of the total world population. Next come Muslims (1.8 billion, or 24.1 percent). The third-biggest category is 1.2 billion people in the world, or 16 percent, who say they have no religious affiliation at all. This does not mean all those people are committed atheists; some—perhaps most—have a strong sense of spirituality or belief in God, gods or guiding forces, but they don't identify with or practise an organised religion.
>
> Hindus make up 1.1 billion, or 15.1 percent, and Buddhists 500 million, or 6.9 percent.
>
> There are 400 million people who practise folk or traditional religions, or 6 percent of the global total. Adherents of lesser-practised religions, including Sikhism, Baha'i and Jainism, add up to 58 million, or well below 1 percent.
>
> There are 14 million Jews in the world, about 0.2 percent of the global population, concentrated in the US and Israel.

So many people have faith, but as the story indicates, a wide variety of belief systems exists. Interfaith dialogue—described by

Wikipedia as "cooperative, constructive and positive interaction between people of different religious traditions and/or spiritual or humanistic beliefs"—could provide a gentle, healthy place for us to pause as we reflect upon our faith.

Why not bring faith into this time of boutique, niche and curated lifestyles we are living? I can cherry-pick texts, ceremonies and rituals that I like from different religions. I can attend a service at a church, a synagogue or a mosque—or even in a forest. I can evaluate whether a religious message comes from love or fear.

What is your faith based upon? What are your personal values and beliefs? What do you believe it means to be human, and what do you believe this life is all about?

Reflecting on our faith is self-empowering. Choose messages, beliefs and practices that come from love and that you feel good about. Get clear enough that you can describe your faith to another. And appreciate that where we are today is just a single point in time on an unfolding journey.

❋ April 25

Today, I marvelled at an acorn. There are thousands of them where I live, and most of the time I step over—or on—them without much thought. Today, though, a single acorn held most of my attention. It was brought into our house by our daughter, and it sits beside me now, placed there by my partner, who said, "This will help you write." So true.

I hold this acorn in my hand as I'm thinking about what to say to you—what is important for me to say to you. I roll it in my fingers, feeling the contours of its shape, the textures, and my mind imagines how perfect its design truly is. Inside this single acorn is a seed for an oak tree, and surrounding that seed is everything it will need to begin the journey from seed to sapling to tree. There is nutrition and protection and an architecture that increases the seed's chances of working its way—or being pushed—into the soil. Once in the soil, the hard exterior of the acorn must soften and yield to the soil and also to the seed so that the latter can extend its roots into the soil and eventually become a tree.

The acorn I'm holding reminds me of Jean Giono's magical allegory "The Man Who Planted Trees." Set in the Alps in Provence during the early 1900s, the short story is an ode to impact and legacy.

> For a human character to reveal truly exceptional qualities, one must have the good fortune to be able to observe its performance over many years. If this performance is devoid of all egoism, if its guiding motive is unparalleled generosity, if it is absolutely certain that there is no thought of recompense and that, in addition, it has left its visible mark upon the earth, then there can be no mistake.

The acorn I hold in my hand makes me think of you and me, perfect at our births, with most of everything we needed to mature. Our character and our destiny are shaped by our actions and can only be fully understood over time—a long time.

You and I, like this acorn I hold, are in the process of becoming.

April 26

Why does society push me to buy services and goods instead of doing things by hand? Why am I rushed to the point that I don't have a chance to absorb what is happening in my life? Today I am sad as I accept the fact that I don't know how to sew the hem of my child's pants.

Such a small detail, in all of the moments that make up my day. However, it is nagging at me. Why didn't I want to learn from my mother when I was growing up? Why didn't school make sure I knew how to take care of this basic need? We could be talking about changing a tire, and my story would be the same.

The bias I have been operating from is changing—from valuing having money to pay for such services, thus giving me free time, to valuing having the skills and abilities to do for myself. Some of you might be more able, at the level that you can fix or make for another, or do one of these things as a profession or as a creative expression. I am humbled by you.

I am stumbling upon the idea that handmade matters. As a story on the Small Business Trends website notes, "When you make something, you leave a part of yourself in it." The story offers such insights as "handmade items are crafted in an environment of joy, honour and respect," they "cannot be duplicated" and "everything is more beautiful when it's made with a heart."

As a society, we are being drawn towards valuing individual expression and products that are "small-batch," "craft," "local" and "artisanal." Perhaps we are seeking to rebalance and learn from our time spent in mass-production mode. As an individual, I know I get more for myself when I buy handmade, and today I realize that the possibilities would go much further if I were to become a maker.

For those of you who make (and alter and fix), I celebrate you and appreciate you. For those in my humble camp of not having those skills—yet—let us consider becoming skilled in a craft, art or hobby that would add richness to our lives and build confidence in ourselves.

✿ April 27

Do you know what it means to "hold space" for another person? I ask because I've noticed lately that most of us seem to struggle with this life skill and gift. Holding space is the act of being a safe place, a container and a witness for someone else. When I hold space for a friend or my partner, it means I keep myself from interrupting or interfering while they share what is important to them. Holding space is a hallmark of emotional maturity, because it requires us to be willing to combat our natural instincts out of respect for the other person.

When we hold space, we consciously put someone else's immediate needs ahead of our own. We create a space for them that is psychologically safe, where they can express and feel everything they are holding. We are fully present to them, actively listening to their words and the way they use their bodies to communicate. We keep our judgments, suggestions, solutions, comments and feelings to ourselves. This moment belongs to them.

This skill is very rare in our everyday life. I've heard from many people that they don't feel listened to by the people closest to them, which creates the paradox of being near but feeling distant from everyone around us. Perhaps you feel the same way. Maybe you have had the experience of sharing a vulnerability with another person, only to be interrupted by their fix to your problem, or to have your moment stolen by them—or worse, had your feelings and words invalidated by an ill-timed insensitive comment. If you're like me, you have been on both sides of this moment.

We can change the way we listen to and hold space for another person. We can give them the gift of our presence and attention. We can clear our minds and hold our feelings in check to offer ourselves as a safe, understanding and compassionate vessel. We can be the person who gives them a deep sense of being heard.

And we can begin offering this gift today.

❀ April 28

You are much stronger than you know. In fact, you have the potential to face any adversity or challenge that may come your way. You have something inside of you, something innate, that comes to your aid when you are facing your darkest moments and that grows in strength with each challenge you make it through.

It is not faith or courage, willpower or conviction—although in some ways, these are all a part of what I believe we all possess. I am talking about our resilience.

Resilience is not about being tough or emotionally thick-skinned, and we are not born with a specific amount of it. Resilience is not about letting things slide off our backs or denying that our pain exists.

And it's not a case where some of us have it and some do not. Our resilience is born with us, and it grows stronger as we express, accept and appreciate each and every adversity we experience. As it grows, it forms an indelible aspect of our character. True resilience builds our mental and emotional integrity as we learn and practice healthy behaviours instead of dysfunctional coping strategies. Being resilient means becoming adept at adapting to life in ways that are healthy for us.

Healthy behaviours, such as processing our feelings (the good ones and the painful ones); accepting difficult truths about others, ourselves and life in general; and showing appreciation for what we possess and acknowledging that our life could be far worse—these are actions that build our resilience.

I needed to learn how to be resilient from people who could teach me. I didn't learn it from my parents, because they weren't taught how to be resilient by *their* parents. I learned how to be resilient by listening to and being with people who had experienced trauma and tragedy in their lives and who, through resilience, adapted to the new conditions of their lives with renewed passion. I learned the lessons of resilience from people who cherished and nurtured the spark of life that had nearly been extinguished.

From them, I learned I was much stronger than I thought I was. From them, I learned I could be resilient.

From them, I received a torch that I now pass to you.

✳ April 29

We haven't talked about "tribe" yet. Does that word resonate with you?

The *Oxford Living Dictionary* defines tribe as "a social division in a traditional society consisting of families or communities linked by social, economic, religious or blood ties, with a common culture and dialect, typically having a recognized leader."

How would you describe your tribe and its role in your life?

Along my journey, I am realizing that "tribe," for me, needs a spiritual undertone; it needs to encompass people who are willing to be open and vulnerable, caring and interested in growing, for me to feel safe about sharing myself.

In modern days it seems to be accepted that we place people into separate compartments—some with whom we share a long history or relationship, others with whom we share strong interests—and they never completely come together as a tribe. This is energy-draining.

A tribe is like water: it will always find the opening. Tribe wants to swirl in a circular motion around us. Tribal energy wants to flow through us and wants us to flow through it.

What if we consider tribe to be a reflection of our highest self— different parts swirling together to create a growing energy of highest good? Consider what your affinity, loyalty and commitment look like, if tribe is this meaningful to you.

To make it meaningful to me, I share myself openly and embody the values we are committed to. I make time for every member. I mourn and celebrate, take risks and support inside of my tribe. I commit to being there for each individual for their lifetime, unconditionally. Disagreements are repaired and our spaces are held inside the container.

In this context, tribe is more like how I imagine it must have been in ancient times: togetherness that blends relatedness, daily life and spiritual practice. Adding or losing members becomes a very big deal, and I walk the earth with a sense of belonging. I wish that for all of us.

Today, try on this sense of tribe and feel yourself walk differently through the day, knowing you belong.

April 30

White Pine
I stood at your base with my feet wobbling and slipping on your roots
  and I could not take in your size
I leaned my back up against your trunk and I could feel that my skin
  was soft and vulnerable next to the ridges of your bark
Tipping my head upwards and backwards, I stretched my neck until
  my eyes were looking through you to the grey sky above
I felt heady and dizzy and reached out to touch you, to hold you, to be
  steadied by you
I felt scared by you—your enormity tipped me to the edge of where
  excitement and fear breathe together
I heard the wind first, then I felt you move and bend in ways I could
  not understand—I felt scared for you
I felt the rain drive into us and I was thankful for your protection I
  did not want to let go of you
Then I saw the ant scurrying towards my foot and I understood

May

🌸 May 1

We have Indian Runner ducks here on our farm; they topple about like six Charlie Chaplins and they do everything together, like a school of fish. They live in a small pen with a kids' wading pool, a water dish and a bowl of food. They spend their days going from station to station in a daylong cycle: they bathe, rinse their eyes, eat, sleep, wander, repeat.

This morning we opened the gate and let them out to give the grass in their area a chance to regrow. We moved their food and water to just the other side of the wire dog fence and left the door open.

We watched from the kitchen window as the group went from station to station, not finding their familiar bowls and pool. They stood at the fence, chattering to each other, trying to figure it out.

I was upset, thinking, "The ducks aren't going to be able to do this. They aren't going to cross the threshold. Now they have no food or water." I could feel panic building within me, my body physically responding to the crisis signals my brain was sending.

And then I saw a younger duck that happened to be standing by the door at the same time that a hen was standing on the open side. They were facing each other. The young duck took one step towards the hen, and he was through the doorway. The others followed. Done. Handled. Change made.

In that moment I realized how much I distrust change. Even though the ducks would be happier roaming free, I was fearful for them. Our relationship to change, be it trusting or difficult, is a major factor in how we feel every day. Sometimes I need to follow someone else to get myself through to a new, better side of life. Life constantly offers us the hand of change—sometimes gently, allowing us to choose, and sometimes deciding for us. There is always fresh water for us on the other side of the change.

What if there is a reason for the changes we are confronted with? What if we allow ourselves to go with the flow of change, rather than treading water or resisting the current? I breathe deeper thinking about how pleasant and relaxing it would be to float and flow.

Reflect on your relationship to change today. I am not talking about change that we initiate, but the sort that comes to us. Notice how it comes to us in many forms, big and small. Try trusting the changes, perhaps affirming, "I am safe in the hands of change," or even "I am excited in the hands of change," throughout the day.

I am rebuilding my relationship to change, viewing it as a friend who takes me to new and better places.

🌸 May 2

Reverend Stephanie Dowrick, an interfaith minister, counsellor and social activist, is the author of *Intimacy and Solitude: Balancing Closeness and Independence*, published in 1991. In that book, Dowrick looks at what some regard as two independent states of being and suggests that intimacy and solitude are not opposing forces but in fact two parts of the same self. Her background is rich in world religions and spirituality, and she uses these perspectives to give us the message that closeness and independence are interrelated, supporting and feeding each other to help us balance our lives and enrich our relationships—beginning with our fundamental bond with ourselves.

As an introvert who has developed an extroverted personality, I find independence and solitude to be comfortable, safe places to be. I can manage my own Inner Critic quite well, and I am at home with my own feelings. I learned at an early age that being vulnerable with others was painful, so I kept my emotions and deep thinking to myself. I became adept at listening to and observing others rather than participating. And over time it became apparent that I feel most at peace when I am alone.

Intimacy and closeness are where I still need to do the most work in my life. I recognize this not only from reading Dowrick's words, but mostly because I can feel that when I am close to others, when I do take the risk to be intimate, what I gather and gain from these close experiences—the lessons I learn about myself in relation to others—make being alone even richer. Being with others gives me more to reflect on, to examine and to grow.

Most of us have a dominant preference—either intimacy *or* solitude—and we tend to lean into the one we prefer and feel comfortable with at the cost of exploring and developing the other. By leaning heavily in one direction, we can become imbalanced, developing behaviours that could make us either standoffish and timid or overbearing and needy.

My invitation to you today is to develop your less dominant self. Spend time with others at levels where you can live on the outside edge of your comfort zone. Or pull within and focus your mind on learning about yourself. Imagine you are rebalancing your inner being as you spend time either being close or being independent.

Your goal today is to find out one new thing about yourself that you did not know yesterday, using the two parts of your self—intimacy and solitude.

May 3

What you seek is seeking you. —Rumi

Let that sink in.

All of what we seek … let the whole list pour through your mind—all your wants, your hopes, your desires—and bring every single one forward.

When I do this, it starts with experiences and material things, followed by time, validation and affection from others. Very quickly, my list deepens to become about values, maybe needs, that I hold as most precious: freedom, love, connection, celebration. There I am touching my most personal self, because it feels dense, rich and solid.

Let them come in big and little waves, fast and slow, tumbling over each other, in groups or singly, loud and quiet, like molasses or soda. Greet them, welcome them. See them arrange themselves into a one-of-a-kind composition, your beautiful music playing for the world. How wonderful it is to let the wants tumble and flow, echo and grow, into the never-ending music of life.

You are meant to have what you want. It is your song.

Fill your heart and mind and body with your song. If it's not a song but a poem, scent or watercolour, let it be. Let it come to you vividly, so you know it and feel it, and that way so will we.

In the words of Jorge Luis Borges: "A man sets himself to the task of making a plan of the universe. After many years, he fills a whole space with images of provinces, kingdoms, mountains, bays, ships, islands, fishes, rooms, instruments, stars, horses and people. On the threshold of death, he discovers that the patient labyrinth of lines has traced the likeness of his own face."

May 4

Boundaries are what I am exploring today. I hear the word "boundary" used commonly in conversation these days, and yet I'm not confident that many people are really aware of what it means or how crucial boundaries are to our own mental health and the integrity of our relationships. For instance, did you know that setting a boundary is an act of self-care? Or that a boundary is about our needs and another person's behaviour? And that, even when we set boundaries with others, we are still ultimately responsible for holding firm to them—we must accept that others may break them and leave us to make sure our needs are met entirely on our own?

Boundaries are experiments in owning our own power to take care of ourselves. In fact, setting a boundary with another person is the ultimate act of self-care because it is built on what we recognize as our basic, non-negotiable needs in life—such as physical space or privacy. A boundary is also a clear definition of what we will and will not participate in, such as safe intimacy or gossip and lying. In this way, boundary setting helps us define—and lets others know—where the borders of our morals and principles lie.

Establishing a boundary with another person is about behaviour only. You can't set boundaries about types of people. In this way, boundaries help us transcend clichés, stereotypes and prejudices to focus on the behaviour we absolutely want to have in our life or simply will not tolerate.

Boundaries become easier to establish with practice. In the beginning, you may find that drawing a line around someone's behaviour is awkward and uncomfortable. That's okay; that's how it is supposed to feel. With time, the awkwardness dissolves as we gain self-confidence and self-esteem and others begin to see that their behaviour, which may have been mostly unconscious, has had an unintended or unwanted outcome for you.

For today, I invite you to think about three boundaries you have. To help you do that, let's look at your life from these aspects: how you need to be listened to, your needs for safe touch, and which needs in friendship are non-negotiable.

🌸 May 5

Sometimes presence and silence are most comforting. Coming close without saying a word is a profound experience. Sitting together, standing together, being . . . together.

I have this experience when I go to our horses. I don't speak, yet they say so much. One turns its entire body to face me, moving in closer to share a breath. Another deliberately stands beside me, both of us looking forward. Another stands behind, not moving. I stand still and silent. I can feel the energy that is me, with the energy that is them, stronger because I do not touch or speak, reach or signal.

Try this today in a natural setting—for example, a park. Let an animal approach you without you coaxing, calling, feeding or smiling. Focus on your own energy, your own breath. When they approach, receive their presence without interruption. Refrain from speaking or giving, patting or asking.

Stay open. Stay in your own energy. Let them give you the moment, as it is in them to do. It will feel far more powerful for you both. This is the gift of presence.

❋ May 6

It is customary for spiritual travellers on the Camino de Santiago—a series of sacred walking trails that pass through several European countries, including England, France and Portugal, before ending at the cathedral of Santiago de Compostela in northwestern Spain—to choose several stones throughout their journey that are then added to stone cairns that dot the route. Each stone is chosen carefully and placed with awareness on the cairn or pile to represent a wish to be granted to the traveller.

What inspires me about this custom is the care and consciousness each traveller summons as they choose each stone. Stones have long been associated with the divine and the eternal, and they have also come to symbolize solidity, stability and groundedness, as well as gravity, depth and simplicity. Stones continue to be carried in the pockets of believers around the world.

I believe our relationship to rocks is one that brings us in close communion with our primordial existence and an enduring future. When we grasp a stone, we hold an ancient piece of our planet and come to connect with a form of life that was rooted well before us and will continue to exist long after we are gone.

Rocks also underscore the deep contrasts in being alive. We see them weather the harshest conditions nature has to offer, appearing stoic in their resilience, and yet we also watch them yield to forces greater than themselves, washing up on our beaches or being ground down by wind and sun into grains of sand. Stones are also symbols or remembrances of where we have been—our journeys.

So for today, I invite you to turn your attention to the stones you see on your travels. Look for one that speaks to you. Pick it up, hold it for a while, then place it in a pocket so that you can come back to it occasionally throughout your day and roll it through your fingers.

Notice how you feel when you touch this stone.

✺ May 7

Successful actors often encounter a paradox: the very role or character that becomes their greatest achievement can also be the identity they're never allowed to leave behind. Maybe you remember an actor named Jaleel White. No? What if I say the name Steven Quincy Urkel? Urkel, as most of you have now figured out, was the unforgettable central character on the 1990s sitcom *Family Matters*. White is the talented actor who created a character so memorable that we would struggle to accept White in any other role.

This is typecasting, and it's similar to what we do with our siblings.

Research suggests that birth order sets in motion in many of us a host of behaviours that form the foundation for how we will relate to our friends and partners as we grow older. Our siblings are the first beings we encounter with whom we must compete for our parents' attention and love, and the ways we succeed in receiving that attention and affection become our methods for attracting love throughout our lives.

Sibling relationships can feel as crucial and complex as an intimate romantic love. Missed opportunities, superficial rifts, never-forgotten grudges, knowing glances and gestures, deep connection and painful separation—this is the day-to-day knife edge our love for our siblings occupies, and the same can be said of our deep bond with an intimate partner. What we don't see, however, is that much of the back-and-forth struggle we engage in with our siblings is rooted in those early points of view formed when we and they were children. What we don't see is that the heaviness and stress of our bonds with our siblings are the result of how we see each other, and that we have typecast them and they have typecast us.

We are locked in a family sitcom—or drama—where none of the characters are ever allowed to leave their roles. For many, this typecasting is unconscious and easy to fix by simply allowing ourselves to accept our brothers and sisters in their updated, evolved lives. However, some of us really struggle to let old, familiar—and, for us, comfortable—roles die.

My invitation for you today is to question whether you have placed your siblings in a role or a box that may be limiting the way you see them. If you dig deeper, you may find that by identifying the role in which you have cast your sister or brother, you will also discover the role you have taken on for yourself.

Just remember Jaleel White.

✹ May 8

When life seems a bit raw, inside or out, a pause can be so helpful.

Look out the window or at your hands, or take off your shoes, and take a moment.

We can give our self comfort. Sometimes I put my hands lightly over my eyes and give my self a moment of darkness. Or let a hot cloth linger on my face for an extra moment. Or take a morning bath instead of a shower. To be as we are, as things are, and give our self comfort is truly beautiful. It's a natural part of life—the ebb and flow of energy. Pausing to get regrounded, even in the midst of chaos, will reconnect us to our centre. Giving our self one minute of silence, deep breathing, touching our feet or holding our teacup until we can have more is worth it.

Be in life, with comfort.

 ## May 9

We are all authors. The stories we create are about ourselves, where we came from, how we arrived at this moment and where we will be in the future. They explain to others the "why" of our thinking and behaviour and the "how" of our choices and actions. Our stories sew together the places, people and events of our lives into a plot that supports the person we believe we are and who others experience. Our life story is both the truth as we know it and as we have shaped it.

In my story I am the social actor, complete with personality traits, behaviours and events that have formed my identity. In my life story I am the motivated agent who describes and labels my goals, values, morals and principles. In my life story I am the autobiographical author who shapes and moulds a narrative that I believe in and that I know is acceptable, lovable, even permissible for my family and the culture I live in.

I am the hard-working, rebellious, first born who values loyalty, honesty and empathy. I am funny, clever, young-looking and wise. I believe in fairness, kindness and hope. I have struggled to love and be loved intimately because my deepest wounds came from those I thought I could trust.

I have learned that the only consistency in people is their inconsistency. I have survived abuse, divorce, bankruptcy and depression. I have come to believe that those events helped me become a stronger, healthier, kinder person.

I am working on creating a legacy of work for other people that builds their resilience and restores their faith in themselves.

This is my redemptive story of my self.

I am the social actor, the motivated agent and the autobiographical author of this story.

Today, I would love to hear your story.

✳ May 10

If I were writing an operations manual for being human, I would definitely include a chapter on the human psyche being made up of many parts, or subpersonalities, that are orchestrated by an Aware Self. I think of them as an all-star team of talented players and their coach.

We all have these subpersonalities, and they love us and want what is best for us. Even so, as on any all-star team, two or more of the players may be at odds with one another from time to time. Or one or more of our parts may fall out of alignment with our adult values. We may notice this happening when we're facing a big decision or life change, struggling with a relationship or being overtaken by a strong, opposing desire. We may feel ungrounded, sense an inner conflict or suspect that something is "off." At such times, it can be very empowering to get to know our team. In the 1970s Hal and Sidra Stone developed a method called voice dialoguing to engage with subpersonalities. I would suggest that this is a method we can explore with a counsellor, and we can journal about it as a self-discovery tool.

We all have between four and eight subpersonalities or parts, sometimes even more, along with the one who is driving the bus of our life, the Aware Self. The better we know our parts, the more we empower the Aware Self to make better decisions and the more we love our whole self.

For instance, we all have a part called the Inner Critic. It isn't who we are; it's but one part. The Inner Critic wants to protect us from others' judgments, but its acts can also compromise our self-esteem and interfere with our relationships with others. In order to make sure the Inner Critic pulls in the same direction as the rest of the team, our Aware Self may negotiate with it, perhaps promising to ask its opinion when making big decisions.

Other common subpersonalities are the Perfectionist, the Bully, the Artist, the Warrior, the Judge, the Comedian, the Martyr, the Lost Child, the People Pleaser, the Addict, the Victim and the Rebel. Each has positive and negative functions; some play a prominent role in our lives, while others appear at specific times and still others are hidden to us. Hidden parts can be the key to unlocking unexpressed talent and creativity inside of us.

Please, please, please have compassion for all of the parts within you; peaceful negotiation is the only way to relate to them. There is no getting rid of or shutting off any of our subpersonalities. (An urge like that could be the result of the Perfectionist and the Bully teaming up!)

As a mature, self-aware adult, I am the steward of my many sub-personalities and *I* will choose which to engage with based on their strengths, matching them to the situation and necessary decision. I can call in my Warrior to protect my Creative Child. Or I can ask my Perfectionist for space while I explore my creativity.

We have an all-star team inside of us, with our Aware Self choosing the players and drawing up the plays, coaching and cheering, managing to everyone's strengths. Take notice of the parts, thank them, and choose your best team for wherever you are in your life right now. You can update the team and call in specialty squads any time you want. You are driving the bus of your life.

✳ May 11

I am so grateful that the day my last partner suddenly announced we were over, I had a previously scheduled doctor's appointment. I don't remember what I said, but the doctor referred me to a social worker in the building.

That session changed the trajectory of my life and the way I experience it. It was the very first time I was listened to without interruption. It was the first time that all the other person said after I told my story was "I'm sorry that happened to you."

I cried for most of the hour during that first visit, and at the end I was blown away by the humanity I felt from being heard and receiving empathy.

Looking back, that first session put me on a path of learning about myself, a path on which new doorways appear to this day. I believe that an experience that is emotional and felt in our body is the most helpful way forward. Cognitive and spiritual awareness need to be integrated in our body to be helpful. To make a difference, knowledge needs to be *felt*.

I have come to trust that our body has a beautiful mechanism that opens us only as far as we can handle, and then gently closes us back up afterwards, leaving us able to function in our life. It is an automatic process that keeps us emotionally safe.

I always feel better when I have a guide in my life, someone trained to listen and observe who is paying attention to me and noticing what I might have missed. My guides are empowering—meaning that they help me find my own answers rather than giving me suggestions. Having a guide willing to walk into the fire with me, keeping the experience purely about me, is a profound gift. Having a witness to my darkness, being accepted unconditionally and respected for my courageous heart—these are gifts for which there is no substitute. Neither my family nor my friends can do this, though their love is so amazing.

I hope you take the opportunity to see a counsellor, psychologist, social worker, psychiatrist or therapist—not once, but as an ongoing experience of developing yourself. It is such a gift! To become, to grow into our self, to expand and learn under the witnessing of a trained other, makes life sweet and rich.

I have had the privilege of working with three different therapists over the last twenty years, each appearing to me in a different chapter of life. I wept as each chapter ended. I am now searching for my next guide, and I am so eager to meet them.

I hope you open yourself up to the experience of therapy. I wish for you to be heard and accepted unconditionally for the great person you already are.

❉ May 12

Harvard Health Publishing, a division of the Harvard Medical School, recently published a guide to increasing our brain's overall fitness. Definitely an interesting read, not least because research has demonstrated that healthier, fitter brains are more resilient to stress, help balance our moods, and seem relatively resistant to diseases such as Alzheimer's. The Harvard tutorial suggests six steps as part of their brain-fitness regimen: eat a plant-based diet, get regular exercise, manage stress, challenge your brain, get healthy amounts of sleep and nurture your social contacts.

It is this last step that I'm interested in today. The relationship between the health of our brains and our willingness to create and build strong social networks is well understood. We human beings are social by nature. We bond together, we group together, and science apparently now understands that we are healthier when we are together. The constant stimulation of the reasoning, conceptualizing, language and comprehension, and emotional regions of our brains that comes from rich, connective social activity is like a superfood for the brain. Put simply, the more social engagement we undertake, the more workout time we give our brains. Treatment protocols for conditions like depression, post-traumatic stress disorder, Alzheimer's disease and anxiety—just to name a few—feature social connection as a passive yet powerful intervention to stimulate brain activity and regenerate cells.

As an introvert, I find this science a daunting reality. While it seems our brains might be selecting (from an evolutionary standpoint) for extroverted behaviour, shy people like me can rest assured that our brains also receive high levels of stimulation simply from being around other people. Sitting among a group, observing them and reflecting on your own inner reactions is a powerful brain workout. Just as you would with physical exercise, be sure to respect your own limits; stretch yourself when you know you can, and only then.

Social, healthy brains build balanced minds. That's our mantra for today.

🌸 May 13

In our uncertain world, it can be difficult to make decisions, especially those with high stakes or potentially far-reaching implications. Because we are swimming in information, you would think decision making would be easier, but it's not; in fact, the abundance of data often leads either to a type of analysis paralysis or an outright abandonment of anything quantifiable. Either way, many of us get stuck just trying to make a good decision.

Liv Boeree is a professional poker player who sees the game as a perfect metaphor for life. As she shared in a TED Talk in April 2018, poker is growing in complexity and sophistication. Gone are the days when players could win simply by being adept at reading opponents or by trusting their gut instincts. Today's game, Boeree says, is "about slow, careful analysis." Top players are master statisticians who understand that poker is a game of probabilities and luck.

Which brings me back to making decisions in our topsy-turvy

world. Life is also full of probabilities and, yes, luck. The first key to making good choices is to be at peace with uncertainty. Depending on how emotionally attached we are to our expectations, uncertainty can scare us to our core or set us free. As a fatalist, I have surrendered control of my life to a force greater than myself. I can make choices that support how I want or need to live my life, but I am under no illusion that I can control how much life I have to live. I agree with Boeree when she says that our gut instincts are useful for decision making when what our gut tells us is based on repeated experience and so long as we don't "overprivilege" what it tells us.

"Should I have that milkshake?" we ask our gut.

"Well, based on the knowledge that we're lactose-intolerant and the last time we had a milkshake we had stomach cramps," our gut advises, "I'd say no." Helpful.

"Should I accept that job offer?" we ask our gut.

"Sure—that would be cool," says our gut. Not helpful.

The second key to great decision making: use numbers. Most of our major choices in life can be quantified if we're willing to do the work. Giving the information available to us a numeric value makes decision making much easier. Numbers can bring to the surface any biases that might be blocking us from making a choice or swinging a decision in a given direction to keep us in our comfort zone. Numbers also firm up our choices when we use them as a way to express our level of commitment.

"Are you coming to the gym today?"

"Sure, I'll be there—later, after I run a few errands."

"Are you coming to the gym today?"

"There's a 75 percent chance I'll get there today; tomorrow, though, is 100 percent."

The final key to making solid choices is to understand that time is a critical factor in most if not all of our decisions. Some decisions have an immediate timeline that helps us decide what to do—choices about our safety, sustenance and health will often require that we choose quickly and decisively so as to keep ourselves alive and others safe. On the other hand, decisions about our life direction, our relationship health and even our success must be seen over a much longer timeframe—it may even be years before we can have any confidence that we decided correctly. The passage of time gives us a valuable, reflective perspective through which to assess the choices we made, the consequences of our decisions, what we learned, gained and lost, and how we grew as a person.

✳ May 14

I was scanning the weekly tabloid covers the other day as I was waiting to pay for a few groceries, and what stood out for me was how many methods, tips, programs, strategies and game plans there are for handling stress. It seems we've covered all aspects of stress and the many forms of pressure we deal with every day.

I had the thought when I began this daily journal writing that stress, and managing its symptoms, would be a major focus of the entries. Then I listened to Kelly McGonigal's research on stress, and I think she has the right idea. With over seventeen million views, her 2013 TED Talk and the TEDGlobal conference are changing many people's perspective on stress—my own included. McGonigal says our physical stress response—sweaty palms, shallow rapid breathing and tunnel vision, for instance—is not just an alert of impending stress, but in fact—and more accurately—our bodies' way of *preparing* us to deal with stress. For decades, professionals like me have been working with clients to minimize or manage these symptoms, hoping to improve our clients' tolerance for the discomfort of their stress response and increase their resilience to stress itself.

It seems we've all been off track. What works best for us is to reframe our stress response—the discomfort—as helpful and beneficial. Our stress response is our bodies' way of preparing us to be energized so that we can face stress with courage and joy. According to McGonigal's research, we all have an important ally that aids us in facing stress. Oxytocin, known as the "cuddle neurohormone," seems to be present, along with adrenalin and cortisol, as part of our stress response. It helps open the vascular system, aids our heart cells in regenerating and repairing stress-induced damage and is our body's natural anti-inflammatory. When oxytocin is in the bloodstream, the stress response transitions from fear to excitement, getting us ready to face the challenge in front of us.

Oxytocin also prompts us to seek support from and offer empathy to those who need our care. A high level of oxytocin means our social instincts are dialed in, making us crave physical contact from family and friends.

When we choose to see our stress response as helpful, we recognize that oxytocin is infusing our bodies, shifting us from the biology of fear to the biology of courage. And by encouraging us to support and seek to connect with others, our stress response empowers us to build our stress resilience.

Our stress response is not to be feared—it is to be celebrated, as it is a sure sign our bodies and minds are transforming us into our super-selves.

May 15

I woke up this morning not wanting to start anything, anywhere. Do you have those mornings too? I scan myself and I can feel that my head is foggy, my feelings are all jumbled up, and underneath, way down in my core, there is lightness, but I can't access it because of all the cloud cover in between.

In earlier years I might have denied all the fog, pushed through anyway and found myself being sarcastic, whiny and probably passive-aggressive with others. Also, I likely would have tried to distract myself by overeating or binging on mindless TV, drinking too much or working out excessively—anything to push what I was feeling away or to the very back.

I realized a while ago that I never had great role models for how to self-care, and I can see now that I come from a line of people who either denied or distracted themselves from what they felt. We never talked about feelings in my house when I was growing up, beyond an expectation that I should always be in good mood—because as a young child, what did I really have to be upset about? Meanwhile I saw my parents rage at each other; separate themselves from the family in depression; or numb out with marijuana, alcohol, cigarettes and work.

For me, the writing was on the wall that I was somehow expected to follow their lead—this was how we were all supposed to deal with our melancholy and pain.

I still believe I was lucky to find myself in a group of people who had similar backgrounds, all of us struggling to find a better way to care for and nurture ourselves. We railed against our facilitators, we revered them, distrusted them, challenged them, cried on them— while they held the line and showed us all what empathy, compassion and self-responsibility looked and felt like. I learned from them the language of emotions, healthy ways to feel and process, and how to connect deeply with others.

As I write to you this morning, in my current foggy state, I know to give myself some space to feel and to let what is really troubling me rise up and clear itself. I know to keep myself in check so that I don't bait others into a conflict or leak my mood onto them. I am aware of my urges to distract or numb myself, and I know to let them pass over and through me. I know that this fog will lift, but I know I'm not able to foresee when and how that will happen. I know that what I'm feeling is deserved and valid, even if I don't know how it came to be.

And inexplicably, all that I have told you I know is helping the lightness within me stay bright. So despite my fog and my mood, I mostly feel grateful and grounded.

🌸 May 16

Holding space for each other is the first step towards creating a deep, respectful listening experience. I realize as I write this that there are people all over the world who are firmly entrenched on one side or the other of deeply polarizing points of view, debate and experience. So holding space as a profound act of listening may sound like surrender.

Entrenchment is the act of creating and living within a psychological bunker, where all that exists inside the bunker is right and must be protected, and everything that takes place outside is wrong and must be defended against. The thing about entrenchment is that at the same time as we are building our own bunker, we are also building bunkers and walls around everyone else. In entrenchment we stop seeing others as human beings and instead see them as support systems for beliefs and views we think are wrong or dangerous. When we are entrenched, we don't hear to listen, we hear to counterattack. And inside our bunkers, we feel self-justified because our identity and personality are closely tied to our views.

Listening, especially deep listening, means we are willing to shift from being self-justified to being self-confident. Confident not in our knowledge or opinions, but in who we are. As a listener, I know who I am as a person and I am open to having my views influenced by new information I hear and take in. As a listener, I crave new information because it helps me grow and relate more to myself and everyone else around me. Listeners do not live in self-built bunkers; they prefer to move freely and openly.

Holding space for another person so that they can share and we can learn means we open and create a safe listening container with our body language and by being present. To build a container with our bodies means we are first standing at a respectful distance, we are open and relaxed, our hands are at our sides, our upper torsos and heads are turned to face the other person. To be present means we have cleared all distraction from ourselves, our phones are off or silent and tucked away somewhere, our eyes are focused gently on the other person (not scanning their bodies or peering into their souls!) and our minds are clear of any competing thoughts (such as "I need to pick up milk!").

To hold space for another is an act of love and respect and kindness, and when we are successful it is so powerful that the other person feels invited to share. They reveal who they are and what they believe, and in our open minds we hear things we have never heard. And with even more listening, we are changed.

🌸 May 17

Let's talk about being attached today. The kind of bond I'm thinking of is the one in which we want to be forgiven for our unintentional errors and mistakes, but we judge others harshly for theirs—because they, of course, were intentionally trying to hurt us. It's an attachment in which we see others as perpetrators and ourselves as victims and we are mostly reacting to things done or said to us.

We've never accidentally cut someone off while driving. We've never bumped into someone on the sidewalk. We've never eaten the last serving or left the milk nearly empty. We've never gossiped about anyone, and we certainly have never jumped a queue, parked over a line or gone through a door without holding it for the person behind us.

Of course we have done many if not all of those things, and most of us have done them unconsciously and unintentionally. We expect that other people, without knowing us, will recognize our good nature and let our transgressions go. After all, it wasn't personal.

Why, then, do we feel justified in prosecuting others for their impersonal slights? Why do we hold on to being righteous victims? Why are we so attached to the belief that people are out to get us?

Maybe, just maybe, it's because we judge ourselves.

While we want others to forgive us and let things go, we hold on to a little bit of self-shame every time we transgress. Rather than see our behaviour for what it really is—unintentional—we judge ourselves. Rather than accept ourselves as inherently flawed, we strive for perfection, frequently coming up short. And because we do these things to ourselves, we also spread such judgments outward to others.

It's time to let this whole cycle go—just let it go. I'm flawed, I make mistakes—we all make mistakes, we all have flaws. I accept that the same is true for you.

That's the beauty of being alive.

✺ May 18

"It was just a means to an end."

My friend made this comment to me as we were talking about her journey from being an employee in a large corporation to being laid off by the same company, going back to school, earning her MBA and starting a successful yet challenging new business. I had asked her if she enjoyed the journey, and this was her reply.

"I was so focused on my goal of being my own boss that, looking back over the whole process, I don't think I paid much attention to each step," she added. "I just buckled down and got it done."

This journey we were talking about, and which was still very much in progress, had taken my friend four years of hard work and self-sacrifice. When I looked back over the last four years of our friendship, I could remember many times when her drive and her focus and the end goal were all she could talk about. It was as if she and the goal were one—which I still see as admirable, yet I wish she had been able to find joy in the process of getting there.

No matter what the goal is, working towards success requires that we hold it as a powerful, attractive vision. We have to summon all of our resources—those within us and those in our sphere of influence—to bring us closer and closer to realizing the goal. We have to make choices that are tough and uncomfortable, often pushing us well outside our comfort zones. We can lose touch with those closest to us as we pour all of our energy into our goal, leaving little energy for others and sometimes even our own personal needs. We soothe ourselves along the way by saying that everything will be better once we have achieved our goal, that that's when our life can really begin.

But that's not living. Every step we take towards a goal is an opportunity to be alive and fully experience a moment. There is a richness to almost every moment that is ours to hold and absorb if we just slow ourselves down to notice. There is learning, appreciation, gratitude, connection and communion sprinkled along the path and available to us. And while achieving many of our goals is, in part, about that singular moment of realization, the truth is that we set goals in order to travel a multitude of journeys.

It's not a means to an end—the end empowers the means.

May 19

The more we wake up to life, the more we realize how important it is to "let it be." Go inward and tap into wisdom our mind hasn't yet met—in our heart, soul or essence, spirit or intuition.

Prayer and meditation do this. They refocus my energy when I am impatient and afraid. I feel better after asking for help. I imagine a powerful, capable force holding all my worries for me, transforming them into gold dust.

A quiet mind allows insights and ideas to bubble up. Quiet allows us to see patterns all around us, to feel our way.

I often thank the universe for the abundance, love and peace in my life. I pray for courage to share my blessings and my self with others. I find myself feeling thankful for a beautiful day, for children, for nature and animals.

I pray for salvation and protection; for goodness, kindness, equality and peace. That we will share equally and, with every person having enough, unlock worldwide creativity and celebration and unimagined beauty.

As an NBC News report put it in October 2017, "When a situation comes up and you're out of ideas and you are helpless, feeling much like you did when you were a baby, prayer can provide some other source of hope. And these meditative acts may be a way of being real with yourself—of locating where you are right now, what you're feeling and identifying your needs."

Prayer and meditation give us hope, and hope is direction for our actions.

May 20

You may have never heard of Thomas Holmes or Richard Rahe, but thanks to their research and work, we now know that there is a strong relationship between the most stressful events in our lives and chronic illness. Back in 1967 Holmes and Rahe were exploring this link, poring over the medical records of more than five thousand individuals. They discovered that their theory was correct—so much so that they developed a scale that ranked life events from the least stressful to the most stressful.

Their scale is still the predominant measure doctors use today to understand how much stress an individual may be experiencing. It has proven to be accurate, regardless of gender, geography or culture, in predicting the onset of serious illness resulting from traumatic stress. Each event in Holmes and Rahe's stress scale is assigned a "life change unit" value, and what doctors seek to learn is how many of these events a person has experienced within the past year or is likely to experience in the near future. The events' scores are added together to determine a person's level of chronic stress.

In Holmes and Rahe's estimation, here are the ten most stressful life events:

Death of a spouse (or child)	100
Divorce	73
Marital separation	65
Imprisonment	63
Death of a close family member	63
Personal injury or illness	53
Marriage	50
Dismissal from work	47
Marital reconciliation	45
Retirement	45

To determine your individual stress level, take note of each event you have experienced in the past year—or expect to happen within the next twelve months—and add up the corresponding figures in the right-hand column. (If you believe an event will occur more than once, combine each occurrence into your total.) According to the Thomas and Rahe scale, you have an 80 percent likelihood of illness if your score is over 300. If it's between 150 and 299, the likelihood is 50 percent. And if your score is below 150, it's 30 percent.

How did you do? Better than you expected, or were you pretty accurate in your self-assessment? Remember how I mentioned earlier that most of our lives can be measured or quantified? This is an example of a measurement scale that can help us in ways that are obvious and unexpected. Obviously, if you feel chronically stressed and you have also scored high on this scale, it's a wake-up call and you need some serious self-care immediately—denial or dismissal of what you feel is not an option anymore. But if you looked at the events listed and none of them have happened or are likely to happen to you in the coming year, perhaps your stress is self-created.

I know our lives can be stressful, but you'll notice that shuttling children to activities, work/life balance, work environment, traffic, interpersonal conflict or even personal finances didn't make it onto the list. I believe there's a reason for this. Much of what we experience in our life as stress is because we make it stressful. Many of us bake our own stress-building intensity into most of what we do in life. Our social code seems to dictate that if we're stressed out we must be busy, and if we're so busy that we're stressed out much of the time, it must mean we're important and achieving.

Look, if this describes you, I'll be honest: stress is not your issue. You are likely attached more to being valued and being seen, and you discovered long ago that to be busy and intense meant you received some type of reward. I know this because for several decades it also described me, but I no longer feel this way about my life. So the hope I hold out for you today is that you discover what truly makes you valued and lovable, and that you can shed your attachment to being intense.

🌸 May 21

I was having a casual conversation with someone last week when, in the middle of them speaking, I noticed I was fumbling with my fingers in my pocket. It was a nervous type of fidgeting, and as soon as I noticed it, I stopped and began to wonder why I was nervous and what it was about this chat that was making me anxious. Thankfully, there was a pause in the flow and I had a chance to self-observe a little more. I noticed that I was standing shoulder to shoulder with the person, with my eyes facing forward and my right foot turned outward— clearly, I was so nervous I didn't want to make eye contact, and I was contemplating moving away from them.

The more I began to notice about my own body language, the more I started to be fascinated by this other level of communication I was putting out. While my words were saying I was interested in chatting, my entire physical being was trying to get away.

Over 90 percent of our communication is non-verbal. I remembered this research finding from a talk I gave to a group of nursing professionals earlier in the year. And here I was, in my own moment of self-realization about what I was communicating.

Hoping to shift my state from anxious to calm, I took a risk and said, "I notice I'm a little nervous speaking to you, and I can't figure out why." The other person checked herself quickly, paused, and then, recovering, said, "I've been a bag of nerves the whole time. I've wanted to come over and chat with you for a while now, and when I saw you standing by yourself, I thought, 'Here's my chance.'"

"Why are you nervous to talk to me?" I asked, already feeling a bit more calm.

"Well, I've heard so much about you from your partner and daughter, I feel like you and my husband would have a lot in common, and he really needs help right now. I guess I should have said that earlier."

Now I understood why I was behaving nervously. While my brain was having this lovely, seemingly random chat, it was also perceiving that this person wanted something from me that they weren't saying. My mind picked up on her nervousness, and in turn alerted me that I needed to be aware. The fidgeting of my fingers was the sign that reached my consciousness loudest, even though my whole body was pretty much in motion to move away. Connecting the dots of what I observed and felt with the reality in front of me, suddenly I was back to feeling calm.

Turning to face her, I said, "Of course. I'd love to help any way I can."

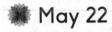 May 22

Close your eyes and feel your body. How is your body feeling today?

My body feels a little worn all over.
Like a favourite shirt washed many times,
In need of appreciation.

Focusing is a method developed by Eugene Gendlin in the 1960s as a way for people to get in touch with felt body sensations that can lead to powerful inner awareness. Focusing is a simple, light way to begin a dialogue with our bodies.

Start with your eyes closed and take deep breaths. Scan the body, not going into anything, simply asking, "How are you?" What parts of our body want our attention? Get a felt sense of the message or the problem in that part of the body.

For example, my hands feel swollen and slow. Looking at them, I see they are willing and honest, keen and humble, in need of moisture and soft touch. They want to hold lightly today, or open and rest. It is uncomfortable to squeeze them closed. Have I been squeezing myself or others lately?

An image of deflated balloons comes to me—purplish black, like a bruise. Soft and gummy to the touch. "Deflated" is the word, and it matches the image of the balloons. I go between the word and the image, the word and the image. It's okay if they change; we just need to follow with our attention.

Ask yourself, "What is this feeling all about?" and "What does this felt sense need to feel okay?" What is one small step we can take towards resolution today?

Feeling deflated resonates with me, after weeks of being excited and full of expectation before a big event. After the event my energy is low, in an ebb. My hands want to be still rather than holding tightly. Something in me says, "I want to be hugged and held today. I want to be still and rest." Today I can treat my hands with care—I can soak them and put on cream. And yes, I can rest.

Be glad when your body has spoken. Thank it. Welcome it. Try to keep the critical voices at bay. The body always tells the truth.

May 23

Today might be a perfect opportunity to surrender. I don't mean the kind of surrender that has us waving the white flag and giving in; I mean a surrender in the sense of consciously releasing, relaxing and letting go—exhaling all of our stresses and the energy we have bottled up. Loosening every place inside of us that is constricted and tight. Surrender today, my friend, is about taking bricks out of walls.

We can release judgments we have made about ourselves and others. We can release the expectations we hold that things in our life must go a certain way. We can release the attachments we have in which we love or are loved conditionally.

Today we can relax our muscles and let any tension in our bodies drain away. We can relax our schedules to create time for ourselves or for someone special, opening a space for intimacy and magic to happen. We can relax our breathing, bringing deep, rich breaths into our lungs and allowing any feelings we have trapped inside of us to rise up and flow out.

This is the day to let go of being perfect, of needing to get it right, of living for someone else's approval or love. This is the moment to let go of the thousand little emotional cuts you have been enduring for quite some time and let them heal. Today we can let go of a personality trait or a behaviour that keeps you small and limits your light. Today we can let go of needing to be right, so that we can become close to someone we love deeply.

This is our moment. Today we can choose self-love. Today we can embrace the cleansing power of surrender.

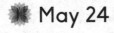 May 24

I've been thinking again today about psychological safety. Do you feel psychologically safe in the groups you belong to, at work and in your personal life?

It seems most powerful if we can make our self feel safe, wherever we go, by defusing our fear of failure and being judged. This is ongoing learning for me, because fear and shame are default responses. I try to focus instead on what makes trying worthwhile. I tend to move very slowly and I still resist change, but I love doing my best. I am blessed to have people in my life who model doing their best and create safety for themselves. I learn from watching them. When I get clear about why doing my best matters in a particular instant, I use that insight to outweigh the death grip that fear of failure has on me.

According to the *Harvard Business Review*, psychology professor Barbara Fredrickson found that "positive emotions like trust, curiosity, confidence and inspiration broaden the mind and help us build psychological, social and physical resources. We become more open-minded, resilient, motivated and persistent when we feel safe. Humour increases, as does solution-finding and divergent thinking—the cognitive process underlying creativity."

Learning to create psychological safety for ourselves is a huge gift of freedom, and at the same time the world gets to experience us at our best.

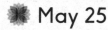 May 25

Doubt is the origin of wisdom. —René Descartes

I'd like to plant a seed with you today. It is a precious new beginning that promises to grow into a fresh way of seeing the world. This seed has the potential to create change not only in your environment but also in the deeper areas of your life and being—the places where change is irreversible and set: your identity and your core.

We can plant this seed together because I want to share the experience with you, to be connected to you, as we both explore what this seed will bring us as it matures and we grow wiser. I want to witness your transformation—and you to witness mine—as the people we've built ourselves to be fall away and we become the people we have always been. I want to nurture this seed with you and, over time, build a community with you where we commune with uncertainty and the unexpected.

We can feed this seed together, giving it our questions, our hopes, our dreams, our mistakes, our successes and our failures. We can nourish this seed with effort and intention and willpower and, as it grows, prop it up against complacency, mediocrity and indifference. And when our seed has grown into a tree, we can both stand under its shade, feeling grateful for its calming sanctuary.

I'd like to plant a seed with you today.

That seed is doubt.

And all we need to do to plant this seed of doubt is to ask ourselves, "What if?" and "Why?"

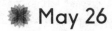 May 26

Unity is being together or at one with someone or something. It's the opposite of being divided. This is a word for togetherness or oneness. —Vocabulary.com

What is your experience of unity?

I was raised in friction and praised for developing a thick skin, trained to thrive in disagreement—not because we were oppressed as a family, but because of an ancestral belief passed down through the generations that it is dangerous to surrender emotionally, agree, acquiesce, admit to needing and be vulnerable. The more self-aware I become, the more similar others become to me. When I look inside myself, I am able to see *you* more clearly.

Unity to me is more than similarity and common ground; it is coming together as one. All of us fitting together like puzzle pieces, each unique, clicking into place to form a larger whole that takes in all of life, all of the earth, all of the universe, all of humanity, all beings, all nature.

I feel hopeful and curious and motivated to finally reunite with a whole. It feels natural for us to be different and original and still click.

Connect with your self today. Listen for a quiet, soft voice that whispers ideas, encouragement and guidance. Get to know your self—how lovely you are. That is where unity waits.

🌸 May 27

I never judge a seed; I am thrilled when it sprouts, no matter the size.

Today I am imagining that money is like the plants growing in my garden. I prepare the soil and dig the rows, and then I water and cover. I talk to the plants, check on them and remove weeds. I get so much joy from harvesting a few sprigs of thyme. I clip chive stems and keep them in a Mason jar with a pair of scissors inside, so that people can clip their own chives for their baked potato. I pick the vibrant green kale leaves, amazed that one kale plant regrows three or four times. Our daughter's basil plant sits by the kitchen sink—we all started talking to it, and its leaves smell like life growing!

What if I were to direct the same level of attention and care towards money? I tend the garden with my family, and it feels like a creation of love. My parents reciprocate my level of care when they visit, and they add their own touch and knowledge, and their experience helps us add dimension and beauty. My parents also have a lot to teach about growing money.

What if my bank respected my "garden vision"? It seems that having my seeds locked away, and eating one every day to survive, is a waste of potential. If I manage each seed so that it grows exponentially and returns year after year, what an exciting endeavour! I imagine sharing harvests with family, friends and neighbours, as we do with our herbs, eggs, garlic and kale. I love to share. It would be amazing to grow money to share.

Money is about flow, and money is about value. It is our garden.

Think about your relationship to money and how it can flow to be a reflection of your best true self and your vision of life. Find someone who models the way you want to be with money. Find positive, soulful help. I got myself started by Googling "money is like a garden," so use a simile or metaphor that resonates with you, and you will find someone like-minded. Grow your own garden, get your hands in to feel the earth, make it your own. Find help that empowers you, rather than doing it for you. We deserve financial flow. We deserve to know how to grow a beautiful money garden.

❁ May 28

"I'm not sure what to believe anymore," she said. "I just don't know what is true."

Do you ever have that thought? More and more these days it seems the truth has become complex and difficult to find, leaving us to expend a lot of our energy playing hide-and-seek with honesty. Falsehoods, lies, fake perspectives, deliberately misleading headlines and promises, public relations pivots, retouched or staged photos, unreal "reality" television—these have come to dominate our cultural landscape, so much so that jadedness and skepticism are no longer traits of the very old. Even some kids in elementary school have abandoned innocence to become hardened skeptics. To survive or thrive in this environment, we have all had to adapt to become master deceivers by the time we reached adolescence.

Which makes the process of living through hardship and struggle even more difficult because the handhold we need to climb out of our personal pits—the truth—is barely visible. But it is there. It is tucked inside of each of us, a muted, timid voice that has lived in darkness underneath the staircase of our souls.

Try this experiment with yourself today to coax out the truth. Take a long look at yourself in a mirror, being sure to study your face and memorizing all of its detail in your mind. Once you have the image set, tell yourself a truth and study your face. What do you notice? Do your eyes and mouth relax? Is there a general calmness in your expression? Can you maintain eye contact with ease? Now tell yourself another truth—perhaps a more personal one—and again notice your face, especially the areas around your eyes and mouth. Look for relaxation and softness.

Now tell yourself a lie—an obvious deception or falsehood. What happens to your face? Do you notice the tightness around your eyes, the firmness of the muscles of your mouth? Did you swallow? Did your eyebrows rise? Did your eyes shift away from your own gaze? Try again. This time, tell a deeper lie, one with more emotional weight, and watch the signs of deception appear on your face.

We all have this truth compass, meaning we all have a way of reaching honesty when we need it most, and like a muscle it gets stronger the more we connect to it and use it to guide us. I did this experiment myself several years ago and I became so reinvigorated by my truth compass that I would try to connect with it as often as I could. I enjoyed the feeling of honesty so much that my truth became my new best friend, and I shifted my life profoundly by bringing it with me everywhere I went. Soon I noticed something more curious happening: with my truth at my side, our partnership grew as we were joined by my self-esteem and my self-confidence. And all together, we acted as a team, unified in our intentions and actions.

And we gave our team a name.

We called ourselves "integrity."

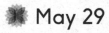 May 29

A pregnant woman with a one-year-old left her abusive husband. . . . She had courageously taken her son and left with little more than the clothes on their backs. She had found an inexpensive apartment and had been promised a job. The job

had fallen through. She had been promised another job but it wasn't due to start for a week. Public agencies told her she'd have to wait fourteen days for assistance. She did not want welfare, just food for a couple of weeks. She was referred to a small grocer who had been forever in the community. When the store owners heard the young woman's story, they immediately offered to help: "Of course we will help. Would you like to just run a tab until you start working? Many people need to on occasion. Welcome to the community." —Jane Middelton-Moz, *Boiling Point*

It is a special experience to feel known and supported by a community. We lived in a walkable neighbourhood in the city, and the lovely woman who cared for our daughter walked everywhere. Our daughter became known to the shopkeepers, and they would often ask about her. It was very comforting to me that she was known in the community.

Living far from relatives, I am learning to set down roots and open myself to new people. I am thankful to people who are "hubs," and it is the traditions in this small community that are making the biggest impact on me: the Halloween costume contest hosted by the volunteer firefighters; the Rotary Club turkey dinner; the library's Saturday morning art class. These activities bring us into the community and get me talking to people. I depend on them happening each year. We have an opportunity to sponsor a gold leaf on the library's new giving tree, and I am excited our family name will be displayed in our community.

Do you have a shop owner or a neighbour in the community who has helped you? Are you known in your community?

Joining in at annual events and traditions in our community and talking to our neighbours are profoundly connected to learning how to stand up for others and how to live in peace.

✳ May 30

In 2018 researchers at the University of British Columbia's Vancouver School of Economics and at McGill University in Montreal happened across some surprising findings when they studied the relationship between geography and happiness. Based on their data, drawn from over 400,000 responses and more than 1,200 communities, it became clear that a rural life was a happier life. There was indeed a geography of well-being.

The scientists noted that major urban centres are more stressful for their inhabitants, creating significant pressures on daily life that are mainly trade-offs for the opportunity of employment. Rural life, on the other hand, offers such benefits as fewer people as neighbours, shorter commute times, less-expensive housing and a stronger sense of belonging within a community. American studies corroborated the Canadian findings, concluding that "the farther away from cities people live, the happier they tend to be."

Okay, that's that. Let's pack up the house, grab the kids and go out to the country! Right?

Well, maybe. It also seems that while there is a strong association between rural living and happiness, moving to a house in the country will not make you happy. If you're an unhappy city dweller, moving to the country may make you an unhappy country dweller.

But perhaps there is something we can glean from the researchers' findings—something useful for all of us, regardless of where we live. A recipe or formula for less stressful living. Tips like the following:

- relocating to neighbourhoods with fewer people per square mile;
- rejigging our careers and work, making it a priority to reduce commuting time to less than ten minutes—or, preferably, ten to twenty minutes on foot;

- choosing housing that costs less than 30 percent of our income; and
- seeking out communities with a strong social identity and fabric where we can belong.

Is this not a matrix of choices that would shine the spotlight on the most important aspect of being alive—our quality of life? Can you imagine if you were to look at your life now and make these adjustments? Wouldn't they bring you a greater sense of ease and contentment? Oh, the possibilities!

🌸 May 31

An article I read in the November 2017 *Entrepreneur* magazine suggested that our brains have an unlimited capacity to respond to new things by creating new neural pathways. So how much "new" are we giving our self?

My capacity has expanded exponentially over the last ten years, in direct proportion to my saying yes to love, kids, animals, a farm, school, writing, yoga and learning to drive a tractor. I remember that, when I first moved out on my own, I could barely plan a meal and I clung to routines. As my feelings of safety in the world grew, I was able to say yes to the possibilities for expansion that were always around me.

Think of a time when you rose to the occasion—when you did something you didn't know you could because it was asked of you or needed to happen. Amazing. Tapping into all that brainpower and surprising our self.

What else are we capable of?

I'm not talking about multi-tasking or doing more. I'm talking about learning, taking a chance, growing our self. The littlest thing counts. The article suggests brushing our teeth with the other hand. Today I'm going to apply for a position on the library board because it scares me, makes me tingly and will help me set down roots in this community.

Build a new neural pathway today. Do something that feels safe yet new. Say yes. Wear your hair differently. Eat lunch somewhere else. Follow a coincidence. Notice the people around you. Are they different from you? Are they good at something you aspire to do? Do they model a behaviour you value? Expansion is always around us, inviting us to tap into our unlimited capacity.

June

❋ June 1

How have you been feeling? Can you feel a flow of lighter energy in your life? Have you been feeling more at ease lately? Have you had more days when you felt grounded in your self?

What about the last five months? Can you see yourself at your starting point and appreciate all of the changes and shifts that have happened for you? Do you see where you worked really hard, where you were challenged and perhaps stuck for a while? What about those days and weeks when it all came together and just clicked, and you soared? Can you see all of your growth?

What have you discovered? What new information has appeared on this journey, helping you to expand your emotional geography?

As you reflect on the recent past, gently turn your focus towards the future, where anything is possible. Can you see the shifts that you have put in motion that have yet to fully pay off? Is your future a picture that is clear and vivid, or is it still unfolding and being moulded by your deliberate, loving intention?

Knowing how far you have travelled already—as well as the steps that are ahead of you and yet to be taken—can you see those footprints leading you to your vision, coaxing you forward?

Let's take a full, deep breath here, and as you inhale, fill your being with appreciation—hold it, gently, and savour this appreciation for you.

When you're ready, steadily let this breath out with a sigh.

More wonder and learning lie just ahead.

🌸 June 2

Whenever I have been most successful, I was working closely with someone I respected, who gave me positive reinforcement, compliments and positive regard. Their feedback mattered to me and I believed what they said to be true. I would come away from time with them feeling excited and happy. It was a physical feeling, like a high, and I would smile and be carried by the feeling for several days. Feeling that good would leave me willing to be bold and creative, and that increased my effectiveness.

An article in *Psychology Today* in December 2015 said, "Neuroscience tells us that when we feel safe our brain releases feel-good chemicals; serotonin, oxytocin and dopamine, that in turn help our performance. We are more motivated, more able to learn and manage challenges." I take this to mean that my number one priority is to feel good about my self, and my body will take care of the rest. We must ensure that our physical safety is in place first; we cannot do anything until it is so.

Who are the people with whom we feel safe and with whom we feel good about our self? I have a dear friend who puts me into that feel-good space every single time we speak or even text. And even when I don't know individuals personally, it feels really good to receive messages from connections on social media from people I admire. Beyond having a relaxed or happy tone, the messages need to be personal, about our greatness and goodness. We are looking for feedback that will make us feel very positive about our self, coming from sources we trust.

Some days we will trust a voice outside of our self more than our own, and that is okay. Whether the information comes from within or without doesn't matter; we simply need it to transport us to the feel-good place. Ask someone whose voice you trust a personal-greatness question like "What do you think makes me special?" or "Why do you think I am great?" We need to hear it. Ask them to text you or call you. Tell them what you are up to. Maybe they will ask you to reciprocate.

I am so grateful you are here. You are talented, powerful, loving and intuitive. Your commitment to your self and to developing your gifts inspires me. We are lucky you are here in this world at this time.

❄ June 3

If hands fulfill the expression of my heart, how hands-on am I in my life?

I have no issue with getting my hands dirty; I'm not squeamish about having them in dirt, water, manure or a sink full of dirty dishes. I learned to eat rice and curry with my hands, and I enjoy the tactile experience of creating sacred food. But when it comes to managing and directing the mental details of my life, I have been fairly hands-off.

Working through the finer details requires focus and attentiveness and care. It takes effort for me to create plans and dates with friends and family. I experience an invisible repelling magnetic force that prevents me from going into the details. I glaze over, go into the back room of my mind and feel the need to pull away. I realize that I can become fairly inattentive to many parts of my life, preferring to soar high above and scan the landscape of the present and the future. I'm not sure when that happened, but I do know that becoming hands-on, literally feeling things, is the way to pull myself back down to earth and to the forefront of my lâife.

Bringing life into the physical realm with my hands keeps me grounded—tasks like opening the mail, making a pile of bills, writing due dates on paper calendars. My daughter may sit all evening with me, reading a book. But if we choose to watch a television or computer screen instead, she creates with her hands, crocheting or drawing, at the same time. I don't think she likes the feeling of floating away that so many of us adults crave. Her hands keep her grounded too.

Look at your hands. Notice what you touch and how you touch. When are you more and less likely to touch? Relate to your hands as your indicator for being hands-on in life.

June 4

I have a hard time admitting this: I'm not a big fan of routine, yet routine makes me comfortable. I really don't like the tedious, repetitive nature of doing this and then that, day in and day out. And despite many attempts at being more mindful of the things that I have to do every day, I still find that boredom and apathy creep in. At numerous points when I have to make a new behaviour into a habit, I get distracted and want to run away or return to the way I was doing things before. At the same time, routines sometimes feel restrictive and adult-like, triggering my inner child to act out and rebel, blowing raspberries at the changes I want to make in my life. Learn the guitar? No. Develop a daily yoga practice? I don't wanna.

But here's the rub: I also know that routine and structure bring me a profound sense of security. In our family and in my relationship, I'm the person who holds the space and the responsibility for a lot of the flow of our lives. As the timekeeper, I set the alarms every night to make sure we're up on time. I fill the cars with gas. I create the work systems on the farm that save us time and energy. I buy the calendars so we can track everyone's schedules. I keep a running inventory of groceries and supplies in my mind, and I make the shopping lists so that when we travel to town we make the most of our time there. I do all of this to keep our lives glued together and make me feel more secure.

Interestingly, being this way makes me live in two very different worlds. To my birth family and many of my friends, I'm a stubborn, reckless person who doesn't like limitations in any form; yet to my partner and children, I'm an overly structured control freak!

With mindfulness, I've become aware that I like my rules for living and I don't like having someone else tell me what to do. I've grown up to be self-sufficient, and deep down, I've learned to trust myself—more than anyone else—to keep myself safe. I realize now that I was overly controlled by one parent and left alone by the other, and that this family dynamic is now inside me as an internalized way of being.

I'm reflecting on this today because I'm thinking that I'm not the only one of us living with some kind of dual nature. I'm learning to harmonize the two mes and lessen the effect of each side's more extreme ways of being.

How do the two yous show up in your life, and what do you know about your dual nature? Find some time today to sit and reflect—to be mindful of the two yous and their intertwined way of living inside of you.

June 5

Which is worth more, a crowd of thousands,
or your own genuine solitude?
Freedom, or power over an entire nation?
A little while alone in your room
will prove more valuable than anything else
that could ever be given you.
—Rumi, "Two Days of Silence"

Silence and solitude are the true solvents of the soul. As I grow older, I've come to appreciate how beautiful and stirring both can be. When I was younger I craved being around other people, sacrificing personal time for friend time and believing that my value as a person was determined in part by how many friends I had, how popular and in demand I was, and how active my social life seemed to be. It appeared, based on most of my friends' lives, that we shared this view and way of being.

My best friend, however, didn't see things this way—and still doesn't to this day. He prefers solitude and quiet time, and over the last three decades of our friendship I've come all the way around to meet him on this point. As teenagers, he and I were very close, but we weren't necessarily with each other all the time. I respected that he wanted time and space to himself, and I filled my need for social connection with other friendships. In retrospect I was a bit envious of how he was able to be by himself so much of the time and how solitude and silence were so necessary to sustaining his quiet, stable nature.

As I said, I have come to look forward to quiet time spent alone. My old triggers of panic or desperation, which were connected to loneliness, have trickled away, to be replaced by a rejuvenation I feel after time in separate stillness. Sitting in sunlight on a step or park bench; taking a walk deep in a forest, or along a beach or shoreline; taking a long highway drive with the radio off; sitting in a comfortable chair, staring into the fire of our wood stove—these have all become enlightening vacations for my mind and soul.

I wish you a moment of pure, still separateness today so that silence and solitude can begin to work their dissolving magic.

🌸 June 6

Self-control, especially emotional self-control, is much more than having grace under fire. In our culture, we praise perseverance and resilience and admire those who can stare down pressure and stress and perform their duties despite personal attacks or character assassinations. We look at individuals who walk with a stoic demeanour while surrounded by overwhelming pressure and we laud them and want to be like them. In their shadow, the rest of us seem like heaving, seething, emotional hot messes.

I know that in my own life I'm in the process of making the transition from being an unaware, emotional pin cushion to articulating and feeling healthy and appropriate levels of sadness, anger, fear and joy. I'm moving from pure limbic reaction to a more balanced, cognitive response. In other words, I've gone from being Dr. McCoy to Captain Kirk, with the help of a little Mr. Spock. This has been, and still is, hard work, and I have to say that as I abandoned my fiery, chaotic McCoy for more calm in my life, there was a period when I was too much Spock and people found me cold, unreal and lacking in empathy. Kirk seems to be the happy medium where I have all my feelings but I can look at and understand them and then choose how I want to respond.

I hope you'll indulge me in the *Star Trek* analogy. Sometimes we will find fictional characters helpful because they act as simple guideposts for modelling a behaviour we're working towards. Growing up emotionally and becoming a self-regulated, responsible individual is important, necessary work. It just doesn't have to be intense and serious all the time.

🌸 June 7

I had the opportunity to go to Alinea, Grant Achatz's restaurant in Chicago, which has received three stars from the Michelin guide. I had read Achatz's autobiography years earlier, inspired by his imagination and vision, particularly the way he uses food to invoke memory.

Cedar branches were lit as part of the dining experience, an ode to his childhood memory of burning leaves in the fall. Green apple peel actually formed a helium-filled balloon dessert, and for me, the whimsy of the creation was a celebration of my childhood, of fun and fantasy and magic. I bit into the balloon, pulled in the helium and had the best giggle as I said the names of my family members and all our animals while sounding like a chipmunk.

When we were first led into the cozy, dimly lit dining room, each table had a huge urn of dry ice that sent fog wafting across the table, misting the most beautiful oranges (sliced in half) and filling the room with their scent. The dim light amplified my sense of smell, and I remember being filled with awe.

Think back to a memory that activated your senses, or a new combination of senses. Where in your body do you feel that memory? Let yourself go there with all of your senses. Feel and smell the surroundings, hear the sounds, touch, look around you . . . take your time to savour the remembering.

I remember when I first saw the oranges; my core—the centre of my chest and stomach—awakened in response to such beauty, and I imagined my body feeling like velvet, as though I embodied a texture of beauty.

Let your senses transport you. Notice how and where your body responds to beauty-filled moments.

❋ June 8

Sometimes I get disenchanted with the world. I decline invitations. I worry about how I am going to protect my family and the magic in our lives from other people's stuff—acquaintances who compete and compare, people who unload their negativity, gossip, anger, fear and anxiety. I am aware of receiving less because I am not in crisis, while being asked to endure showboating and drama. I worry about feeling trapped in a roomful of egos and stories.

Sometimes I drag myself out to functions, because the activity sounds fun or because my partner is going. Sometimes I force myself to say yes, thinking it's the only option. Quite honestly, I would rather be with my self! Otherwise I come away disappointed, drained and sad that my overtures of friendship and sharing were ignored or rebuffed, that I had to spend time with people who have not done work on themselves.

Does that sound familiar to you?

I know that the others' behaviour is unconscious. I know it isn't personal, and I'm getting pretty good at holding my ground to avoid succumbing to my own insecurities. And I know the size of my reaction and the amount of energy I give are directly proportionate to the measure of self-care and self-love I need. When my cup is full, the drama isn't nearly as dramatic, and I don't need love and attention from those who don't have it to give. Many times these are family members, partners and friends who "should" have this to give, as part of our relationship. We all know it doesn't work this way. I must fill my own cup to walk lightly in the world. In doing so, I hope others might be encouraged to do the same.

Another form of self-care I feel extremely grateful for is group therapy. My own group was a diverse bunch—all ages, interests and ethnicities, totally unlike one another in most ways. Yet these people showed me their souls and I showed them mine. We let one another speak. We had empathy for one another. We witnessed one another's deep hurts and healing. We took responsibility for being triggered. We created a safe circle in which we could fully be ourselves. I could— and did—say anything, be any way, dress any way, express my feelings, yell, cry, giggle . . . because I knew I could apologize and I would be forgiven. I knew my circle would respond truthfully to me. They too would show me their true selves.

Group therapy is the most profound experience, other than my relationships with my partner and my kids, that I have ever had. It's how I wish the world worked. It isn't a natural way of being at first, but once people get the hang of it, it's how we want it to be everywhere. The world needs group therapy.

We fill our cups, learning what we need. We say no, we set boundaries—sometimes with grace, sometimes not. We find safe places to explore who we are, to release, to expand, to be nurtured. This is the journey.

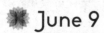 June 9

How are you when no one is looking? Are you feeling sad? Angry? Happy? Afraid? We all feel these feelings. Everything else is a thought.

I wish someone had told me this when I was little. I never knew I had so many of all the feelings in me. I didn't know that feelings build up inside our body if they aren't allowed out. And feelings can occur in layers, all of them true—sadness layered on top of anger, anger on top of fear.

I was the last to know I was angry. Being witnessed and supported by a professional as I release feelings stored inside is a great healing gift. I urge you to get to know your feelings. It is a relief to let out the truth. You are beautiful in your feelings.

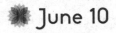 June 10

Truth does not fight against illusions, nor do illusions fight against the truth. Illusions only battle with themselves.
—Helen Schucman

I battle with the illusion that I need more, when I know the truth is that I have everything I need. It is a new practice to focus my attention and energy on this truth, since I have always pursued "more," for sport and for survival. It has been the bane of my conversations, meditations and ego identity.

Going deeper into this truth of mine, that I have everything I need, there is stillness, and I imagine that beyond the boundary of stillness is peace and freedom too. I have had glimpses of that feeling, usually when I stand in meditation with the herd of horses that live here. And I have shared that feeling with the rest of the day, bringing it with me, not leaving it behind.

Standing in this truth today, my cup is full. The day is about discovery, a gift to open. I have everything I need. I am breathing that in as truth.

What illusions are fighting inside you? What truth exists inside of you? Choose to believe the truth living inside you today.

❄ June 11

Are you aware of the influence of music in your life? The songs that affect us deeply are the ones that tug at our insides or tickle our hearts. The music that makes us feel grounded and centred is different from the music that takes us up into our heads, or makes us cry with sadness and loneliness or scream in anger. It can be a subtle nuance, this distinction between head and heart.

Music's beauty can inspire awe and reverence; in gratitude for the skill, the gift we are hearing, we usually slow down and take a deep breath, and feel better for having listened. That good feeling usually lasts well into the day.

One of the songs that touches my heart is a winter song. It pulls at my love of freedom, of nature, of big open spaces and of my ancestry. I love it so much.

Enjoy music. Choose music deliberately to make your heart feel good. In doing so, we learn more about our beautiful self.

❄ June 12

We all have an ego—our constant mind buddy that lives inside our heads, doing the hard work of making sure we avoid potentially vulnerable situations. Some of us even have large, hypervigilant superegos that see the world as full of risks and dangers and keep us safe by developing "ego games"—elaborate, practised and layered strategies to keep us in control and out of any danger our ego might perceive. Eric Berne, a pioneering transactional psychologist, wrote about these strategies—with names such as "I'm right and you're not right," "Poor me" and "Me too"—in his 1964 book *Games People Play: The Psychology of Human Relationships*.

We all have some level of ego game going on in our relationships with others. Think about it for a moment: have you ever been a martyr, a victim, got the last word in, fought to be right or exacted revenge on someone for a slight against you? Of course you have.

Ego games are natural and normal for most if not all of us. I don't think we can ever erase them completely from our minds until we do the work of getting to the bottom of understanding, then finding a healthy way of fulfilling, the need the ego games satisfy for us. With that in mind, the trick is to be aware of our own ego games so that we make a conscious choice about when and where we enrol others in our games.

I find I'm pretty clear about when I'm starting to engage in an ego game because I can recognize that my mind is generating all kinds of thoughts about how I might be less than, or more than, the person in front of me. This active witnessing of my mind allows me to see all of it without having to claim or react to every thought it creates.

Then, almost immediately, my stomach starts to churn and I notice myself biting down on my lip or chewing the inside of my cheek—both are early signs of irritation and frustration for me. I've come to trust signals like this, knowing that they foreshadow a game about to begin.

I've learned that these early physical symptoms are my best guides to pause, reflect and then adapt or change my behaviour. I tend to look at them like flashing red lights at a four-way intersection, and with a heightened awareness of my thoughts and emotions, I approach the next moments with extreme caution. It has become a tool for me to regulate my feelings, and the more I use it the more trust I have in myself.

While ego games are normal and natural, and most of us use them to get our needs met, they are superficial, unkind and self-centred at best, and dysfunctional, malicious and narcissistic at worst. Ego games freeze and destroy intimacy—there's no better way I can say this.

Well, maybe there *is* another way: most of the everyday conflict we have in our relationships is the result of our egos and ego games!

There it is—that's the whole knotted ball of string.

✻ June 13

Today, I'm extending a simple invitation to you and to myself. All I ask us both to do is to look at ourselves in a mirror and say "thank you." Say it as often as you like, out loud or silently, in your head. Let's say "thank you" as many times as we need to until the message starts to sink in, our bodies relax and we really steep in the gratitude we're expressing for ourselves.

That's it: say "thank you" to yourself, while looking into a mirror, until you hear it, believe it and feel it.

Thank you.

✻ June 14

The Oxford Living Dictionary defines "originality" as "the ability to think independently and creatively."

We walk more lightly when we discover our originality, as if we have wings that lift us.

What is your relationship to originality?

I am aware of a paradox inside me: I allow myself to be original, on the condition that others agree with, approve of or join me. It takes self-confidence and resilience to want to be original for our self.

The feel-good aspect of originality comes from having an awareness, an idea, an appreciation, an "aha" moment that is our own sacred ground. Being my self feels so good and is so freeing.

Sink into your originality. What do you believe makes you original?

✻ June 15

The consciousness that says I am is not the consciousness that thinks. —Jean-Paul Sartre

When you are aware that you are thinking, that awareness is not part of thinking. It is a different dimension of consciousness. When we yield internally to this new dimension of consciousness, if action is possible or necessary, action will be in alignment with the whole and supported by creative intelligence. If no action is possible, you rest in the peace and inner stillness that comes with surrender. —Eckhart Tolle

With more and more access to people and news, I am extremely motivated to practise looking inward to determine whether or not action is calling. Most of our thoughts, actions and reactions come from the outside. They propagate further worry and do not feel aligned with our inner values. Consider that campaigns that vow to "fight," "win a war against" or "end" stem from an outer reality.

In contrast, when we go inside to stillness, the next action to take, if any, always presents itself gently, as a whisper, as loving language. Inner guidance is filled with love and light, and it culminates towards resolution of the outer.

As more and more of us go inward, our actions will become more love- and light-filled, and this is what will heal the world's great troubles. It's what will keep us safe. It's what will fill us with joy and peace. We may not always be immediately clear on how inner guidance helps to heal our outer world, but my experience is that inner guidance always leads to unimagined and exponentially larger results. This is where faith comes in. Focus on awareness of your inner world. Let your actions come from within.

June 16

The *Oxford Living Dictionary* defines "normal" as "conforming to a standard," though it seems these days that "normal" has come to mean conforming to *the* standard—implying that there is one way of being, doing, thinking or feeling, and demanding compliance.

Today I'm asking myself: Where in life am I holding "normal" as a standard? Where am I holding my self to be what is considered normal, in a limiting way?

How much more appetizing it is to be able to choose our own norms than to conform to those established by others!

I am grateful and excited that labels are dissolving in our world. Woman and man, homosexual and heterosexual, are no longer ends of a single spectrum, but only two of many ways of being. I love that people—at least in some safe parts of the world—get to declare their own gender identity and/or sexual preferences and forgo labels completely. I am thankful to the LGBTQ+ community for its courage to model healthy norms, and I pray that life becomes more welcoming.

Millennials—those born between the early 1980s and late 1990s—are another great example. They question the de facto standards or norms of buying a home, buying a car and staying in one job. They are refusing in droves, thus redefining norms for money, success, mobility, independence and freedom.

Do we have to put a certain percentage of our earnings in our savings accounts? Do we have to go to college to be successful? Do we have to go to church to be faithful? Do we have to see our family regularly to be loving? Do we have to serve appetizers to be great hosts? Do we have to defer to the school principal to be respectful of authority? Do we have to buy gifts on birthdays? Do we have to be legally married to be married?

We might feel a little lost in a world without norms, as they've been with us for so long, embedded so thoroughly into our society. Even if we choose a norm for our self, to gauge our own changes and progression through life, it seems confining. The more we act according to our own values and beliefs, the more we will see confining labels and standards dissolve. We will act with kindness and from love, and we will act because it is our true expression.

More open language might be "right now I choose *x*." I might choose differently tomorrow, or the same way; it depends on so many factors. Like in a good yoga practice, we never come to the mat in the same way. Each day I bring different strengths, awarenesses and challenges.

Free yourself of norms. Choose in the moment, from your values and what you believe.

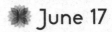 June 17

The more real you get, the more unreal the world gets.
—John Lennon

Isn't that the truth? Have you noticed that as you move towards becoming your real self, the most genuine you possible, the people around you and your world generally seem increasingly artificial? When we make a commitment to being truthful, first with ourselves and then outwardly with others, we run into all kinds of socially acceptable camouflage and deceit. As our hearts open to honesty, our eyes open to see people hiding their feelings, lying to caretake our feelings, or withholding from and micromanaging us in an attempt to control our behaviour. Once we are awake to and grounded in truth, we see that the rest of the world is careening out of control in the pursuit of fantasy.

That realization is shocking enough on its own, but I also remember feeling a profound aloneness at first, thinking, "Great. Here I am, committed to being genuine, and I'm all by myself again because no one can relate to me anymore." I start to eat healthier foods and smaller portions, and suddenly I see aisles of junk food and packaged meals and enormous servings in restaurants—and the ads for pizza and desserts on television take on a more sinister tone. I make a commitment to live more minimally, and suddenly big-box stores packed with clothing, furniture and gadgets seem to be taking over the world. I work on my relationship with money, and everywhere I turn I'm encouraged to spend or someone is trying to give me more credit. I choose to be more environmentally conscious, and almost immediately I see how blind other people are in their relationship to our planet.

When we step out of the general flow of the world and stand on the sidelines to achieve lightness, that is exactly when we see how much chaos and confusion and stress and heaviness exists in the flow.

Adapting a phrase from Helen Schucman's *A Course in Miracles*, authenticity and consciousness reveal all that is unlike themselves.

Today, let's just notice this trend and choose to see these opposites as a sign that we are on the right path for ourselves.

✳ June 18

I'm reading and researching today about emotional triggers, especially the ones that can ignite our anger. I came across some interesting research that suggests our anger is evoked by two fundamental triggers: a violation of expectation and a blockage of goals. The writers go on to suggest that our anger is not only based on our identities, or how we see ourselves, but also on our cultural conditioning—those conditions or events that our culture agrees are acceptable to trigger anger.

Children, especially infants and toddlers, are easy to anger when something or someone is in the way of getting what they want in that moment. This type of anger trigger stays with many of us as we grow older and becomes the root of why we're quick to rage when another car cuts us off in traffic or we're blocked from making our bus or train by a throng of commuters.

Violation of expectation is a bit trickier because it is born out of the way we see ourselves relative to others, the way we wish to be seen and treated, and the meanings we assign to people, behaviour and events. We are meaning-making machines, weaving symbolism and narratives with everything we do and everyone we meet. The meaning we ascribe to something also comes gift-wrapped with feelings or emotional attachment, which serves to give the meaning more flavour, creating relevance and importance and urgency. So seeing someone wear white after Labour Day triggers irritation and judgment, we get mad at having to wait endlessly for Netflix to load when we're just trying to enjoy our deserved downtime, and we're incensed when our supervisor mispronounces or forgets our name.

While much of the anger management training that is available is concerned with distraction, or rationalizing or minimizing the intensity of our anger, it seems to me that we're missing the nugget about how anger is triggered—and similarly, how all our feelings are evoked and are able to grow. And that rather than work from the outside in, we need to work from the inside out. Meaning and attachment.

June 19

I am very aware today of my compulsivity—of my breath becoming shallow, my frustration building, my head buzzing and wanting me to eat something or make a coffee (years earlier, it would have been a cigarette, and later in the day today it might be a glass of wine).

In his book *Bradshaw On: The Family*, John Bradshaw defines "compulsivity" as "addictiveness"—but he broadens the meaning beyond alcohol and drugs to include the inner emptiness we try to fill up with any mood-altering behaviour.

Today, when I noticed my compulsivity, I put on my boots and went outside. That was a great break in pattern. I wasn't sure it would make the feeling go away, but I did it anyway. Yesterday I listened to the voice that promised I would feel better after the coffee and the early lunch and the four leftover treats from Easter. I did not feel better.

Compulsivity is a common feature of everyday living; it covers up and pushes down our feelings and thus our truth, because we are afraid of facing our feelings. All of our relationships—whether to people, food and drink, time, work, entertainment, religion and spirituality, exercise, sex, shopping or sleeping—will lighten once we come to terms with how we use them to distract our self from our feelings. Recurring compulsive thoughts or ideas can similarly keep us from feeling what is truly happening inside of ourselves.

It is good to be aware of whether we do this. Notice today whether you are compulsive, and how that looks in your life. Try to notice how you are feeling and what you are thinking when compulsivity pops up. Our ability to separate from the behaviour long enough to be aware of it and look at it is a super-positive step of being conscious. We need to be gentle with our self when we discover what we are doing. We need to remember that this behaviour is occurring because we are feeling lost inside and we are turning to an activity to soothe our self. It's amazing if we are able to recognize this. We might still proceed with the activity, and if we do, that's okay. Our awareness is what's important. We have made a great beginning.

When we have a new awareness of pain and need inside of us, therapy that delves into feelings can be life-changing. Please consider emotionally based therapy as a way to take another learning step towards understanding your self and what you need.

As we heal our inner self, imagine letting go of all the distraction and consumption and activity that is superfluous, until what is left is a meaningful and enjoyable life. This is the good path we are on.

🌸 June 20

Your life is a story that does not begin as a blank slate; instead, it comes imbued with themes, characters and plots—essentially, a narrative you inherit.

The narrative we are given at the beginning of our lives might take the form of a dominant narrative—that is, a story told from a perspective that reflects the interests of the dominant culture. Or it might be a cultural narrative, which tells a story from the point of view of a nation or an ethnic or minority group within a nation.

It is helpful to look at our life stories—the arc through the beginning, middle and end—through these narrative lenses so that we can choose to accept, modify or recreate the narrative for ourselves, thus altering the rest of the story to go according to our individual hopes and beliefs. This is an extremely empowering way to reclaim our lives.

It started for me when I moved to a property filled with wildlife, including snakes, and I questioned why I couldn't care about the snakes as I did about everything else there. I had inherited a fear that was not mine, and slowly, as the universe gently gave me snake encounters I could handle—two slow and distant baby snakes sleeping curled together, and a pretty emerald-green one—I was able to admire and care about these creatures. I realized I didn't want this snake-fearing subplot as part of my story, because it conflicted with the rest of my larger story of returning to nature and embracing an untamed life.

On the other hand, the prairie part of my ancestral story—the tales of the open land, the women, the horses, that I have heard and imagine still—I have chosen to keep in my narrative because it resonates. My travel adventures around the world, though they made me appear courageous, were actually me re-enacting my parents' bravery and individualism. I choose for myself now, at middle age, to set down roots and tend to them as they grow deeper. The Canadian cultural narrative I was born into—the tendency to apologize for our very selves—I decline. Instead, I choose to embrace a "cultural creative" way of life.

Despite our freedom as individuals, we must be aware that the things we do are in resistance to or in support of existing family, ethnic and cultural narratives. The more aware we are of these lenses, the more consciously we can pick and choose to create the story that uplifts and inspires us.

✸ June 21

According to a 2016 article in the *Harvard Business Review*, more than 75 percent of our time at work is spent in groups or teams.

Do you enjoy participating in teams? Do you feel uplifted in groups?

Collaboration is usually not as effective as we intend, primarily because the group is not psychologically safe for people to participate fully. Google's study, Project Aristotle, revealed that groups with psychological safety and strong narratives excel.

As the *New York Times Magazine* related:

> What Project Aristotle has taught people within Google is that no one wants to put on a "work face" when they get to the office. No one wants to leave part of their personality and inner life at home. But to be fully present at work, to feel "psychologically safe," we must know that we can be free enough, sometimes, to share the things that scare us without fear of recriminations. We must be able to talk about what is messy or sad, to have hard conversations with colleagues who are driving us crazy. We can't be focused just on efficiency. Rather, when we start the morning by collaborating with a team of engineers and then send emails to our marketing colleagues and then jump on a conference call, we want to know that those people really hear us. We want to know that work is more than just labor.

How can we make ourselves safe psychologically? We can get clear about why the group matters to us. We can focus on the content of the group more than the group's response to us. We can bring our curiosity. We can assure our own safety by not judging ourselves or threatening ourselves with failure ultimatums.

When there is psychological safety, a group not only succeeds, it creates a highly rewarding experience that people want to repeat. It all comes back to our amygdala—the part of the brain that processes emotions; when we feel safe, our brains are open to reflection, learning, change and creativity. When we are afraid, our brains close, we put on defensive masks and our egos are very much in the driver's seat.

Too much of our lives is spent in groups and teams for us to suffer through it, stay quiet or wear masks any longer. We matter. People in our groups matter. Our reasons for participating in the group matter. Let us focus there.

June 22

Are you one to whom animals come?
Do children say, "I like talking to you"?
Because you wait, you stand still, you stay quiet, you are awake.
To receive without moving, to hold open,
Chosen to witness their greatness and beauty.
Be still. Be one to whom our most innocent come to show themselves.
Your cup will fill, because you allowed it to be empty.

June 23

How we accept others,
Flaws, imperfections, mistakes, easily explained.
Or are they?
Is the grace, understanding, forgiveness, tolerance, space
We give a real place? Reserved only for some or open to all?
Open to us too?
It is one or the other. We are open or we are closed.

To choose open,
Gently start small, something we have already to give.
A smile, a yes,
To another or ourselves.
Today might be our best.

June 24

In *Women Who Run with the Wolves*, Dr. Clarissa Pinkola Estés writes:

> I was lucky to be brought up in Nature. There, lightning strikes taught me about sudden death and the evanescence of life. Mice litters showed that death was softened by new life. When I unearthed "Indian beads" fossils from the loam, I understood that humans have been here for a long, long time. I learned about the sacred art of self-decoration with monarch butterflies perched atop my head, lightning bugs as my night jewelry, and emerald-green frogs as bracelets.
>
> A wolf mother killed one of her mortally injured pups; this taught a hard compassion and the necessity of allowing death to come to the dying. The fuzzy caterpillars which fell from their branches and crawled back up again taught single-mindedness. Their tickle-walking on my arm taught how skin can come alive.

There is raw beauty, vulnerability, in the natural world. Soul. Meaning. Value. Growth. Sacrifice and effort are worth it.

Will you allow yourself to be untamed and unwilded? For a while, take yourself to a place where a dog can be unleashed. Walk in a ravine or in the woods. Get low to the ground. Watch nature happen. Smell leaves. Put your hand on a tree trunk and feel its energy. Climb and descend—come out of the straight line for a wee bit. Indulge your urges to take off a shoe, hug a tree, cry with gratitude, giggle, touch, sit on the dirt or get your pant legs wet.

Your own wildness will respond, your intuition will stir, your soul will smile.

🌸 June 25

My best friend invited me to celebrate our birthdays at her favourite place in the world: on Georgian Bay in southern Ontario. She booked us into a remote Airbnb on a small island accessible only by boat.

When the boat came to pick me up, I saw a truly wild woman at the bow, holding the boat line. My friend was barefoot, her hair was blowing back in the wind, and she wore a bandana, a bikini top, shorts and an ear-to-ear grin. She jumped onto the dock, tied up the boat and greeted me with a look of pure exhilaration.

Later that weekend I would walk behind her in silence on this rock island we were exploring, while she held a long walking stick and poked the grasses for rattlesnakes. That image will stay with me forever, and I remember thinking that she walked like an Indigenous grandmother—an "earth walker," as another friend says. One who is humble, alert, respectful, wise, self-assured and very much alive. My friend melted my heart in that instant, for she had again shown me her true essence, her true spirit. She has done it many times over the years—when music moves her body and she can't help swaying to the rhythm, when she belly-laughs so hard that only squeaks and gasps come. These are endearing memories of sweetness. Standing on a million-year-old piece of granite, the wind nearly blowing us over as we take in an endless horizon, she was not only sweet, she was powerful—an awe-inspiring Mother Earth.

We are lovable, good people in everyday life. Sometimes, in the right environment, our spirit takes over. I always get goosebumps, and tears well up, when another's true essence comes out. It is an honour to witness, and I trust that my reaction is my own spirit responding. Namaste—the spirit in me sees the spirit in you.

When we put ourselves into environments that call our spirits forward, our inner beauty, inner power and holiness shine through. A time when we can "just be," knowing who we are and where we come from, and feeling a natural ease with ourselves and the world. If you know this part of yourself, encourage it to come forward through music and poetry and nature—your happy places that open up unbridled creativity. If you are new to meeting your spirit, ask a friend you trust to describe your spirit to you. They will have a sense, a knowing, of your spirit. Ask them to describe it using their senses, imagination and intuition.

You have the power to call upon your spirit to guide you through the day, help you make decisions and help you stay grounded. What a beautiful way to live—by inviting your spirit to take you by the hand.

June 26

To me, "surrender" means to lower my defences and let myself be seen, to give up pretending, to admit I am afraid. My defences are what keep me in fear and attract fearful people and fearful situations.

When I surrender, my fear melts away. I become aware of who I am as a person: kind, sensitive, gentle, intuitive, trusting, happy, innocent—the person everyone sees except me.

When I surrender to not knowing, a space opens for knowledge and for people with knowledge to flow to me. When I surrender to life going at its own pace and I stop forcing things, I let go of the invisible weight I carry and I slump with relief. I am left with an ease that will attract ease. Like attracts like.

When I surrender to being cared for and loved preciously, it becomes so, and I am left to dwell in love and hope and goodness. We receive from people who are open—children, especially. Their light touches us and we are better for them being here. Unburdened, unaware, surrendered to love.

Surrender is good. When we have lost touch with ourselves, when we feel tired, sad, worried or in despair, it is a good time to surrender, to say, "I don't know. I feel tired. I feel afraid. I feel despair. I need help. I need love. I need care. I need protection."

Opening up to our neediness, surrendering to needing, truly being with how much we need, brings an exquisite lightness of being that is hard to describe. It brings a knowing that everything is all right. From that moment, we will know what to do.

Surrender often. As ego and defences return, surrender again. Let us fill ourselves with surrender, again and again, so that it becomes grace.

❀ June 27

We have a tree in our front yard that is over a hundred feet high, with a trunk that takes three adults to encircle arm to arm and spreads across our yard with big, sweeping boughs. It is majestic; there is truly no other way to describe it. My partner and daughter, sensing the tree's feminine energy, have named her the Grandmother, and each will greet and speak to her with kindness and reverence. "Good morning, Grandmother." "How beautiful you are today, Grandmother." "I hope you are happy, Grandmother."

We found some photographs of our farm that are difficult to date precisely, but that seem to have been taken in the 1930s. In one picture a family is sitting in front of the house on a summer's day, shirt sleeves rolled up, their tanned faces smiling. Everyone is relaxed and light. And in the far-right corner of the photo, there is a young Norfolk pine tree, barely six feet tall. The branches are longish and curled slightly, like a young child's hair, and the trunk, while rigid and straight, is barely the thickness of an adult's wrist. This young tree looks full of promise. Planted twenty feet back from a corner of a fieldstone wall, the adolescent tree has all the space it needs to expand and grow.

On closer inspection it becomes clear that this adolescent tree and our friend the Grandmother are one and the same. More than eighty years have passed since the photo was taken, and the youngster has grown to fill the entire corner, pushing out at the stone wall. The boughs are all more than thirty feet long and reach across our driveway to touch our garage. The Grandmother is the tallest tree on our farm, and she can be seen at the top of the forest line from more than a mile away.

The photo and the Grandmother remind me of longevity and perseverance. I look at either of them and realize that the speed at which my life seems to move is really only fast to me. The rest of the natural world has a constant, slower rhythm and our experience of time is a reflection of how we choose to see it.

❈ June 28

I'm of an age that I can remember galoshes. Do you remember them—those rubber overshoes with the big zippers that men and women would huff and puff to pull on over their dress shoes to protect them from the rain or snow? I can also recall that all trucks had two-wheel drive and carburetors, and in the winter it would often be too cold for them to start. I can remember that the first laptop I ever owned had eight megabytes of RAM and a one-gigabyte hard drive, and it seemed I would never need all that computing power or storage space for my files.

I can also recall that people carried transistor radios, and then boom boxes, and then Walkmans or Discmans if they wanted to listen to music on the go. I remember cars with eight-track tape players, and TVs that relied on rabbit-ear antennas. Then came cable, and we changed channels using push-button converter boxes attached to the receiver by long cables, before wireless remotes were finally made available. Most coffee tasted bad, people chewed away a space in the lids of their takeout coffee cups so they could sip from them, and donut shops always smelled of cigarette smoke.

At each point in my life, I can also remember thinking that that moment in time was perfect and that we had everything we could ever want or need. Our houses were big enough, our cars carried more people and everything we owned had a function—and if it broke down, you fixed it. I remember feeling very content.

I'm thinking about this in a kind of wistful way today, because I appreciate how far we've come in some ways, while also being conscious of what we've lost.

I can see that we have gained in convenience, ease and efficiency, but we have lost the knowledge of how things work. Most of us live at a level of comfort that our grandparents could only dream of, yet we've lost their sense of community and contentment with simple things like playing cards and chatting to neighbours.

They were happy just to be able to hold a mug of hot coffee, while we are frequently disappointed if our coffee isn't at exactly the right temperature.

We must remember that the most important aspect of life, next to survival, is contentment.

We need to arrive at a place where we are simply content with who we are and how we are living.

🌸 June 29

Can we be comfortable in silence? Are we willing to be in moments of silence with others? Will we wait for another to finish speaking, even when the pace of their speaking is halted or slow or they are searching for words?

We can look into their eyes as they are speaking and watch them. We can see that they are present and with us. We can wait for them, if they have been pulled into the trance of remembering their own story.

How silent can we be? Can we greet friends, colleagues, family or children and wait for them to speak first? Are there instances when we can communicate using methods other than speech—for example, with a smile or the touch of a hand?

Silence is a gift for us too. Silence can be sweetest inside of noise because it requires us to focus, which quiets our mind. How quiet do you like your silences?

Consider that the depth of life happens in the spaces between words.

❀ June 30

I am blessed that the people closest to me are well balanced in their feminine and masculine energies. They listen. They wait. They are responsible with their emotions, energy and words. They are deliberate—and they can seem slow. They have great capacity for love and laughter. They trust in the goodness of people. They trust themselves. They feel safe in the world.

These energies are inside each of us. Do we understand and allow them?

As Allie Horner writes on her blog *Adventure Knocks*, "Feminine energy is one of feeling fulfilled and free within the self, and love illuminates her path from the inside out. She is the energy of beingness. [Masculine energy] is the energy of action, but loving and open and faith-based action."

Feminine and masculine energy are a balance inside of us, to inspire and then flow. We are all we need.

July

❋ July 1

When we have nothing to say,
And we wait,
Life fills the moment for us.
That is beauty.

❋ July 2

I know for sure when I love another. I trust the feeling wholeheartedly.

I know what love feels like in my body when I am near someone I love. It makes my hands tingle, my head buzz and my eyes well with tears. I feel a gentle, warm pressure on my chest. I don't have to touch to feel this love. It comes from simply being in their presence. This is true of people as well as animals, trees, ideas, music and places that I love.

At first I thought my list was too short, having only one thing of which I am sure. Maybe it is good that there is only love on my list. I am happy with a life dedicated to feeling love.

What in life do you trust absolutely?

Think about what you have dedicated your life to. Is it worthy? If it is, you are blessed to know it. If it is not, you are also blessed to know it.

✹ July 3

I was on a plane the other day, flying to a conference. After we had touched down, the flight attendant announced that there were eighteen passengers on the plane who needed to transfer to other flights. Everyone else was asked to remain seated to allow the eighteen to gather their luggage and leave the plane first.

When I looked up and down the aisle, I saw more than fifty people standing, ready to walk off the plane.

Inconsiderate? No, I don't think they were all lacking kindness or consideration.

Inattentive? Possibly, but it's unlikely so many people weren't paying attention to a very clear, reasonably loud request that more than two hundred others also heard.

Indifferent? Yes. I think some of the people standing were indifferent to the needs of those who had to get off the plane first. Perhaps they even justified their actions, telling themselves that they too had places to get to urgently.

Deceitful? Yes. When I looked at the faces of those standing, I noticed that many wore expressions of mild shock and embarrassment that they were so exposed to the rest of us.

You see, the folks who really needed to leave the plane genuinely looked the part—they had their tickets in their hands, they were anxious about time, they were checking their phones frequently and looking flustered. And I counted eighteen such people.

The rest were standing there, looking firm and determined to be off the plane first. They were lying.

Why lie in a moment like this? What could be so important, or at risk, to trigger a person to deceive in such an obvious way? What mechanism of thought inside their minds overrode their basic understanding of the truth?

Some of you reading this may make the distinction that the extra thirty or so people standing in the aisle were being opportunists—they could see an opening to leave the plane early and they took it. Bravo for them, you may be thinking. But that distinction is also a lie—in fact, it's a lie created to cover an already existing, uncomfortable lie.

The simplest way to live lightly is to live truthfully. To clearly know the difference between honesty and deception in ourselves. To feel truth in our bodies as a sensation we learn to trust. And to make choices from that truthful place that we never feel uncomfortable about, doubt or regret.

Despite what we are often told, to live truthfully doesn't take courage. All it takes is self-love.

✳ July 4

If you could bring five things with you to a desert island, what would they be? They'd probably be your most valued possessions—things you would miss or never be able to replace.

If you have lost possessions dear to you, I am sorry, and I hope that reading today will help you celebrate the memory of those items and give you new insights into yourself.

Today there are three things I would want to bring: a pair of handmade blankets, one from each of my grandmothers. One has a pattern of colourful crochet squares, while the other is a soft, creamy white cable knit. Our family calls them the "Grandmaman" and "Nanny" blankets respectively. They represent my ancestors to me, the two different sides of my heritage, and I appreciate the hands that made them.

The third thing is our home. I love our home. It is a dream come true after many years of living in the city in beautiful small spaces. We now have space and light, comfort and wilderness, safety, privacy and freedom.

Beyond these three most treasured items, I typically wish for things to give me a sense of myself I don't yet feel—confident, beautiful, successful, grounded, creative, smart, talented and original. If I have these boots or these dishes, I will embody the person I want to be. Hmmm, great trickery here! I use my awareness to tell the difference between wanting a possession because it reflects who I already am and what matters most to me, and wanting a possession to become what I feel I am not.

Reflecting upon our relationships to our possessions, which things are most significant and meaningful, and why?

Possessions that matter most to us reflect our values. Think about what our most loved possessions represent to us. Dwell on the feelings our most cherished possessions give us: comfort, joy, safety, nurturing, love, belonging, expression, freedom.

Is there something more that we need to reflect our values and make a great life? Are there items missing that we would bring to that desert island?

An inventory of our possessions and wish lists is freeing, because it helps us focus our precious time and energy on what we want most. It helps us understand why we have what we have. It might open a new door if we already have what we want most.

❋ July 5

By now, we've come to understand that we cannot control another person or their behaviour. We've tried to cajole, invite, manipulate, leverage and coerce others in our lives into doing the things we want them to do, and in most cases, it really hasn't worked out for us. At the same time, others have tried to get us to do things we haven't wanted to—or didn't like or feel comfortable doing—and that hasn't made us feel good about ourselves.

So we know that we can't control others and that we don't like being controlled, but have we *accepted* that we cannot control others and their behaviour? After all, there's a vast difference between knowing a truth and accepting it. Knowing and understanding something as true lie at the surface, or on the perimeter, of our awareness. We see it, we get it, but we don't like it, and we may rail against it or resist it. To accept a truth is to embrace it fully, letting it in so deeply that it washes out any and all objection, tension, discomfort or expectation to the contrary. We've arrived at acceptance when we are at ease and at peace with a truth.

I'm writing about this today because I realize that I still hold on to expectations about how some people in my life *should* behave. Just realizing that I have attached "shoulds" to these people means that, at some level, I don't accept the way they behave or who they are, and that I still wish that they would be different. I also see now that much of my tension and conflict with them is because I have set them firmly in roles. And it is these roles, packed with the meaning that I have given them, that have created my attachments, expectations and "shoulds." I see now that I have some rigid prescriptions for how parents, siblings, partners, friends and co-workers ought to behave.

I have some deeper work to do to get to acceptance and see the people beneath the roles I've assigned them. I want to do this for them, of course, but mostly for me.

I don't like living with the heaviness of expectation and the longing that people behave in certain ways. I don't like the feeling of wanting to control people so that they become just the way I want them to be.

I can't grow living my life that way.

❀ July 6

I watched my partner give a cashier a points card—I don't mean to scan it; I mean my partner gave it to her to keep. The cashier was in disbelief at first—this gesture came right out of the blue—but my partner looked her in the eyes and smiled, then walked away as if it was no big deal. The woman's day was brightened by this random act of kindness. I marvelled at my partner being so present in the moment

with her, then becoming aware of having something to give and sensing it would be well received.

Spontaneous kindness feels as powerful as the spark of an engine,
generating a lightness, a giddiness, an energy between us that promotes connection and possibility. It lives in the eyes. It is a timeless
feeling of joy, peace and love. It lights us up and galvanizes our energy
and enthusiasm, making us feel great for days or even longer.

Being present. Being an observer of people. Being an observer of
self. The rest is as easy as following the sparkles.

July 7

**Humanity does not differ in any profound way; there are not
essentially different species of human beings. If we could only
put ourselves in the shoes of others to see how we would react,
then we might become aware of the injustice of discrimination
and the tragic inhumanity of every kind of prejudice.**
—John Howard Griffin, Black Like Me

I call it one of my growing-up moments—when I first realized that
difference and prejudice were not just about whites versus everyone
else. For a long while I was taught that prejudice, bigotry and racism
mainly described the system of preferred and superior status and origin of white male Europeans over women and all other races. I remember a kind of cognitive dissonance in this—feeling a sense of shame
at being white and European and yet, inside my being, seeing and
accepting everyone around me as certainly equal to myself. As a teenager, I became aware that the way I saw the world and others was not
the same way that others experienced the world, and that the colour of
our skin or the cultural heritage we belonged to dictated how we were
treated and how we saw the world.

In my twenties I saw bigotry and racism within communities—

people judged and mistreated because they were too white or too black, because of their sect of faith or because their lives had been predetermined by their birth caste. And still I saw people as equals and began to appreciate how similar our stories were.

In my thirties and forties I became aware of how much difference and separateness there was in our world—how many voices had been silenced, how many cultures erased and rewritten, how many people had been disappeared. At the same time, I marvelled at how much all of us shared universally—how our stories, struggles, songs, religions, family structures and feelings were connected. I could see that we are more the same than we are different.

And now, in my fifties, I see something new: our true enemy is not the other, but the pain inside all of us that is connected to being seen and told we are different. It is the significant wound or chronic hurt we hold in our minds from times when we were made to feel so different that we began to believe we didn't belong.

Our enemy is the moment when knowing that we were all the same was replaced by the thought: "I can't belong because I am different."

What if we went back to that place or moment inside ourselves? What if we journeyed back to our own innocence and saw the truth again?

July 8

In prosperous countries the world of work is always in transition, evolving to reflect people's wants and needs and their search for fulfillment and purpose. For many people, work has become a reflection of their talents, values, social norms and networks. Relative work security and economic growth have empowered people to challenge the status quo and demand such innovations as flex hours, the option to work from home, maternity/paternity leave and shift schedules that allow time to pursue personal interests.

Those with an entrepreneurial bent are finding ways of earning beyond being an employee, replacing the paradigm of working forty-plus hours for someone else with techniques that "attract" the kind of lifestyle they desire—for example, by returning to trades as careers, generating Airbnb income as they travel for part of the year, opening an Etsy store online, or making their household more self-sufficient by creating and trading.

The day we reached the point of outsourcing care for our children, pets and home in order to work, I began to question what I valued most. I started observing when our children were most content, I took note of my daily headaches and backaches, and I reflected on how time with friends meant eating and drinking—code for numbing out.

Now evidence of climate change, war and social injustice are fuelling my desire to live on my own terms. Predictions of automation and AI, continued scandal and corruption in government and corporate leadership make work less real to me and push me to be more demanding in everything I do. I feel myself being nudged into taking risks and challenging my own conformity, because it really seems up to me to take care of myself and my family. My illusion of security is certainly growing thin.

The people in my small northern community are inspiring me to think differently about lifestyle and money, and I feel more hopeful. I watch them knit together seasonal jobs to fill the year, or start family businesses where the role or title is irrelevant. Early retirement and part-time work are being topped up with starting online businesses or foundations, becoming board members, buying property, accessing grant funding, growing your own vegetables and raising backyard chickens. It is exciting to see what people create when they have time, control and freedom.

We can rebalance scales so that impoverished people have options other than disreputable, dangerous or illegal jobs to provide for their basic human needs. Becoming financially self-sufficient myself has got me thinking about how I can help others to do the same. I've had to come out of scarcity thinking to truly see how much I have—and how much I have to give. It feels like a new life power I am learning how to use.

The erratic, unsettled and dangerous times we live in may be just what we need to take back our freedom. Our world of work is a huge part of life, one that offers opportunities for us to consider how we might take back control over our time and effort so that we can have the lives we want.

July 9

You cannot see the light in the light. You have to see the light in the darkness. This world does not exist all in the light.
—Rabbi Rayzel Raphael

The most difficult aspect of life to accept is the existence of darkness and pain, hopelessness and despair. It is disturbing and confusing and makes no sense to us that our world is also this way. We don't accept it, even though the truth is all around us. Some of us work very hard to filter out or wall ourselves off from experiencing any pain at all. With our eyes shut and our fingers in our ears, we want all the darkness in our world to be erased and we hope that every conflict can be avoided or solved in favour of peace.

I see this every day. I have clients who insist that I help them have conflict-free marriages, or that I take all their anxiety away or give them a pill that will give them a life without depression. My partner will turn off the radio when the hourly news comes on or will walk out of the room when the television news airs. I have friends who always want to be positive and happy and will leave a conversation or walk away from a moment that becomes difficult or heated. And the internet and bookstore shelves are full of blogs, books, tips and how-tos designed to help us escape the pain of real life.

But none of this is working for any of us. And it seems that the more energy we put into denying or running away from the pain, the more it seems to grow. "That which we resist persists," as a colleague of mine used to say.

I don't believe the answer or the way through is to live as though darkness doesn't exist; I think we need to accept and appreciate darkness and lightness together—and that life is made up of both. They are not balanced perfectly or equally. We are not predestined to feel only one, but both, and sometimes together in the same moment. What makes reality rich is that it is composed of both lightness and darkness, joy and pain, transcendence and suffering.

To fully appreciate living lightly requires that we accept that we also live in darkness.

❋ July 10

I'm going to live my life in thin slices today. Would you join me?

Imagine these thin slices of joy: the feeling of your pillow as you first awoke; that first sip of water, coffee or tea this morning; the warmth of a hot shower; hearing a great new song or a favourite familiar tune on the radio; hearing people laugh; having someone smile at you or give you a hug or a warm handshake.

Or imagine these thin slices of anxiousness: running to catch a bus or a train; hurrying to get yourself and your family out the door on time; the early moments of your first day at a new job; meeting a new friend; taking the risk to share something personal with someone you feel you can trust; making a mistake.

Or imagine the thin slices of irritation: an alarm that didn't ring; an elevator that stops on every floor; a long, slow-moving line at a government service counter; the telemarketing call that came just as dinner was ready to be served; the person who veered into your lane on the way home tonight; the train that was so full you had to stand the whole way home.

And finally, imagine the thin slices of melancholy that can occur inside light moments: walking back to the car alone after putting your young child on the school bus, feeling the weight of responsibility the driver has for delivering the children safely; thinking about a friend who is going through a tough time; wishing family visits were different and wondering whether the effort will be worth it; moments of loneliness when a friend doesn't see you or hear you.

Our lives are happening in moments that are thin slices for us to taste, see, hear and feel—morsels of emotions and thoughts, actions and reactions. I know that when I share with a friend how my day is going, or I reflect back on it at the end, I too often see a plate with only one large serving of good or bad. I'm realizing that this is a trick my mind plays on me and that in truth, my day—every day—is full of these thin slices of moments for me to savour.

🌸 July 11

Regular periods of silence are required for what we seek.
Watching. Waiting. Breathing. Listening. Feeling.
Regular. Periods. Of silence.
Silence connects us to the energy of life.
In stillness we can feel it
In our hands and the tops of our heads,
In our body temperature and sensations.
When we get to know this feeling,
It acts as a signal:
Intuition, guidance and holiness are present.
These moments are where our truths live.
Ask our question, feel our need, dream our dream, pray for help.
Feeling grateful to be heard,
Silent and not alone.

✺ July 12

Intuition is often explained as one of two general modes of thinking, along with analytic reasoning. Intuitive thinking is described as automatic, fast and subconscious. Analytic thinking, on the other hand, is slow, logical, conscious and deliberate.
—Valerie van Mulukom

It fascinates me to consider that intuition and analytical thinking operate in tandem. Because they use different brain processes, we don't have to choose one or the other—they complement each other, and when we are making a decision, we are wise to call upon both. Sensory inputs inform our intuition, remind us of relationships and activate empathy. For instance, whenever we encounter a person or a place, we get an immediate "gut feeling" based on the sensory data we take in. This intuition can be a powerfull ally to our analytic thinking.

Reflect on a decision you've yet to make and try using both modes of thinking together. Use your analytical skills to gather the information and comparatives, and then activate your intuitive mind to bring the subconscious cues to the surface—these might have come from a visit with the person or to the place in question.

Mastering two levels of decision-making skill equips us much better for the world we live in today, where empirical information is not always fully available or fully accurate.

✺ July 13

If we look at life as circles of people with shared intentions, we can draw upon the circle's connective and generative energy—flowing, receiving, accepting, intending. Circles provide a transformative structure by which our views and ideas are lifted into a greater whole. Circles are like a bubbling sauce on a stovetop; just as spices build layers of flavour, ideas and people add depth and power to the circle's intention. All are accepted into the whole, melted into the whole, to become transformed into fulfilling intention.

A circle is a beautiful form to put life into, one in which we can create intention and govern our lives in synergy with others.

A non-profit called These Numbers Have Faces uses a concept called "impact circles," whereby donors form a circle around one African student and pay for their tuition, books and leadership training. The goal is to help develop a generation of ethical, just and effective leaders in Africa.

Forming a circle around a person, cause, project, community or even the whole world to assure its well-being is, to me, the pure essence of mothering. Our daughter has been surrounded by family members who support and encourage her love of baking through their gifts. We watch our daughter smile and connect with them because she feels seen and known. Beautiful.

Forums, communities and interest groups typically organize as circles, bringing together those with like minds, passions, interests or hobbies. The level of support when there is a mutual interest, helped by a common language and enthusiasm, is incredible. Rather than try to convince friends and family to share my love of horses, I started joining online equestrian forums. Internet forums offer an easy, immediate and no-cost way to find like-minded people around the world.

Our Percheron horse Shorna had an emergency illness recently, and the vet unexpectedly told us we might need to euthanize her that same day. My online community—people I will likely never meet in person—rallied around us and sent messages of love, support and healing. They could understand the depth of our angst and could contribute knowledge and experience and stories because we share a love of horses. A neighbour we didn't know came right to our home with supplies, blankets and tons of advice and experience, and she saved

Shorna's life. She said the same thing had happened to her Belgians and she wasn't giving up. I felt exquisitely supported and more. I felt love and an energetic power. And Shorna lived.

If we put our lives into circles, momentum builds, and we never have to be alone. Consider an intention you have that matters to you and join a circle that shares your intention. Give yourself the experience of circle energy.

❋ July 14

Withholding or oversharing information can reveal our problem with boundary setting. Healthy boundaries give our sense of ease and peace in life a quantum boost, and in our interactions we learn to focus our energy on managing our own state, rather than trying (impossibly) to manage others'.

In thinking about boundaries, I realize how little I share during times of crisis, when I am focused on the critical decisions and actions that need to be taken. People who are directly able to assist are involved with me very intimately, yet it may take several days, or even longer, before I share what is happening with my friends and family. Because of this I find myself sharing and recounting and reliving the episode after the fact. And others are left to experience, process and resolve the shock, the ups and downs and the resolution of the story in one telling. The whole process feels draining to me—both because I don't enjoy reliving the experience and because I have to answer questions so that others can fill in the gaps in their knowledge.

My withholding the information in real time has blocked loved ones from sharing in my life and being connected to me. When I'm in crisis mode, I withhold information by default, to control my environment as well as other people. This tendency is rooted in my childhood—adults would pin their emotional needs onto me and I felt unprotected and unable to separate myself from the other. Without healthy boundaries, I am blocked as an adult from experiencing the support and love of others; I am simultaneously on the defensive while I go on offence, patrolling for non-confirming ideas or behaviours. It is exhausting and draining for me *and* for the people around me. While my withholding behaviour is most evident when I'm in crisis, I always behave this way.

At the other end of the scale are people who overshare, speaking compulsively and repetitively to relieve or soothe themselves without showing any awareness of the other. They shift their state by using the energy of someone who allows their energy to be drawn.

The way through is to practise setting healthy boundaries. For the most part, withholding and oversharing are done unconsciously. By making ourselves aware of our state, we can intentionally empower and enhance ourselves, our relationships and our interactions.

For me, healthy boundaries start with being aware of my own feeling state and being self-responsible for my needs, energy and actions—and seeing all of these create a bubble around me. When I meet another person, they have their own bubble. Healthy boundaries allow us to be together with our own bubbles intact. We can connect and interact, each of us having our unique experience in life, in parallel, free to choose for ourselves. Sounds idyllic, doesn't it?

Yet not everyone we meet in life is self-aware or self-responsible. Some people open their bubbles and their energy and emotions spill out, looking to flow into another. Or they pull energy away from another to fill themselves up. We can't manage or control such behaviours, but we *can* monitor, care for, advocate for and trust ourselves. In a moment of crisis I can be aware that I am feeling sad or fearful, that my emotions are heightened and that I am tense from lack of sleep and an adrenalin rush, so I can be responsible for my actions. I can let people know this is the state I am in. Ultimately, it is *my* responsibility, not theirs, to steer myself back towards a healthy, positive state.

Sleeping, eating, resting, getting support, taking breaks, asking for help, surrounding myself with helpful, positive people—these are all ways I use to get myself back. I shift my own bubble.

Mastering our own bubbles is a wonderful way to live. Awareness is the key factor. Instead of assessing others to make ourselves safe, let us first assess our own states and see to our own needs. That way we will be able to be with others, maintaining our energy. Acceptance, empathy, community, forgiveness, peace—all become possible when our emotional safety no longer depends upon the other.

🌸 July 15

When I was a teenager, I remember being fascinated with the wave-forms that appeared on the screen of an oscilloscope. In my high school electronics class, I first saw them and learned what it meant to lengthen the peaks and valleys, stretch them horizontally or alter the number of waveforms I could see on the screen. Something inside me just resonated with the idea that waves are a universal truth—that all of life comes and goes and happens in waves—our thoughts, our moods, our relationships, our work and everything in nature.

I was reminded of this yesterday as our daughter created her mood tracker for the month in her bullet journal. As we were talking, she showed me what she was preparing for the coming month, and then she opened her journal to the previous month. Looking at her progress, achievements, habits and moods over the past thirty days in picture form, I was struck by how many waves she had drawn. We went back further, exploring more months, and discovered even more waves.

When I asked her if that was what it felt like every day—that she was on a wave—she answered, "No, I'm so focused on all the little things every day that sometimes I feel like I'm moving, and other times I feel stuck. It's only when I look back on the month in my journal that I can see that I'm never really stuck."

Isn't that the truth? I know that I can get so drawn into every moment of my day and week at such a micro level that I can't see how I'm always travelling on a larger wave. It's like having a kind of amnesia—I struggle to remember whether I've had a good day or a great week. I know there were some good times and some hard or difficult stretches, but were they connected in some way? I don't know, because I can't remember.

It's only by looking back with the help of a visual reminder like a bullet journal that I can see the waves of how I am living. I can see in an instant that the early part of the month was a high point for me, and that somewhere around the tenth of the month I started to feel more uncertain and my mood dipped. Then it flattened for a few days and now it is back on the upswing.

The value of this graphic look at my life is that it helps me create a more truthful narrative of how I live. Understanding that my life always moves in waves allows me to have greater awareness and acceptance of the low points and more appreciation and gratitude for the high points. I can crash the thought that I'm ever stuck—even in the plateaus—because I can see that my life is always moving. This too shall pass—this is the truism of life—a life of waves.

❋ July 16

Have you ever had the feeling you were about to be fired? The sensation is an unshakable combination of dread, fear and lightness all wrapped up into a ball. It starts the moment you walk into the office and notice that some of your colleagues are a little more distant than usual. Then, just as you're sitting down, there's a call or a knock at the door and a few mumbled or softly spoken words along the lines of "We need to have a chat."

I've had four distinct careers in my life—not just jobs, but careers. Amongst all the jobs I've had, I've been fired twice. The first time, I was young and there was a heated confrontation that resulted in me storming off, swearing and feeling angry, scared and, truthfully, ashamed. I knew my boss didn't like me and that being fired wasn't about my performance but had more to do with my not being one of his favourites. So I marked it down to a personality conflict, decided he was wrong and moved on.

My second firing was tougher. Again, to be honest, I was at a low point in my life—just divorced, a single parent—and I needed the job but didn't like what I was doing or the company. I was hanging on to the job, conscious of my mediocre achievements and hoping that I would one day work myself out of the rut.

Two weeks before Christmas, the owner of the company took me out for lunch, and before the glasses of water arrived, he said in a low voice, "This experiment is not working. You won't be coming back to the office after this lunch." He handed me a severance envelope, told me the lunch was on him and got up and walked out of the restaurant. I was shocked and embarrassed. I felt found out, angry, scared and sad.

I think what made getting fired the first time easier to overcome was that I was clear that the issue belonged to my boss. My second firing was all mine and squarely on my shoulders. It took a few months to find a new job, and a year or so to fully own my truth about the situation.

In a weird but real twist of circumstance, two years later I met my previous boss again. This time I was facilitating a therapy group and he walked into the room as a new member. We looked at each other and we both smiled. I walked over to him and gently said, "Hi, good to see you again. I just want to say thank you for firing me." His smile deepened, and then his head drooped slightly, and looking up, he said, "I gave you the nudge I knew you wouldn't take yourself. And now I need your help."

Firings are endings, yet all endings are beginnings. We must choose to see them that way. What we make them mean and the stories we create about them are what give them all their power. This is our unique ability as humans: each of us gives our own meaning to the events in our lives.

❋ July 17

Imagine that your mind is like a beehive—thousands upon thousands of independent yet coordinated processes happening simultaneously, constantly busy, constantly assessing, adjusting and acting. Sounds like a lot, doesn't it?

Our minds are constantly working, observing and processing, judging and creating. All this activity creates a busy-ness that, like a beehive, can be very loud and chaotic. For most of us, this ongoing chatter in our heads seems to recede over the course of our lives because we learn to function despite it. It's like driving to work with the radio on in the car—we pay attention to the song and drive mostly by habit.

Those of us who want to live lightly can do so by turning down the volume of our minds' inner activity and developing the skill of observing, rather than reacting to, our minds' busy-ness and activity. When we can be our minds' observer, it's like listening to our thoughts as if they are coming from another person standing beside us. We hear the thoughts, but we don't act on every single one of them.

Such brain skills are the essence of mindfulness practice. Jon Kabat-Zinn, who created a course of mindfulness-based stress reduction in 1979, defines mindfulness as "the awareness that arises through paying attention, on purpose, in the present moment, non-judgmentally." In creating quick, personal connections with strangers at a bustling international airport for my CBC television series *Hello Goodbye*, I found that clearing my mind prior to every conversation allowed me to focus fully on the other person's words and actions. With mindfulness, I'm relaxed and keenly aware of who is in front of me. My mind is free of distraction and ready to absorb what they say. With mindfulness, I calm the beehive.

Mindfulness helps us build tremendous mental resiliency and offers such far-reaching benefits as decreased stress, better and clearer judgment, greater feelings of fulfillment and contentment, and increased serenity, empathy and self-compassion. All of these are critical to the building and growth of rewarding relationships.

When my mind is at rest, I create an observer's point of view from which I can see what my mind is working on and how it's working—"Oh, there's that thought that I need to call my friend. And there's another thought about the teller at the bank—she looked sad. I wonder why? Oh, there's another thought about my hearing—am I really going deaf in my right ear?" All this activity and much, much more is humming at a pace I can handle and is there for me to observe. I can choose how I want to act and respond, and I don't have to react to everything I think.

✳ July 18

Make yourself vulnerable,
Before life chooses for us,
And time runs out.
Why be vulnerable?

I looked a stranger in the eye and said hello. It was a most uplifting reward to receive their hello and warm intention in return, after taking a chance to be vulnerable.

The creators of the *Sickboy* podcast and the SickWish gala—Jeremie Saunders and his friends Brian Stever and Taylor MacGillivary—embody vulnerability. In the podcast, Jeremie—who has cystic fibrosis, a genetic disease that affects the lungs and other internal organs—Brian and Taylor engage in conversations with people who are dying or living with degenerative diseases. The idea is to end the stigmas attached to such illnesses and help people deal with them. *Sickboy* speaks out loud what we all know already: that our time on earth is limited and fragile, that change is constant and that we need help.

We don't need to confront a disease in order to choose to be vulnerable. Choosing to be vulnerable gives us the experience of being seen and loved for who we are. There is really nothing else like it. Will you look for openings to be vulnerable today?

❉ July 19

While we consider our next move, let's pause and take a few deep breaths.

> *Do it because*
> *We want to,*
> *So that we feel true to our selves.*
> *It matters to us.*
> *It is holy to us.*

Any other reason is a head-created illusion—an "in order to"—that distracts us from our truth, for our own sakes.

I asked my family if we could share the chore of making dinner. My partner and daughter each took two nights, then we added a pizza ritual and a leftover night. That left me one dinner a week to cook. I can't believe the lift in our spirits, our creativity and the yumminess of the food, made once again with love.

Everyone wins when we dismantle our "shoulds."

July 20

Hesitating, stopped by old paradigms,
I tell myself it must be a certain way or not at all.
So, I choose not at all.
And that "no" sits and ferments in my gut,
Not going away but working away inside me.
The tiniest microbes turn sour milk into yeast, a living, growing
*   organism*
That becomes beautiful offerings, of yoghurt, bread and cheese.
A micro baby step, to admit I am blocked.
I want to be unblocked more than I want to block.
When the balance tips that way, momentum is ours.
We are free, if only for a moment.
To make the call, say yes, post a flyer, press "send."
The tiniest actions turn into conversations, books, projects, launches,
*   customers, partnerships, reconciliation, peace.*
I make my tiny actions in moments when what I want more is to be
*   unblocked.*

July 21

Sometimes I struggle to find the right words to say to someone after they have shared something personal or difficult with me. I can feel my own sense of loss, angst, frustration or even excitement as I understand and relate to what they have told me—and it's these strong feelings inside me that block my brain from knowing what to say. The pauses and silences can be deafeningly loud, and later I may reflect on the encounter and wish I could have said this or that.

These moments weigh heavily on me and can stay with me for quite a while, which is why I want to work on this for myself. I really believe it is something I can grow through.

Some days I really wish that empathy were taught in school as a necessary life skill. Do you know what I mean? Have you ever struggled to find the right thing to say to someone—someone who desperately needed or wanted comforting?

I strongly believe that once we're brave enough to confide in another person, to take the risk to share what troubles us or what troubles are in us, what we want most is to feel heard and understood and be assured that we are not alone and that we are lovable. Opening up and being vulnerable is, without a doubt, us being our most courageous.

Some of us comfort others by saying words or doing things that comfort us. I have friends and family who offer well-meaning solutions, or try to distract me with jokes, or try to make me feel better by sharing a story about a time when they have felt an emotion more powerfully: "Hey, I know you feel sad, but listen to this—see how much sadder I felt here."

I have to say that none of that works or is helpful.

However, over time I am learning that what really does work is allowing some of the pauses to blossom with simple words of affirmation like "yes," or by looking the person in the eye. Honouring the moment and their bravery, I make sure I stay with them, as if we are in a very caring bubble of space and time together. If my own feelings are triggered, I am cautious not to steal the moment or upstage their feelings. I refocus my breathing and promise myself I will attend to my feelings. This is called "bracketing" in therapy speak; the ability to remain present for another person with the promise of attending to our own needs as soon as there is space and time.

I suppose I'm learning that empathy boils down to togetherness. And that the silences that happen while someone is being vulnerable with us are opportunities to show them "You and I, we are together."

❋ July 22

Sometimes I react to people around me who are giving ultimatums, manipulating, gossiping and being negative. I put on an exaggerated mask of optimism and joy—inviting, forgiving, silent in the face of misbehaviour or anger.

At the other end of the spectrum are people who are joyful, empathetic, kind and self-responsible. Around them, my ego may be threatened, and I sometimes get defensive or resentful, feeling as though I am being controlled and judged. In response, I may rebel, shut down or protest. It can be enough to make me want to destroy and be mean.

In either case, if I were to catch myself in the mirror, I would see a disconnect on my face and in my eyes between the mask and the authentic me. That disconnect is how I know my reaction is a coping mechanism that, while protecting me, puts me out of balance and takes me away from who I am.

When I am willing to be direct and authentic with people who are acting out—to disagree out loud in the face of anger or manipulation, to draw a line at behaviour I will not tolerate—I step into emotional expression of my own. Rather than pretending all is well, I can be stern and angry. I can draw a boundary line and I can stand at that line and wait for them—if I care about having them in my life—on healthy terms. I can wait at the line for my whole life because it doesn't cost me anything to do that.

With self-responsible people, I am learning that when I focus on what we are working on together, what we care about as a vision, I put myself back into my power, into my "adult." Once I'm grounded in my power, I can contribute, I can open myself and we can share beautiful time together.

When I am in reaction to another, it means I am out of balance in myself. If I step into the same emotion as the other person, as a conscious choice, it balances me on the inside and it balances my connection with the other person. It's an ongoing journey, but I feel proud of myself and confident of who I will be inside my relationships.

✳ July 23

The other day, I was reading some articles about what was happening in politics in the area I live in. As I read on, I noticed that my ego was sounding off with judgments and criticisms about one of our local politicians: he's narcissistic, what he says sounds ridiculous, he's governing out of fear and he's manipulative. My ego's output of negative reactions was a like a constant drip, drip, drip of what was wrong with this man. And as is often the case, my body started to tighten up in reaction to what I was thinking. My jaw clenched, I started to chew the inside of my cheek and my stomach began a slow, steady pattern of whining and grinding.

Clearly, I was starting to get wound up and my ego kept opening the tap—"This guy is a lousy leader, he's making us all look stupid." Then suddenly, I had another thought: "Look in the mirror." I paused to reflect on who I am, and then the questions began to appear: Where am I self-centred? What am I afraid to say so as not to appear ridiculous? Where in my life do I seek to control rather than lead? What are the ways in which I am indirect and try to manipulate others to get my needs and wants met?

The mirror I was looking into was showing me something I know and hold to be true. Where I judge others is where I have the most work to do myself. My ego's sounding off about this politician was my mind's way of revealing to me who I am.

I'm trying to work that out right now. I feel like this insight needs to be on a T-shirt or a wall mural. Or, crafted with spray paint, it needs to be tagged on railway cars and in alleyways for all to take in and see. Then the truth lying at the root of all our behaviour would finally, undeniably, be brought to the surface: What we judge is where our work begins.

Or something like that. Consider it a work in progress.

🌸 July 24

Plans change. People cancel. Weather affects travel. I am needed at home. Things feel hard. And I fall, literally—I slip, I trip, I bang into, I fall. These are the things that happen when life says no.

Instead of digging in deeper to get back on track, forcing things or picking fights with happy people around me, and instead of trying to figure out what is going on, I can believe that life is working hard to get my attention. I can choose to help life help me. I create an intention to listen, to hear what life wants to tell me, to be grateful. I pay attention to who *does* call, to what *does* happen.

I am listening to life today. I am gratefully open to the guidance life has for me.

🌸 July 25

If there are qualities that form the foundation of living lightly, one of them would have to be self-compassion. I can't emphasize strongly enough how a healthy, kind view of ourselves underscores our perspectives on others and their suffering. Self-compassion also helps us gently navigate the day-to-day disappointments, mistakes, misfortunes and pains that are inherent to real life. Every time I encounter a setback, self-compassion reminds me that I am not perfect or infallible, and life is not always perfect or ideal.

We all struggle and suffer, some of us much more than others, and it is this fact that opens the door for us to practise acceptance and kindness. I think one of the ironies of our modern world for many of us is that while our lives have become much easier than those of our grandparents, we have less capacity or tolerance for suffering than they had. Technology has delivered on its promise to make our lives more convenient and stable, but in the process we have become a people that does not expect to suffer. So when we experience setbacks, upsets or negative thoughts and feelings, we tend to exaggerate, overattach and overidentify with them. If we are suffering, it must be because we're unlucky, we made a terrible mistake, or in some way we are deeply flawed.

Self-compassion's power to transcend suffering begins with the deep realization that we can never truly separate or fully erase struggling from living—they are intertwined. No matter how hard we try or how diligently we work, we can never escape the fact that life is difficult for all of us.

So when we see that our food banks are stretched to their limits, when we see more and more homeless people on the streets, when we hear about rising rates of mental illness or terminal disease, or when we see human beings fleeing places where basic survival is threatened, we can take all of this as proof of life's difficult nature. And the same is true when we feel ourselves steeping in negative feelings, when we make mistakes or when things are disappointing, challenging or incomplete.

We lighten as soon as we accept. We lighten when we view our own suffering and another's with kindness. We lighten when we feel compassion for everyone who struggles to live. And we are enlightened when we breathe in self-compassion.

🌸 July 26

I have a few things I would like to achieve or realize before I die. They're not large, legacy-like accomplishments; they're simple, personal things that up until now have proven difficult to work on. And with each one, I'm at that point where I'll give it a good attempt and work until they happen.

Here's my list:

- I can't sit in a lotus position or put my head on my knees while touching my toes. Flexibility has eluded me.

- I have a guitar and do not know how to play it. I've never been able to get my hands to be limber enough.
- I cannot cut a piece of wood straight and square to save my life. There seems to be a disconnect between what I see and what I do when it comes to cutting wood.

When I reflect on the sum of my life to date, I am more than happy with who I am and what I have achieved. It's been a tough, heartbreaking road at times, though I've often been the beneficiary of a tremendous flow of things just going my way. I am content in all aspects of my life; I can honestly say this to you while also knowing that my contentment is deepening, or simplifying—depending on how you see it—to a place where the smallest acts or things are delicious experiences for me.

And yet these "incompletions" dog me because, despite my attempts, I have never overcome them. Prior to writing this today, I was in a place where I was willing to just let them go. I'd released myself from the expectation of ever being able to do any of those things with any reasonable success. Having no expectations equals minimal disappointment—that was my philosophy. I judged them as silly and inconsequential. "Who cares if I can't cut a straight line or make gains in my physical flexibility?" I said to myself. "These are meaningless pursuits." The rub, however, is that I also know at a deeper level that these three things hang with me because each of them represents an outer or upper limit of personal growth that I've been unwilling to work through.

Working on my flexibility is super-painful for me, so I can only make gains slowly and incrementally, through daily and diligent effort. And the progress is too slow for my mind and too painful for my body.

Learning guitar is much the same, with the bonus that the first time I took lessons—at the age of twelve—my instructor taught guitar through shaming and blaming, which turned me off and drove me away from wanting to hold a guitar ever again.

And cutting wood is connected to the overall shaming I received from a parent who was gifted at building anything but seemed to struggle to show a child how to do things the way he did. I am left-handed, and he is right-handed, so when I couldn't get something right, he would make a remark about me being left-handed and then step in and do it for me.

Does this explain why these three things haunt me? The skills themselves are relatively easy to master, but the processes are laden with heavy baggage that I either must work through or release myself from.

Do you have things like this in your life? Things you know you could do, want to do, but for deeper reasons have never made happen? Are these things loaded with painful experiences or meaning, or will achieving them require you to rock yourself out of your comfort zone?

I think today we can both take the first step towards making them happen or letting them go forever. Are you with me?

✹ July 27

There are many changes I would like to see in the world—environmental sustainability, social justice, peace and abundance for all—that would require some significant paradigm shifts before they can happen. In *The Structure of Scientific Revolutions*, Thomas Kuhn wrote, "When I researched paradigm shift, I found a fascinating model from science of the 1960s that defines a paradigm shift as 'a change in the basic assumptions, or paradigms, within the ruling theory of science.'"

The website Thwink.org builds upon Kuhn's model, suggesting that until the root cause or truth of a system changes, no new solution or resolution will ever be embraced. Systems are unequivocally committed to equilibrium, and changes that upset that balance cannot be accepted. Activism has been focusing on new solutions and pressing for change, rather than looking at the root cause for the system existing as it does.

Let me illustrate how I put these concepts into play in my personal life. Fifteen years ago, I stopped smoking. I had started at the age of thirteen, and for the next twenty years I was physically, emotionally and mentally addicted. Then one morning, I woke up as a non-smoker.

This may sound like an extreme shift, and it is. But it's a true story.

When I think back on this major life change, viewing it as a paradigm shift, I see that there was a fundamental change in the root truth I held about smoking. At thirteen I believed it helped me fit in socially. It helped ease my social anxiety, giving me something to do at a party, something that made me look busy when I was standing alone. I used smoking as a protective social shield, and I achieved my goal. Over the years, smoking became less socially acceptable and I found myself forced into unpleasant and inconvenient designated smoking areas. I think that, on a subconscious level, my truth about smoking changed when I had to promise the landlord that I would not smoke inside my lovely new brownstone apartment. Smoking was now alienating me socially, *adding* anxiety rather than easing it.

My basic paradigm remained the same: I wanted to maximize social ease and minimize anxiety. I became a non-smoker because smoking came into conflict with my basic paradigm. It didn't take any effort or willpower for me to give up smoking, and I didn't even suffer withdrawal symptoms. My system made the change immediate, without resistance, to protect my root goal. I haven't had a cigarette in fifteen years. While my mind tells me I would love to smoke again, I know my system would reject it.

To achieve the personal change we want requires that we find the root truths that drive our system. We recognize these truths when there is nothing more beneath the root—no further answer to the question "Why is that?"

Find the root truth to an aspect of your life you want to change. Start with the intention of finding the root truth, and then let it work inside of you and bubble up. When something presents itself, ask,

"Why is that?" to pull any sub-roots. Continue until you have reached the root truth.

Once we know the root truth underlying an aspect of our lives, our resistance to change will also become clear—as a threat to that truth. How very empowering to understand our innermost workings!

❉ July 28

We are well into the second half of the calendar year. Your plans, visions and imaginings—how are they? We've talked about them as seeds or young plants or sprouts in a greenhouse.

How about your relationship to your life? Does it feel healthy and strong? Is there flow? How do you feel, closing the seventh of twelve months?

How we receive what life is giving tells us where we need tenderness, breath, gratitude and silence. Return to those four things over and over again. They will always serve us well.

Breathing, in silence, grounds us in life, centres us. Let us breathe deeply until we feel the breath coming in from our belly, until the exhale sounds like relief, like a sigh. We will feel a deepening of the breath. There we are.

Now we are connected to ourselves. We can relax into "all is well." Let's stay here, open to love, open to flow, open to goodness and wellness. We are open to life when we breathe consciously. We have our breath, our beautiful exhales of relief and surrender.

Imagine yourself sending beautiful breath to your life, to your hopes and your loved ones—and yourself. Bring that beautiful breath with you today, nurturing your life. Hold all parts of your life with tenderness, as precious. Imagine wrapping your life with love, connecting it to a flow of love.

Bring tenderness to your thinking, to your roles, to your schedules, to your plans.

❋ July 29

"Life always works out for me."

I recently adopted this affirmation. I love how I feel when I say it—natural and humble, yet powerful. It means that no matter how life goes, I will be okay. I work this statement into conversations where I can say it in a matter-of-fact way, and I say it to myself too. It is very boosting for me; I feel myself stepping into the words.

Try saying the phrase and then following the good feelings that the words bring on. Our brains believe all our words to be true, so let's use the words we want! And let's hope that people around us will use this positive, affirming language—it signals we are on a matching vibration with them. Like attracts like. Be happy when people around us succeed and are happy, when life is working out for them; it means the same is coming our way.

Let's welcome the day we hear someone say the phrase first, or when we say it and hear a "Me too!" in response!

❋ July 30

We sometimes find it hard to believe, but from a purely scientific perspective, we're still animals. Nothing of significance has changed in us or about us since our earliest records of civilization some fifty to seventy-five thousand years ago. Over all that time our brains haven't gotten any bigger, nor are our mouths or ears larger. And our bodies are still adapting to the idea of standing upright.

I'm an animal and you're an animal. Which means that, deep down, we are mostly under the direction and control of our animal selves. We are reactive, impulsive and unpredictable. We're ruled by what we feel and perceive to be our immediate needs. All the norms and rituals and codes of civilization—and on a more specific level, our culture, our religion and even our family or our individual beliefs—are just dressing on the salad. Everything we do boils down to survival and belonging.

Having said all of that, there is an interesting development that is aiding our evolution from instinctive, reactionary animals to highly cognitive, conscious ones. Our brains contain a prefrontal cortex that allows or enables us to make choices that serve us beyond our basic needs. Because of this region of the brain, we can reflect, we can derive meaning, we can interpret, we can question, we can be introspective and we can be responsive.

All these extraordinary abilities take practice, hard work and perseverance. In fact, without our deliberate, constant and conscious intervention, our minds will default to what is easier and simpler: our basic, reactive animal state. In that place, we will:

- take things and people personally;
- let our feelings and impulses rule our behaviour;
- react with emotions that are disproportionate to the trigger; and
- recreate and re-enact dysfunctional patterns to get our needs met.

Look around—isn't this at the centre of our world's chaos and stress?

It's time to wake up.

❀ July 31

Have you experienced an injury or illness that requires rest, recovery and rehabilitation, and possibly medication? I have, and it amazed me to think that, in a society as consumed with numbing out as ours is, we are so vehemently resistant to healing remedies.

During a six-week stay in hospital, I met a team of doctors whose job it was to convince me that taking medication was okay and that I wouldn't become addicted. They also emphasized how important the medication was to my recovery. The fact that such pain teams even exist shows me we are in denial when it comes to our own self-worth.

I was then released to go home and recover over the next six months. I remember that, despite the pain team's assurances, my mind resisted the medications—I took doses that were lower than prescribed, or even went without until the pain returned with a vengeance and I was forced to make emergency calls. And instead of devoting the time to resting and recovery, I composed endless "to do" lists in my head, dramatically pushing myself out of bed to vacuum or to bake. I was driven to be productive, at the expense of my own recovery—and to the anguish and annoyance of my family and caregivers.

I couldn't accept that they loved me, for myself. I resisted the idea that I had their love without having earned it. And, capable of great love and spirit, they could see where I was blind and how my feeble attempts to produce belittled me.

Are you being told to rest or slow down? Do you have a prescription or health regimen you've been told to follow? Do you intuitively know you need to take care of yourself?

There is a lightness that others hold for us. They see our worth, even if we do not. We are deserving of love simply for being here.

August

✻ August 1

I am so grateful that, when we fight,
I know in my heart you aren't going anywhere, and neither am I.
That knowing gives me freedom to be in my feelings until I am clear,
And I don't rush into empty apologies to be free of the feelings.
Safe to stretch my boundary for love,
To risk my heart and go deeper,
Burying myself in love.
Deeply fulfilling.
Caring, receiving, surrendering, trusting.
For we are worth it.
I want to know how big my love can grow,
Whomever the person—another or ourselves.
Let love be an epic adventure of our heart, our body, our soul and mind.

✻ August 2

In 1988 a survey of more than a thousand American men and women revealed that most people felt happy with the idea of making about $30,000 a year. Adjusted for inflation, that $30,000 becomes just over $64,000 in 2018.

Meanwhile, a survey of millennials conducted in 2016 (meaning the participants were between twenty-one and thirty-seven years old at the time) revealed that earning $80,000 a year would make them feel happy—and an additional $30,000 was widely thought to result in an even greater quality of life.

I use the term "sipping thoughts" for these kinds of responses, because questions like "How much more money would make me happy?" typically come up as we are sipping our morning coffee or tea. "Just a little more," we say. "That's what would make things right."

It turns out not to be so. And research by psychologist Daniel Gilbert demonstrates that we're not only quite lousy at determining what would make us happy, but we tend to feel as happy making an additional $30,000 a year as we would if we decided to walk for thirty minutes a day!

Isn't that a kick to the corporate pants and a piercing of the assumption balloon? I don't know about you, but I was certainly late to discovering this truth. For years I chased raises in pay as though they would propel me towards my ultimate goal of being happier. I believed more money would mean more pleasure.

It never did. Instead I found that the more money I made, the more tied to the job or career I became and the less time I had for myself and my loved ones. My quality of life was on a steep downward curve, to a point where carving out the time just to go outside was difficult or near impossible.

Years later I'm much more content with my life. We made the choice to move away from the city to a rural area where the median household income is below $40,000 a year. Big-ticket items like housing are much less expensive in the country, and where I was spending up to three hours a day commuting to and from work in the city, I now work from home. We have a farm with animals we raise, so now there is no need for a gym membership—I walk and haul things for at least an hour, seven days a week. I'm outdoors for a good part of my day, in all kinds of weather, and I can honestly say to you that I am happy.

In life, as in economics, there's a law of diminishing returns, and I believe that if most of us were to be truly honest with ourselves, how much money we need to make caps off at a much lower number than we imagine—especially when we measure it against the quality of life we want to enjoy.

🌸 August 3

In the Pulitzer Prize–winning novel *All the Light We Cannot See*, a blind French girl finds comfort in what she explores with her hands, while a teenaged German boy escapes the horror of war through what he hears coming over the airwaves of the radio he operates. Author Anthony Doerr spent ten years writing the story of the two main characters and their separate yet similar experiences in France during World War II. While she cannot see at all and absorbs the war and the German occupation through what she touches and hears around her, he sees too much to process and escapes his reality through memories of his childhood and foreign radio programs his fingers find on the dial. The novel is epic and rich in its language and tension.

Reading it has made me realize, though, that much of my world is unavailable to me because I tend to choose to take it in only with my eyes. If I were to be judgmental, I'd say that relying on my eyes as my sole filter for the world is lazy. It's certainly just easier. But while our eyes are amazing receptors for information, they are limited in what they can tell us.

I think that, for today, I would like to become a sensory explorer. I would like to sit quietly somewhere with my eyes closed and tune my hearing to the sounds around me—their rhythms and tones, pitches and flows. Which voices stand out? What do they sound like?

I want to touch a wide variety of objects today with the goal of soaking up as many textures and vibrations and temperatures as I possibly can. I'll seek to identify as many foods as I can simply by their scent, and touch my tongue to many of the things I know by sight but not by taste: a leaf, a metal pole, perhaps a handful of earth.

How rich could my world become with all my sensory receptors stimulated and in information-gathering mode? How would my brain ignite with all these signals building new neural pathways of experience?

What would I learn to newly love about our world?

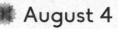
August 4

Bare feet on warm rock.
The smell of minerals activated by the drop of water from a wet
  bathing suit, lying tummy down.
Waiting for that cloud to pass.
Wet to dry. Cool to hot.
Moments of contentment in between.

August 5

If we stop trying to convince—
Selling, smiling, pretending to agree—
And start listening,
What a relief that would be.
Both of us in yes,
Aligned because we are free.
Powerful. Lasting. Authentic.

August 6

We talked about the art of making a fire earlier in the year. Today I am reminded of the awesome moment when our breath causes flames to appear. Blowing on embers—randomly at first, resisting the paper and the barbecue lighters I could use as shortcuts—then focusing the breath to reach behind the wood, drawing closer to aim for wee splints of kindling. Then, watching as flickers form a bowl to hold the flames. Amazing.

Blowing and nothing. Blowing again and again and again, and suddenly—*poof!*—rises a flame. As though it had been waiting for me the whole time, testing to see whether I would stay patient, stay focused. How easily I can give up when I don't see results right away, when the fire ends at the edge of the paper it's been following. But experience helps me to trust that those red-hot embers mean something. They mean life, growth, fire waiting to be fed. How many of my dreams are alive and growing, waiting to be fed?

I blow harder, my confidence bolstered, only to see the flames flatten under my breath. And then, *whomp!*—they reappear, taller and wider. My breaths aren't hurting the fire; there is no such thing as too much. This little fire is solid and it's spreading. How many times do I temper myself for fear that another will leave if I am too much, rather than being myself and trusting that true love stays? It grows and gets bigger when I am fully myself.

I put a larger piece of kindling along the largest flame. Fire accepts my offering and follows the edges. I put a grown log on the top, the tiny fire now nestled between two moss-covered logs and the one above. I have fed and led the flames, and they are growing and ready for me to stand back, admire and close the door to preserve their heat. To build a true fire, the full logs must be in place from the start. I plan for this, never questioning that the full fire will arrive. When I look at my vision for my life, do I have the logs in place, with the kindling in the centre, so that when the spark catches, it has a larger environment to grow into? Have I made space for my dreams to grow into my life?

The Boy Scout motto applies here: "Be prepared." Be prepared for goodness to happen. Make a fire today.

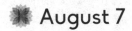 ## August 7

Sharing, cooperation and trading are a big part of the culture of a farm community. We may jump in to help bale hay, lend equipment or share information and learning—recommending a great supplier or warning against a not-so-great one. Using time, knowledge, skills and labour as currencies is an interesting way to explore value and to express ourselves creatively.

Recently I decided I would offer nature-assisted counselling programs in exchange for help with the farm. Using time and service as currencies, I am tapping into an abundant resource where I live and I'm making my services accessible to all at the same time.

Exchanges like these require us to value ourselves as well as others. It feels exciting and good to be in a conversation of abundance and plenty. Bartering is a leveller, in many ways.

Consider your skills, your knowledge and the resources you would enjoy offering, and have fun thinking about goods and services you want. Maybe a trade could satisfy you and another. Maybe you could launch your skills exchange as a prelude to—or instead of—starting a company. We are open to what is possible when we view life as an equal trade.

✹ August 8

When was the last time you enjoyed a great big belly laugh? I mean the kind of laugh that stops you in your tracks and takes your breath away, leaving just a hiss or a cackle in your lungs.

That kind of laugh is so important to our well-being. It can come in a time of grief or stress. It can come when we are alone. And that good feeling carries us through the day and lets us know there is always relief for us on this ride called life.

The Mayo Clinic tells us, "Laughter induces physical changes in the body that, in the short term, release feel-good chemicals and can have longer-term benefits by releasing neuropeptides that fight stress and inflammation."

Find your laugh today. Intend it, ask for it, think about it. Take a moment now and remember a great laugh you had, in vivid detail. What were you laughing about? Why was it so funny? What did the laugh feel like in your body? We deserve to laugh. It is important to our physical, mental and emotional health. *Knock! Knock!* . . .

✳ August 9

Could there be someone you need to ease up on a bit today? Perhaps you've been harbouring a small grudge over a tiny indiscretion, or they've made a mistake that has put you out of sorts. Whatever the case, thinking about it winds you up. Before it becomes a thing you end up holding on to for the next few hours—or even the whole day— why not let it go?

One of the most important lessons I have learned is to not take anything anyone does personally. This doesn't mean I'm not affected by what others say and do—of course that still happens. But my reactions are short-lived and fizzle out quite quickly because I know that nothing another person does is ever really about me.

I read this first in Don Miguel Ruiz's book *The Four Agreements: A Practical Guide to Personal Freedom,* in which he weaves the wisdom of the ancient Toltec people of Mexico into four principles for living an authentic life:

Don't take anything personally.
Don't make assumptions.
Be impeccable with your word.
Always do your best.

The principle of not taking anything personally *really* became a life philosophy for me during my years participating in and facilitating therapy groups. Group therapy is like a family gathering on steroids. Over the course of many, many hours together, sharing the personal, painful and honest parts of their lives, participants become so familiar that they start to seem like siblings or parents. It was in groups that I witnessed how one person's actions or comments could—completely unintentionally—trigger a huge reaction in another participant. In groups, I learned that my behaviour had impact, and that in trying to advance my own agenda, the things I said and did had the ability to hurt others.

My wish for you today is that you let go of a grudge. I get it, you're hurt and upset, sad or disappointed, but I can promise you that whatever occurred wasn't personal. And the longer you hold on to this feeling, the more hurt you inflict on yourself. We all say and do things that innocently cause pain for someone else. We do this because:

We're having a bad day and our misery loves company.
The other person reminds us of a difficult person or a challenging
  relationship.
We're navel-gazing so intently that we don't know they exist.
We're protecting ourselves in the only ways we know how.
We're trying to control others because we like or love them.

These are the main reasons we do things to others unconsciously, but I can tell you that there are many more causes for our words and actions. So let's not judge, nurse a grudge, plot revenge or gossip about something that someone else did or said.

Instead, let's let it go and concentrate our energy and focus on bringing ourselves back to being content and living lightly, one moment at a time.

❋ August 10

It takes a fight, an explosion, for me to realize with great clarity that the upset isn't about this moment, and neither is it about my partner. It is about mounting tension from all the people and exchanges where boundaries have been crossed and I have remained silent. Eventually that tension begins to overflow, resulting in arguments with my children and my partner. If I look back, I notice a mounting negativity, and I recognize that I've been indulging in soothing behaviours, such as wine in the evening, too much screen time and eating unhealthily.

And here's the thing: I put the people I love most—and myself—through this treatment so that I can remain pleasant and accommodating to the rest of the world.

By speaking our truth and holding our boundaries with grace and lightness, we can remain light-filled with ourselves and with our loved ones at home. Doesn't this sound magical and wonderful?

Practise these two things and notice the difference at home. If we do it for them and for ourselves, we then become a model for others. This is change from the inside out, gently rippling within us and the intimacy of our homes, and then more widely to the world outside. It is the only way to light and health and love.

❊ August 11

We can't control someone else's behaviour.
We can't control another person's thoughts or feelings.
We can't control the outcome of anything.
We can't control the expectations of another person.
We can't control the stories people create about us.
We can't control the feelings other people have for us.
We can't control what a person believes.
We can't control a person's dreams.

We can consciously choose our own behaviour.
We can be conscious of and responsible for our thoughts and feelings.
We can adapt to and accept the outcome of anything.
We can set and manage our own expectations.
We can create and author our own story.
We can align our words and our actions with our intentions.
We can develop a practice to deepen our own beliefs.
We can open our minds and hearts to allow our dreams to flow.

✸ August 12

Life is meant to be peaceful and joyful. It really is.

Ask yourself: If life is not peaceful and joyful, where do we have attachment and thus expectation?

Surrender. Ask for help in letting go. Focus on what you do want, on what is underneath the attachment. That essence is the right place to focus on.

This is the way back to peace—every time.

Now breathe, so happy you are here, right now.

✸ August 13

Take a moment for thanks.

It doesn't matter where we are or how we are feeling. It doesn't matter if we are at our best, or even if gratitude is true in this moment. We know we are grateful, so let's take a moment now.

Let's take a deeper breath and close our eyes.

Thank you. Thank you for life at this time. Thank you for the good in my life. Thank you for the opportunity to experience love. Thank you for the good that is coming.

Add to these thanks. Add your pets, your favourite people, favourite foods, your own beliefs, until you are smiling and feel tingly. That's how we know when we are connected to life.

✸ August 14

How much clutter can you tolerate? I know that for me, clutter in and around the house and around our farm tends to linger and gather as the parts of one project flow into another. I see small piles of things here and there and let them lie until I just can't take it anymore. Sometimes, if I'm close to my limit on how much mess I can handle, I may scurry around at the end of the day and tidy up, hoping to infuse a little order and make things seem just a touch more serene. Once a week I make sure to do a more thorough cleaning—not because I'm that organized, but because I don't like having to play catch-up and spend hours washing and sweeping just to get everything back to an acceptable baseline.

Similarly, about three times a year I embark on a few days of deep cleaning. My family stands back as I go through the house—room by room, closet by closet. I load bags with items to donate to charity and scour the farm for all of the remnants of the previous season, which I load onto the truck to take to the municipal dump. These are big, reorganizational cleans where I bring the events of the last few months to a close and get prepared for what lies ahead. The goal I have for each big clean and purge is to lighten up our living space and, by association, lighten the way we live in the spaces.

This is especially true of living on a farm because the essence of homestead farming is to create systems and make each of them as efficient and simple as possible. You only have to haul five-gallon pails of water through deep snow every day for one winter before you start thinking about how to make that task simpler.

Outside clutter is like inside turmoil, and while we have tools, solutions and regimens for clearing away dirt and cobwebs, grease and grime, we seem to come up short when our inner world is unkempt. Like our environment, our minds get clogged with junk that needs to be cleaned out. There are thoughts and beliefs we've held since childhood or early adulthood that just don't serve us anymore. We may also have behaviours that we need to shed because they just don't fit who we are today. When we look inside ourselves, we may discover that our inner houses are in need of a deep clean, a level of attention to keep us in order and allow us to feel more at peace.

🌸 August 15

Love isn't a state of perfect caring. It is an active noun.
—Mr. Rogers

Decades or minutes into love, we won't ever completely know the other. And that is the point. Our quest to know them is noble, and it fuels love because it is an active state of being, as Mr. Rogers says. It keeps our relationships alive and growing.

Free from assumptions, there is so much room to fall deeper into love. "I never knew" is such beautiful, connective language. Hearing someone tell us they know us better than themselves or hearing someone talk about us a way that assumes ("she is always like that") is confining and limiting. Can you feel it?

Whether in romance, parenting, friendship or nature, bring an "I never knew" attitude today. Ask someone why they do what they do. Ask if we have it right. Listen and observe, with the intention of learning.

It is exciting to imagine what our active love will make possible.

🌸 August 16

When we have an idea or an inspiration, a new insight or a deeply personal new awareness, do we share as soon as possible? Do we share with everyone we know? Do we ask for opinions, input and advice?

An awareness, an idea, a feeling, is precious and fragile. It's something to be held, protected, nurtured and kept in quiet sunlight for it to take root. Shared too early, there is a chance the roots will not take, as the winds of well-meaning advice, questions and opinions alter it or blow it away.

When fear or upset are shared, they become wounds, red and irritated. The composition and intention of your relationship with another are changed, which is unfair to both.

Consider a pause on sharing, whether inspiration or upset, and instead hold it inside. Let it settle until it reaches your essence, and clarity will come from within you rather than from outside. It will provide you with conviction and power and ground you in love.

❋ August 17

I have a love/hate relationship with walking. In our current culture of fitness monitoring, with devices like Fitbit, it seems we've become turned on to the idea of not simply walking, but of measuring our walking progress. Yet if we look back only two generations, we'll find that people walked large distances every day—mostly because cars were expensive and rare.

Having European parents who grew up after World War II, I was raised with the leftovers of this reality and would take a brisk afternoon walk every Sunday with my family, doing my best to lag behind and slow the pace. I hated it.

In my twenties and thirties I lived in the centre of a busy city and folded walking into my identity as an urban hipster. I proclaimed that cars were evil machines meant for lazy suburbanites and seniors—neither of which I had any desire to become, and yet did become (the former, at least) in my forties. Now in my fifties and living on a farm, I again walk everywhere—this time, carrying buckets of food and water, all the while dreaming of ways to reduce the number of steps I must take to keep all our animals alive.

The other day I happened across an interesting story on the radio. It involved a Tibetan woman living in exile in Nepal who, at ninety-two, walks three kilometres every day. She's had two knee surgeries and says that her walking, which takes her about an hour each day and which she has done for more than thirty-five years, is a religious experience, and she only forgoes it if she is extremely ill. Her practice, called *kora*, is the Tibetan Buddhist ritual of walking around holy sites and objects as a sign of respect and reverence.

To truly walk *kora* is to engage all three fields of human action—the physical, the verbal and the mental. Buddhist devotees of *kora* walk with determination, reciting mantras while simultaneously imagining and developing a higher purpose, one that benefits all sentient beings. I was humbled and inspired by her story—humbled by her dedication and perseverance and inspired to see the enormous potential that walking with purpose could open up for me.

So today I begin a practice of *kora*. I'll begin by walking along our country road for an hour or so, listening to and learning all the lyrics to Joni Mitchell's *Blue* and *Both Sides Now* albums, and wishing you all the experience of lightness and deep love.

🌸 August 18

Disappointment. It's such a tough word to look at, isn't it? Nobody enjoys being disappointed, and for some of us the feeling is so uncomfortable, even hurtful, that it makes us feel like we're not seen or loved. Many of us may try to soften the blow of hearing a *no* by doubling down on our efforts, in hopes of finding a workaround or a backdoor hack to get to a *maybe*. And while on the politically correct surface we may not believe in a world of winners and losers, choosing instead to think that everyone deserves a prize for trying, none of us really wants that consolation prize.

I see the impact of people not being okay with disappointment everywhere: overindulged or self-righteous adults and children; watered-down, milquetoast accountability within relationships and families; prolonged, needless suffering out of misplaced attachments; and hyper-crazed spending and amped-up, stress-building pleasure-seeking.

One of the truisms of being a mental health professional is that I have the job of giving people hope and helping them build resilience to disappointment. I'm often the first person they encounter in their life who firmly says no to something they are doing or saying. Many first-time clients who hear this *no* are so frustrated that they leave in search of another counsellor who will offer them a *yes* or a *maybe*, just so they can escape the feeling of disappointment.

The important thing about being disappointed is that we understand and accept that what is making us uncomfortable—this belief that we are unseen or unloved when we don't get what we want—is mostly in our heads. Yes, there are some of us who have experienced cruelty and abuse from others, but that is not true of most of us. The majority of us just never learned to be okay with not getting or having what we wanted, when and how we wanted it. We can feel the upset of disappointment without making it mean that we are less worthy, or unlovable. Learning to be okay with disappointment builds our mental resilience and helps us to grow in empathy.

How can we grow to accept disappointment? The first step is to practise saying no to all the things in life that we believe we deserve because they will make us more visible and lovable. We can do it. I have faith in us.

❋ August 19

The haka is a type of ancient Māori war dance traditionally used on the battlefield, as well as when groups came together in peace. Haka are a fierce display of a tribe's pride, strength and unity. Actions include violent foot-stamping, tongue protrusions and rhythmic body slapping to accompany a loud chant. The words of a haka often poetically describe ancestors and events in the tribe's history.

Today, haka are still used during Māori ceremonies and celebrations to honour guests and show the importance of the occasion. This includes family events, like birthdays and weddings.

What a relief it would be to express emotion as freely as through haka.

Haka give physical expression to emotional energy. They are an illustration of the power that lives inside you and me—putting a face on energy, movement and sound reminds us of our power.

Do you know someone who lives with that intensity? Someone who is physically moved at times by life? Children express their energy this way—physically, in beautiful dances and wild facial movements. At times they vibrate with the energy of life, buzzing to move, hungry for all life has to offer. I smile thinking about them just now.

Two of the people who are closest to me have maintained this hunger for life. In times of great excitement, they rub their hands together or clench their fists in the air, wear huge grins and yell, "Come on . . . let's *do* this!" Their eyes sparkle and they plead for me to join in their excitement, to raise the vibration level even higher. I always regret it when I decline.

We all need these outward expressions of liberty, of passion, of love, of celebration and appreciation of life. Find these people, big and small, who would do haka, who express the joy of being alive. Raw emotion shakes off labels—it's neither happy nor sad, it's just pure energy. What a blessing to feel and express a surge, like a wave, before it becomes a specific feeling, later to have a name and a meaning attached to it. Let's allow ourselves to join in—to smile, to laugh, to clap, to scream, to cry, to stomp, to twirl, to make faces, to stick out our tongue.

Watch a haka ritual dance. Its sacred intensity and power live inside us. Once we feel the vibration first-hand, life energy will find ways to express itself through us, attracting high-vibration people and experiences for us. This is living lightly.

❀ August 20

Do you have a happy place—a physical place where you love to be? Picture the details as vividly as possible—the what, where, when and why—and then ask yourself: How do I feel? How am I different when I am there? This feeling about a place offers a huge clue to our essence and what we are like on the inside all the time.

For years I longed to live in nature and had a picture in my mind of being in a field, feeling sunshine on my face, seeing a bright blue sky and hearing long grasses whisper in the wind. I wanted it so badly that it would bring me to tears. While I waited to find this place, I worked with the idea that my dream might be more a *symbol* of freedom, beauty and creativity. As it turned out, not really: the object of my longing was an actual place that I am writing from today, fifteen years later.

Delving deeper into my vision was helpful. So was putting myself in natural settings as often as I could when I was still living in the city. I discovered that the ultimate prize, for me, was an actual field of long grasses, with glacial rocks strewn about, gurgling streams, incredible vistas and lots of trees. I believe this land will play a big part in my life going forward. Our dreams and visions and happy places might be a literal translation, especially if they involve nature.

Is nature calling you? Consider giving your happy place a bigger role in your life, as an ode to your own sweet nature.

❀ August 21

Let us unpack love a little bit more...

Love does not require a relationship, a physical form or reciprocity. Love needs no condition to be.

How amazing.

How are conditions part of your love? Think of a time when you loved unconditionally. How are those experiences different?

Do you focus your attention on the *act* of loving, or the result? Do you feel fulfilled through the act of loving? Do you need the other to respond? Do you love consciously, aware of your intention, deliberate in your acts? Do your actions express your love—are they aligned and in sync?

Let's get clear about who we love and why, so that we can be intentional and deliberate. Living together, being related or being alike or in community is not love, it is a condition. Love does not need any condition to be.

Can we remove all conditions for our love? That entails being willing to travel deeper into our psyches and see many conditions we may not realize we have attached to love. Releasing love from all conditions is a process of awakening. Here are some of the conditions that I have, unconsciously and consciously, put in place that block my love, and to which I am now awakening:

- It needs to be safe first for me to love.
- I need to be in a certain mood to love.
- I can't be too busy, too tired, too stressed or too anxious to love.
- I *know* I love you—that is enough.
- I yell at you, even though I love you.
- I judge you, even though I love you.

All of that has me wondering whether I really do love myself and other beings. Isn't it amazing that love can fit through all these blocks? And that all this energy that is going into blocking could be going towards love?

Conditions are not love. Love is light. Love comes from freedom, soul, flow, oneness and joy. Conditions block our flow of love.

Awareness matters. Being in this inquiry makes space for love. Love is gentle, understanding, kind and forgiving. It will squeeze through the tiniest space to reach us.

I start with love for myself today. I tell myself, "I love you." I remove any conditions. Whether it feels true in the moment is not important. Love does not require us to believe. I say it as love's agent. Even better, I say it in the mirror.

When I say "I love you" in the mirror, I say it fast, so that I don't have time to go into my head. And a smile happens. I walk away, and then return to the mirror and try again. Sure enough, I smile again— my body is smiling in response to the words "I love you." I don't need my head to believe it, or to do it right or to practise or to question it. Love works any way.

I love you. Start there.

 August 22

Yesterday, I had one of those realizations that sink in softly. Not a hard, hit-you-in-the-side-of-the-head eureka moment, but a slow, creeping, whole-body sensation of knowing. Our family dog passed away a few days ago, and in grief my partner had reached out to a friend who sees into the world of spirits. Our friend's words of soothing about our dog were: "He is all around you, he is there with you, just beyond what you can perceive."

I thought about this for a while and, while walking back from our field, I had a sensation that the dog was beside me and then was passing me to walk on ahead the way he had always done.

My logical brain offered, "Oh, this is just a memory, like when a person loses an arm or a leg and they have a sensation that the missing limb is still attached." But it was more than that. I strongly felt his presence beside me not only in that moment, but later as I walked up the stairs to go to bed and felt him standing on the landing above me, waiting for me to join him.

Then yesterday, I was walking up our driveway late at night with only the glow of the inside lights of our farmhouse to guide my steps.

273

As I stood a short distance away from the house, I could see the hum of all the activity inside—our children mingling with each other, preparing food and laughing. I watched them performing the simple, repetitive actions of everyday life: pouring a glass of water, opening the fridge, flipping through a magazine, teasing each other.

I realized I could see them, but they couldn't see me. The reflected glare of indoor lighting against the glass of the windows prevented them from watching me watch them. I was there with them, just beyond what they could perceive. And then the warmth of the realization started to flood into me: this is what death could be—this may be what it means to leave this life and enter a new one.

We are always together and with each other in every moment, and some of us are just beyond what the others can perceive.

And this realization seemed to ring true to me in an "all the water that has ever existed in our world is still here" kind of way. What if all the life that has ever been is also still here today, but in different forms and in different realms of perception? What if we are never alone, but always with those who love us? What if what truly separates us is simply what we can perceive?

I know I would want to make it my life's purpose to become more perceptive.

August 23

Go gently today. Pick one thing, anything at all, and do it with love. Do your very best, with all your attention and joy.

What a relief to focus and give our best for our own selves to enjoy.

How do multi-tasking and doing our best go together? Do they? In the work world, I learned to compromise, prioritize, trade off, phase in and phase out, stage, test, pilot, beta test, be agile, build capacity, fail fast and do more with less.

Wow. Even as I write that list, I notice I am holding my breath!

Deep breath in, big exhale out.

The experience taught me to be with imperfection, to let go and detach. I learned that my capacity is elastic, able to stretch and contract as needed. I learned to create in stages, as an ongoing process. I learned to say no gracefully, knowing that there were acceptable explanations for failure and imperfection. But I never felt fulfilled from these lessons. I never felt pride or excitement. I never went home and shared with my family about how much more I could do. I was learning to produce measurable results, not heartfelt growth or connection.

Any growth that took place during my work days came from practising doing my best. I looked for personal meaning in the tasks that might seem menial or empty, and I came away with a passion for being of service. In time, everything I did at the companies I worked for was connected to being of service: being kind with strangers, being authentic and transparent when selling a service, accepting rejection gracefully. I looked for ways to delight, to be thoughtful and proactive, to hold boundaries with customers and earn their respect for doing so. I would find satisfaction in practising the art of being a good person— to myself, to clients and to my employer.

Children naturally want to do their best. They like to focus on one thing at a time, even if that thing is running, making messes, exploring or adventure. I like to encourage this focus because of the deep satisfaction, confidence and esteem it builds.

Multi-tasking is especially exhausting and unrewarding because it involves a never-ending list of "to dos." Concentrating on a single mission, such as spending time with a pet or preparing to host visitors with the intention of giving them a fabulous experience, is what sends my body and my heart headlong into the task.

Look for opportunities to compare the results of doing your best with those of multi-tasking in all areas of life. Notice how each approach affects you and consider designing your life to have more of whichever approach you prefer.

✿ August 24

I used to laugh at the idea of buying holiday presents months in advance. It sounded like so much work to me to be shopping all year round. Now I'm learning it is far more work to condense holiday preparations into one month—or one week! And I realize how in the moment I feel when I see an object and think of someone enjoying it as a gift in the future. How loving!

Whether for a year or a lifetime, the intention of love and kindness can bring the holiday spirit into the everyday. Think how special the holidays can be when they're the culmination of efforts and intentions that have been percolating for an entire year or even longer!

Picture hampers of food, boxes of tested and curated recipes, handmade and homegrown gifts with lots of time invested in them, crafts and languages learned, books written, songs recorded, seeds planted, wine and cheese cellared, family reunions and musical bands meeting to practise their groove.

Let's give our celebrations the time they need to manifest into something bigger . . . into a beauty-filled way of living.

✿ August 25

Have you ever noticed that there are some days when you just don't have the mental or emotional space or the bandwidth to hear another person complain? You want to be compassionate, and you remain hopeful that you can shift your mood to be a great listener, but you just don't have it in you. Your jug is empty; there's no capacity to be loving of another person.

I know it doesn't feel good to be this way, and sometimes we end up adding this incapacity or unwillingness to help another to a basket of our own self-judgments—in other words, we may start to believe we're not that solid a person.

This isn't so. Everyone has limits to their kindness and understanding, and the more we know about our own capacity to care, the better we can become at taking care of ourselves. All our generosity, benevolence and empathy begin with ourselves. An empty self has nothing to offer; a full self overflows with an abundance of understanding and caring. When we reach our limits and our loving feels scarce, this is the surest sign that we need filling up.

I'll admit that I'm not that great at filling up my soul. I'm still learning what I really need and learning to distinguish between something that satiates me and something that truly builds my capacity to love. I find it hard sometimes to name, verbalize and ask for what I need; it seems like I'm fumbling around in the dark, trying to put Band-Aids on my soul to stem the flow rather than adding anything of substance. But I keep trying because I've learned that my sharp moods and my resistance to love are yellow flashing lights warning me of a developing emptiness.

I know that when my soul is full and my love is flowing, I am able to hear another person's complaints for what they are: a sign that their soul is feeling drained. Their complaint is a cry for help or a warning that they are nearing their empty point. And when my soul is full, I am compelled to love them, to offer what I have inside myself to help them fill up. Today, this is what I'm really learning about love.

❀ August 26

Our focus on living lightly can also illuminate that which is not light, whether inside or outside of us.

I want you to know that feeling heavy is more than okay; it is a sign that we are processing life—we are digesting, percolating, decomposing, absorbing, releasing, settling. It isn't enough to affirm our way to feeling whole. We cannot sidestep the awareness that what lies beneath can be rage, anxiety, fear, shame or grief.

As I focus on opening myself, some of our beloved pets have become sick, I have repeatedly stumbled and bruised my body, and people around me are going through hard times. It is very disconcerting to my mind to intend peace, only to be interrupted by illness, death, intensity and crisis. That word "interrupted" is a clue that my ego is judging and assessing, preparing to defend against life. I feel myself wanting to pull away until my feelings pass or I can rebottle them. I made a choice one day instead to join my family in their joy, even though I did not feel it inside me. I told them I was upset and didn't know why, and they welcomed me as I was. I felt a most beautiful and generous luminosity in their acceptance and love. They didn't need me to pretend or hide or cover up.

Not everyone will be able to welcome or embrace a heavy state. We can be tempted to focus intensely on the sorrow or loss, on the story that keeps us separate and feeling the pain. But it *is* possible to bring our feelings into the light. To find not only those we love or who love us, such as a best friend, a relative or a spouse, but those who are light enough, strong enough in their boundaries of self to embrace without absorbing, and to find the stillness of acceptance that we seek. The ones who will be honoured by vulnerability will be the ones to teach us. It may be a waiter, a counsellor, a neighbour or a dog. People who have embraced their own heavy will receive us with respect for our willingness to be humbled by life.

The story is not required; only the state of your feelings. Bring your intensity and your pain on a walk in the sunlight that unconditional acceptance offers. Be in the company of a joy-filled person who is responsible for their own energy while you are grieving or aware of anger and rage inside. It was difficult for me to say yes. My ego really wanted to be alone, even to lash out and dim the joy around me. To offer your heavy state to the light is to choose vulnerability, and that will always lead you to love. It will provide you with comfort and relief—a soothing balm—to be accepted and seen in your raw state. I wish this for you, and the peace that comes after.

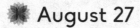 # August 27

What are the lightest words you can think of?

> float
> bubble
> fizz
> pop
> sheer
> vapour
> mirage
> clear
> feather
> snowflake
> sunny
> serene

Can you keep going, retrieving lighter and lighter words from your mind's vocabulary and your life experience? Can you fill a page simply with words that evoke lightness? Please try. Here's another favourite of mine: ease.

 # August 28

Can you remember a time when you experienced a first in nature? When you saw your first mountain, perhaps, or felt tropical humidity on your skin or the hot sand between your toes on a beach? Or when you witnessed the expanse of a grassland plain or the wonders of a jungle? On a more personal level, what about the natural world around you now, where you live? Is there anything that people who visit marvel at? Do they see something beautiful and amazing—something they have never seen before?

I'm thinking about this today because I had this exact moment with someone yesterday. I live in a place that is rugged and wild, with numerous freshwater lakes and pink granite cliffs. We have four distinct seasons, with all the accompanying flourishes of colour and extremes of temperature. As I write this I can hear the hum of dragon-flies and the buzz of bees and cicadas. The winds, drying out from the moisture of spring, are foreshadowing a baking-hot summer.

Yesterday I met a man who was visiting our town for the first time. Originally from Southeast Asia, he had never seen so much fresh water and had no concept of a forest made of broad-leaved hardwoods and needled softwoods. As I watched him cautiously dip his toes in the water, unsure whether to go in, he turned to me and asked, "Is it safe to swim here?"

"Sure," I said. "It's very safe. There's nothing in here that would harm you."

"I've never seen so much water like this," he added. "You are very lucky to live in such a beautiful place."

"Thank you," I said, sure that I had no part in any of the beauty he was seeing and feeling. Then I took a little risk and asked him, "Tell me more about what you see. Is there anything that is new for you?"

He seemed surprised by my question, and yet his eyes widened instantly, and a smile opened on his face.

"There's so much here that is new for me," he said. "So many new things, it's like I'm a child again."

We spoke for a few moments more and then, with my encouragement and assurance, he dove into the water and I watched him surface, shake his head and laugh. A while later he came over and sat with me and asked if I would like to see what he had collected in the area. He opened a leather shoulder bag, unwrapped a small handkerchief and revealed his treasures: a pine cone, a maple key, a shard of pink granite, dried moss, a wild blackberry, a small mallard feather and a curled length of white birchbark. He looked up at me as he gingerly lifted each item from the cloth to show it to me.

I looked at them with my own eyes at first and had the thought

that these were things I saw every day and they really held no fascination for me. Then I had the presence of mind to pause and look at
them with fresh eyes. And borrowing from his excitement, I found a
childlike place in my mind that allowed me to see his collection with
new wonder. Then I remembered that I had had this moment before
with both of my children. I remembered their wide-eyed amazement,
the pure depth of sensory engagement that comes with true discovery.

And then I had another thought—a big thought: wonder is
always available to us. That is my invitation to you today. Allow wonder to find you.

🌸 August 29

Who repeatedly tells you their problems or gossips about another
family member?

Who tells you they wouldn't be able to live without you?

Who might slip into a dark place, or rage at you or cut off communication?

Who is bitter or resentful because of what they've gone through?

Unfortunately, these behaviours often come from close family
members such as parents or siblings. These are our closest and most
challenging relationships. We can be great with other people, be successful and achieve personal growth, then in an instant revert to an
angry or hurt child in the presence of a family member who is not
emotionally available to us because they are consumed by their own
stories and their pain.

It can be extremely difficult to be light and authentic in the presence of these individuals; we may be tempted to hide our own joy, needs
or personality, thus giving them all the space. But it helps break the spell
when you intend to be content—truly making choices that put you at
peace, truly living in pursuit of your dreams. You can control this effort
to live a fulfilled life. And as they go into the automatic motions of gossip, negative words or complaints, you have the right to gently say, "I

want to be here with you. Can we talk about something lighter?"

You may need to ask more than once. You may need to say it each time you meet. If you say it early, it is easier to stay gentle. Assume that they do not know how to speak lightly, that they haven't had any practice at it. Model it for them. Talk about the weather, children, movies. Tell them why you love them. Remember a happy time for them. Keep the visit short if you need to, to stay loving.

Things won't change immediately, but they *will* change. Family members who have not been taught as children to be content, who haven't had their self-esteem built up or who have never been loved well, are starving. Fill your cup first, then gently offer them small amounts they can digest. What a gift you offer in setting these boundaries and putting your own self first.

August 30

A passage from Eckhart Tolle's book *A New Earth* tells a story about "the monk with sweaty palms."

> Kasan, a Zen teacher and monk, was to officiate at a funeral of a famous nobleman.
>
> As he stood there waiting for the governor of the province and other lords and ladies to arrive, he noticed that the palms of his hands were sweaty.
>
> The next day he called his disciples together and confessed he was not yet ready to be a true teacher.
>
> He explained to them that he still lacked the sameness of bearing before all human beings, whether beggar or king.
>
> He was still unable to look through social roles and conceptual identities and see the sameness of being in every human.
>
> He then left and became the pupil of another master.

Do you act differently with the different groups of people in your life? Clients tell me they can't be emotional or spiritual at home or among friends who reserve certain activities or topics of discussion for others. Work adds another layer of pretense: the formality of professionalism, which further alters our language, appearance and behaviour.

I catch myself withholding information at times, saving it for those who I judge will understand or relate to it better. My energy level varies depending on what group I'm with. Even in shops, I can put on my "acceptable" customer demeanour.

These masks or partitions restrict our energy, dividing our own selves into smaller bits that lack authenticity and fullness. I start to feel ungrounded and long for a sense of home when I have divided myself into many small pieces.

Tolle says we are feeding our ego defences when we play these multiple roles, strengthening the ego to be even more separate. What we are working towards is closeness and a coming together, so we need *all* of ourselves, whole and complete, as we journey through life. It may mean that we have fewer circles and need to move into one circle in which we are free to agree—and at times, disagree.

Imagine being our full selves everywhere, needing to manage only our own state without having to manage walls or distance. Think of the energy that would become available through being whole and complete. Imagine the experiences that would arise as we bring our full selves to all people we meet.

❋ August 31

Have you thought about going back to school? Learning for the pure pleasure of it? What would you choose to study? What kind of learning environment would bring out your best?

I obtained my psychotherapy certificate at the age of forty-five, and it was a completely new learning experience for me compared to working towards my bachelor's degree in the early '90s. I was very much in the driver's seat this time, choosing the school based on the experience and curriculum I wanted. The program was part time and involved hands-on learning. I found it incredibly refreshing that instructors spoke to all of us as though the future had already happened, using such terms as "when your practice is open" or "when you have clients like this." Assignments and cases were reviewed with curiosity and a collegial tone, rather than the top-down pressure of grading, and passing or failing.

There is a deeper learning I crave still, for the artist and creator in me—a part of me I left behind as a child. Learning to work with my hands and still my mind, learning for the pure joy of tactile creative expression, with a gentle teacher to show me the tools. I still hesitate and procrastinate, afraid to commit or make a mistake or get into something I might not love or be good at, yet I know my soul will wither should I fail to ask what it would like me to do.

It is helpful for me to consider all that can happen over the next twenty years if I work backwards from 2040, by which time I'll be in my early seventies. I can have a real impact on my community; I can be part of change and conservation. I could open a gallery, a restaurant, a school. There is time for all of this to happen.

If we think of our lifetimes in ten- or twenty-year blocks, there is plenty of time to change course—multiple times. Personal expression, whether as a hobby, a business, a contribution or something else, fuels our primary purpose for being here: to enjoy the experience!

Consider opportunities for further learning that is unrelated to work but is all about a dream or a passion. Be open to the idea, and you may pick up on unexpected clues and connections that will feel like a gentle unfolding of your own story. Don't worry about how to do this just yet; simply be open to the possibility.

September

✺ September 1

Are you addicted to your phone or your computer? I don't mean addicted in the traditional sense, but in a more modern way. Are you compulsive or impulsive—or both—when it comes to your electronic devices?

In 2017 the consulting firm Deloitte surveyed 4,150 people in the UK aged sixteen to seventy-five. The study found that 38 percent believed they were using their smart phones too much. Among young adults (aged sixteen to twenty-four), more than half said so. A remarkable 79 percent admitted to looking at their phones in the last hour before sleep, while 55 percent said they do so within fifteen minutes of waking up.

There also seems to be a strong correlation between moderate to heavy app usage and such conditions as insomnia, anxiety and depression. We also know that app developers, with the help of consultants in behavioural psychology, are designing interfaces and games that stimulate the reward centres in our brains, triggering us to pay attention to their products more frequently and longer.

The other day I found a series of apps that are specifically designed to help us become aware of and change our behaviour with our electronic devices. These apps, called Mute, Moment, Space and Hold, are designed to help us curb our enthusiasm for our electronic devices. Hold is specifically aimed at students, and helps them reduce their device time by trading tangible rewards for keeping their phones in their pockets.

My favourite, however, is an app called Forest, which begins by having me plant a virtual tree that continues to grow if I don't quit the app—and, by extension, as long as I'm not engaging with any other apps. Forest offers up such prompts as "Stay focused, be present" and "Put down your phone and focus on what's more important in your life." It keeps me off Facebook, Instagram and other time wasters and rewards me by helping me build a virtual forest of trees, each one a symbol of my focused time. At the same time, Forest works with tree-planting organizations in real life to fund ongoing reforestation projects around the world. To date, more than 370,000 real trees have been planted by Forest app users. That's a lot of focused time and a lot of fresh air being created for our planet!

Find Mute at justmuteit.com; Moment at inthemoment.io; Space at space-app.com; Hold at holdstudent.com; and Forest at forestapp.cc.

🌸 September 2

Our lightness of being is closely tied to how free we believe we are in our daily lives. I'm not talking about the escapist sort of freedom— the running-away-from-it-all kind that can be great in short bursts. I'm talking about our being free to express who we really are.

In most democratic cultures, "freedom of expression" is a fundamental guarantee, and it has been my experience that some democracies are more open to their populations expressing themselves freely than others. That's why we see such a huge swing in the happiness scores reported by citizens of different democratic countries around the world.

To be who we are, to move freely, to express freely and responsibly, to have agency over our lives and work, to love whoever we love, to worship openly, to be free to live and, more currently, die when we feel we must—these are some of the freedoms that bring about true lightness in our being. And while much of our life is governed by external forces and rules for living (some of which we can work to change), I think we should talk about our internal self-governing mechanisms because I believe that most of us have decided on or chosen lives for ourselves that, without our knowing it, restrict our freedoms. We choose convenience over nutrition or well-being; we choose the chance to earn more money over doing purposeful work; we choose status over balance; we choose luxury over quality and beauty over substance; we choose excessive consumption over gratitude; and we choose screens over connection.

We have built for ourselves restrictive, heavy lives that close around us like boxes, and some of us have even gone a step further to market and promote this type of living as something to aspire to, rebranding an excess of anything as a true indicator of a life well lived.

When we buy into this modern mantra, we are not free. And if we are not free, we cannot hope to be light. And if lightness eludes us, we will long and pine for escape.

🌸 September 3

I need more time looking out windows.
I want time alone to do nothing—not to read, nor watch, nor write.
To sit and stare at nature and remember special times.
This is the road back to myself, I believe.

🌸 September 4

I keep forgetting that we are the last to know.
That the dogs and frogs and horses and pigs know the grand master plan.
I am the one who is wondering, waiting, questioning, praying.
While all the others play in the light, just beyond what we can see.
Human is not in charge, not superior, not master, not first.
I, actually, am last.

The animals know. So does the land.
Yet I keep thinking and talking and deciding as though I know.
Maybe I can ask. Maybe I can observe. Maybe I can listen.
That feels like a much better way.

September 5

The shortest path between two conflicted points of view is a straight conversation. I learned this lesson last weekend when a good friend, whose politics are diametrically opposed to mine, sat down with me to catch up and chat. When we were younger, so much of our conversation would be taken up with lobbing facts back and forth to prove the rightness of our respective opinions—and the wrongness of the other's.

As we grew older our arguments became more complex, and underneath our words I could hear the workings of our belief systems being aired. I'm not proud of it, but the discussions did get personal— we often called each other names and branded the other as the enemy. While we remained friendly, the chasm between us grew. Our views had become more important than our relationship.

Time has blurred that which was once clear, and our most impassioned debates have come to seem superficial. Last weekend my friend asked, "Why do I have to be wrong in order for you to be right?" I paused and thought about what he had said (truthfully, I'm still thinking about it now). All I could offer in reply was "I don't know."

I don't know anyone who likes being wrong. I know people who are okay with making mistakes and who are willing to experiment and take risks in many aspects of their lives. But being labelled as wrong— and more importantly, being proven wrong—based on what we believe is a very difficult pill for most of us to swallow.

I'm talking about preserving a relationship by developing the skills of empathy and listening. I'm talking about having a different opinion from another person and respecting their thought pro-cesses—and them—simply because they are a person. I'm talking about becoming more resilient, even accepting of differences of per-spective and life experience.

I'm talking about giving up our hold on the view that our lives are a prescriptive recipe for how others should also live. I'm talking about having straight, honest, respectful chats with others that are about learning rather than trying to convince the other.

The straight truth is that no one is right or wrong.

September 6

How about making today a slow day?

A slow day is one in which you make a deliberate attempt to reduce the amount you do to just one or two things. You've likely heard the expression "curl up with a good book"; that's a great example of a slow-day activity. It's not important what you try, only that you limit yourself to one or maybe two activities.

Slow days give us a pause during which we can dive more deeply into something we love or have been wanting to get to for a long time. They give us the opportunity to experience a richer sense of accom-plishment as the extra effort we devote to a task or a passion yields a deeper appreciation for the rewards.

We can clean out a room that, up until now, has been sorted and re-sorted; we can read a newspaper from front to back—*all* of the sec-tions; we can take a fresh look at our living space and move the furni-ture around to create new views or retreats for our family or friends to gather; we can learn a new skill or experiment with a recipe. I try to plan a slow day at least two or three times a year, and sometimes I find that my body and soul will tell me I need one sooner than anticipated, especially if I've just had a long stretch of multi-tasking.

In a slow day we work our mental or physical muscles—and possibly both—to engage more fully in the experience of being alive. We consciously choose behaviours that help us better appreciate the minutes and hours in a day for their depth of quality. We focus on stretching the time in our day rather than packing activity into each moment.

A slow day is about exploring our inner creative and reflective voices. Slow days grow our patience and our ability to be present to ourselves in moments. They deepen our self-learning and self-loving, which are gifts we give ourselves. They are gentle reminders that there is always an abundance of quality time all around us and that every moment can be—and is—precious.

September 7

What are some of your favourite things?

Mine are very tactile—a round coffee cup, soft slippers and boots, a woven tapestry that hangs beside the bed, the way my leg muscles feel after skating or swimming. These things ground me and give me moments of pleasure, and I feel connected to life through them.

What are some of your favourite things—things that connect you to life?

September 8

Do you know someone who has gone deep into themselves? Someone who lives in a way that is untamed, wild and free?

Take a moment to imagine such a person. They can be anywhere on earth—they may be someone you invent or a character you have read about.

I think it is very healthy for us to know someone like this. They can inspire us, teach us and guide us, showing us how to awaken to our dreams. When you encounter a person like this, find a way to connect with them. Introduce yourself to them. Write to them and tell them, "I am yearning to be free, as you are." They will understand. They won't be intense or heavy or symbolic. Instead, expect an ease and lightness; if you detect these things, you'll know you are talking to the right person.

Can you feel freedom coming closer? There is nothing for us to do except admire and acknowledge the freedom of spirit we see in others. In doing so, we call our own forward.

❋ September 9

What is your idea of perfect happiness? Stolen moments in a hectic day when you can soak in peace and quiet? Sitting around a long, communal table with friends and newcomers, sharing delicious food, conversation and laughter? Catching the sun dappling and shimmering on the waves of your favourite body of water? Or could it be a moment of pure surrendered bliss with someone you care for deeply?

What is at the heart of your understanding of deep love? Is it being lost, safely, within another? Is it a rock-solid confidence that your heart belongs unconditionally to another? Is it something that is both fragile and resilient at the same time? Is it your hand being held, a kiss that always melts, or the familiar way a smile takes shape or a body moves in an embrace?

What is your idea of ultimate lightness? Is it running and sensing that the rhythm of your strides and your breath are in total sync and that your feet are barely touching the ground? Is it that moment when your life suddenly changed direction and you cast off or broke free from the bonds of a restrictive job or a suffocating relationship? Would it be the feeling that you could float high above the earth with joy and total freedom, having triumphed over a challenge or realized a lifelong dream?

Can you see the pattern surfacing here? Can you see where the richness of being alive truly occurs? It's in our experiences. Rarely does an object alone bring us our greatest sense of happiness or ultimate lightness. It seems that, as beings ruled by our senses, thoughts and feelings, what we remember and crave most are those moments when we feel most alive. Numb our senses for too long and we begin to feel tuned out, turned off and closed in, and we begin to reminisce about when we last felt alive—and we entertain fantasies of future freedom and escape. We even dream in experiences, as our unconscious mind weaves threads of meaning and message into pictures and then releases them into our conscious mind so that we may connect with our dormant desires.

Today let's pursue experiences rather than possessions. Let us both undergo a review and distill all the activity in our lives to arrive at those pure experiences we absolutely must have—the ones that are non-negotiable, the ones that make us feel truly alive.

🌸 September 10

Doing yoga today after a long time away, I felt my body open and let go, and I started feeling so wonderful. Then I heard one word:

"Choir."

I have been focused on strengthening my connection to my inner guidance these days and feeling a little impatient about "doing it right." So what a laugh it was to hear a single word from deep inside of me— surprising and a little lacklustre, given my ego's desire for the complex and heavy!

Then I remembered how much I love to sing. I don't have any real singing experience to speak of, but the few times I have sung in a church or at a retreat were very emotionally uplifting and took me to a joy-filled place inside myself. I had forgotten that.

As we open ourselves up to living lightly, let's consider that we might be attached to the idea of a complicated or deep path, or an expectation that we must invest hard work or sacrifice to be worthy of true lightness. Such thinking is counterintuitive to the meaning of living lightly, yet I find it's easy to slip back into this attachment to a hard life.

Let's keep in mind that our soul messages will likely be short and sweet. Guidance may come as symbols, coincidences or smells. And we will know it is right because it will feel light! The more relaxed we are, the more easily this direction will flow, so take a dose of lightness and enjoy being guided on an awesome life adventure.

✺ September 11

"I'm not going to let my tumour define me or my life. I won't give it that much power."

These words, spoken by a woman I met at the airport one day, resonated with me for weeks to come. She had recently been diagnosed with stage 4 brain cancer and was due to have surgery three days later to remove a large tumor from her brain. "There's a difference between feeling pain and suffering," she said. "I'm not going to suffer."

While I could understand intellectually that pain and suffering could be separate—or separated—I'd never witnessed anyone pull them apart. Especially when it mattered most. In the days and weeks after our wonderful conversation, what stayed with me was a question: How much of our experience of pain is really our unconscious choice to suffer? I, for one, have an unrealistic expectation that my life will be pain-free, and I've become conditioned and accustomed to believing that when pain appears, it is a sure sign of a problem. In my mind, pain is a symptom of something that's wrong, so when it begins, so do my suffering and worry.

I am inspired by people who have transcended suffering while living with physical, mental or emotional pain. From conversations with many of them, I've learned that their decisions to end their suffering came or appeared on the other side of their darkest moments of despair. It's as though despair is a staircase we must descend before we can rise above suffering.

And we *must* rise above suffering. While we have no say in when, or how much, pain happens in our lives, we are in complete control over whether we suffer with that pain. The truth is that our quality of life does not hinge on what happens to us; it is created from the meaning we give to events.

We are, after all, meaning-making machines. Some of us will experience pain, will make that mean that our life is under siege and will suffer; others will experience that same pain, create a different meaning and rise above or sidestep suffering to preserve our quality of life.

This is one of the most powerful choices we can make in being alive.

🌸 September 12

How would you describe your relationship with food?

Food is a huge part of life, and it's vital that we assess whether we are in a healthy, fulfilling relationship with it or if change is needed.

I would describe any healthy relationship as featuring love, connection and nurturing. In this case I would say it requires that we love food for being itself, that we feel connected to food and that we feel nurtured and at our best when we are with it.

I have always loved food—the tastes, the smells, the textures and memories made with food. Yet for the first half of my life, I was unconscious about eating. For that matter, I was unconscious about *everything*. As I awaken in my life overall, I am also awakening to food.

When I am paying attention, I can feel my body respond positively to food, always in my chest and core areas. It's like a tingling sensation, a peppy wake-up feeling. I imagine reactions like "Wow! That is awesome! It is alive food! I want that food. I love it. Give it to me now!"

I even imagine them said in a Cookie Monster voice. I also notice that I eat when I am tired, I eat as a reward and I eat to suppress my emotions when they are running high. I find that I always feel more joyful and healthy when I am *enjoying* food, as opposed to *using* it.

How do you describe your relationship with food? I am not asking about how much you eat, or how much you weigh, or whether you are in control or eating healthily. I am asking whether you and food are in love. Do you love food, and does it love you?

Look at food today and what you love about this life-giving partnership. Have fun! You may learn about your other relationships, because the way we are with food is likely an indicator of how we are in all our relationships.

Bon appétit!

🌸 September 13

When we react to criticism, it usually indicates that we're acknowledging an element of truth in what we're being told. And if we can focus on what feels true in that moment, it will save us a ton of energy we would otherwise waste on resisting, defending, pretending and being angry.

Our egos don't like criticism one bit. But when it is given to us directly and in person, it can reveal a blind spot about ourselves that is extremely helpful to know about. It may be delivered in an anger package or a heated exchange; it may come in a calm, planned and unheated manner. Either way, this person is invested enough in us to say something. People only share criticism with people they care about. And if you are anything like me when it comes to being direct with others, you can imagine how much courage it took for that person to tell you the truth!

Criticism shared directly can truly help us open unknown parts of ourselves. We may not like the way it is delivered, and that is okay. It still will be a gift for us, once we feel safe enough to unwrap it.

September 14

At times in this book, I'll write a note that is deeper and that I hope will persuade you to join me in considering something I'm learning or exploring. At other times, like today, I may write an entry that is more prescriptive. It's not that I like telling you—or, for that matter, being told—what to do, but I realize that there are moments when I need nudging, and you may need nudging as well.

Today I'm inviting you to be more generous than you may typically be. In fact, I'm inviting you to be randomly generous and extend kindness and consideration to others in small, inconspicuous ways—as many as you can muster. Make someone a beverage as you're making your own. Compliment a friend. Buy or make two lunches today, put the second in a bag marked "free" and leave it in the office fridge. Say hi to someone you see every day but have yet to acknowledge. Share your newspaper with a stranger. Pay for the coffee or tea of the person behind you in the drive-through lane. Invite a group to join you in the crossword or the sudoku at lunch. I could go on and on, but I think you understand my meaning.

The point of today is to be a personal beacon of generosity and kindness. It's a social experiment of sorts—one in which you and I are the test subjects and the goal is to compare how light we feel at the beginning of the day and at the end, and to understand the impact of being generous to others.

September 15

In what I think is one of Tom Hanks's finer films, *Philadelphia*, there's a line that the young defence lawyer played by Denzel Washington repeats several times during his cross-examinations: "Explain this to me. Explain it to me like I'm a six-year-old." I remember hearing these words for the first time and feeling that they comprised one of life's biggest truths. Later, in university, the KISS rule ("keep it simple, stupid") became a phrase I would hear over and over. And again, those words struck me as delivering a profound message.

One day, while walking between classes with a professor, I shared the story of a pub crawl that I had taken part in a few nights earlier. I said, "We had so much to drink that we were inebriated." My professor turned to me, and in a very direct yet kind way, said, "Intellectuals get inebriated. The rest of us just get drunk." His correction made me feel both embarrassed and relieved—I had been putting on airs to impress him and make myself look smarter, and it turned out to be an empty attempt to make something simple sound more complex.

These moments have stayed with me throughout my life and they remind me of that powerful truth: living a life of lightness and contentment is not sophisticated or complex. It is quite simple. Simple enough for a six-year-old to understand. I think we overcomplicate life by believing that it is an unsolvable mystery, a timeless riddle or a highly personal, knotted-up ball of circumstances, events, manoeuvrings, slights and codes that we must sort through and unravel. But the truths that really bring us contentment and peace are basic and universal:

- Be kind—to yourself, those around you and your environment.
- Life is tough for everyone. Some of us accept this and some deny it. The second group tends to suffer more.
- Know the truth—especially your own.
- We are born to learn, feel and move—resist any of these and dire consequences will follow.
- "I" is for taking responsibility, gaining awareness and owning our experience; otherwise, life is really about "we." And we are not separate from any other life form on this planet.

These truths have been told, written and shared around the globe for most of our history, and I suspect they will be with us for as long as people maintain their attachment to the idea that life must be complex.

✾ September 16

I learned a new term this week: "sober curious." It was coined by the British writer Ruby Warrington, and it describes a desire for "unlearning the habit of reaching for a drink on autopilot in any and all social situations."

The topic of living lightly has lured me directly into some areas of my life where heavy shitstorms were raging, and more and more I am falling in love with the idea of being connected to myself. My numbing-out habits, such as wine and food and social media, while under control, are really on my radar this month, provoking me more and more. Rather than issue a head-on declaration of war or abstinence on these things, I have been gently removing other, less provocative parts of my life to see what happens.

Yesterday, after a full day at home with my family, we sat together on the couch with dinner and pulled out our books. Our daughter loved it. By 7 p.m., as she went to take a shower, I realized how long the evening was! Two more hours until bedtime, and I had no deadlines or deliverables to occupy my time. We had already done lots of family things together, including baking muffins in the afternoon, so I was done for the day and fully satisfied.

At this point I was struck by a memory from summer vacation when I was about ten years old. I remembered how long the days and nights felt, even if many of them were spent sitting on the curb, just hanging out. I'd wander in and out of the house, maybe walk to the store for a Popsicle, watch the clouds and paddle and float for hours in the pool. I remember saying I was bored a lot, but now I recognize that I was grounded—just being myself, with nowhere I had to go and no urge to rush or make myself busy or artificially full or happy. I was laid-back, quiet, even-keeled. I'm grateful my mom didn't fall for the "I'm bored" bait.

I share this memory with you because last night felt similar. I wasn't up or down, I wasn't stressed out or fatigued and I wasn't multi-tasking or getting ahead on things. I just sat there with my book and the people I love most, and when it was time for me to go to bed, I fell asleep. That's it.

How long and rich life is when we can remove the artificial highs and lows. "Sober curious" is about that, to me, and I think it's applicable way beyond alcohol consumption. No all-or-nothing labels or punishing regimens, just a curiosity and noticing what happens when I remove certain things from my free time. Giving myself space in my free time and feeling what happens. I like it. I hope you do too.

September 17

The Grass So Little Has to Do

The Grass so little has to do –
A Sphere of simple Green –
With only Butterflies to brood
And Bees to entertain –
And stir all day to pretty Tunes
The Breezes fetch along –
And hold the Sunshine in its lap
And bow to everything –

And thread the Dews, all night, like Pearls –
And make itself so fine
A Duchess were too common
For such a noticing –

And even when it dies – to pass
In Odors so divine –
Like Lowly spices, lain to sleep –
Or Spikenards, perishing –

And then, in Sovereign Barns to dwell –
And dream the Days away,
The Grass so little has to do
I wish I were a Hay –

—Emily Dickinson

During late autumn, on our farm, the grass is beginning to slow down. Since late April I have cut it every week, walking for up to four hours behind our lawn mower, covering a landscape that occupies nearly five acres. Many of my neighbours and family have exclaimed that what I'm doing is lunacy and that I should make quick work of the chore by buying a riding mower. But I don't find it a chore to cut the grass—for me, it's a type of communion and a labour of love.

I love the feel of the grass. I relish the fresh-cut aroma as I move over each new section. I look at the grass and observe which parts of our farm lawn are healthier, which parts are growing more wild and which parts feel more carpet-like. At this time of year, as I cut and walk through the grass, I see the monarch butterflies and grasshoppers flitting and leaping just ahead of me; our chickens trail behind, feverishly pecking at the soil to expose the grubs and worms. I'm fascinated by all the activity and movement that happen just beneath the surface of the grass. It is a geography of communities that are invisible to me most of the time.

I love to walk barefoot in the grass, especially in the late afternoon or early evening when the grass feels its plushest and most alive. My partner and our daughter lie on the grass and stare up into the big wide-open sky above, watching clouds or tracing the slow circles of the hawks as they rise and fall on the air currents. The grass feeds our horses, and I'm always amazed at how these large, gentle creatures gingerly pick at the blades—or, more often, grab them in their teeth in big sideways swipes.

Have I tempted you to restore, rekindle or reconnect with grass? I hope I have, because I can't think of a better way today to say yes to being lightly alive.

🌸 September 18

Today is a good day to reflect on our living-lightly journey thus far. How are you feeling? Have silence and breath made their way into your daily routine? Do you like this gentle way we are exploring?

Your yes and no are both welcome; if we are together today on this page, there is cause to celebrate. We have come through some discoveries and found some gentleness along the way.

September always feels to me like a second January, another beginning to the year. Some of that is because of where I live, where the seasons start to change and endings are in the air. Growth goes underground, less visible and quieter, silently sprouting and taking root.

It seems like I am just beginning to get a sense for how living lightly applies to me—what it feels like, what it makes possible for me. For months I have been cycling around in my life, feeling where the heavy lies, experiencing moments of stillness—and every now and then, of connection—that I adore. I love living in a grounded way so much that it feels like the most important thing for me to focus on— connecting to myself and allowing myself to be guided forward, being true to that same self everywhere.

Today I wish for us to spend the rest of the year connecting to ourselves, gently breathing and making space, staying grounded. I think you are amazing. I think about you every day, imagining how you are doing and sending light your way.

See you tomorrow.

September 19

Yesterday, on the radio, there was a phone-in conversation about the leading reasons why people leave their jobs. Insufficient wages, limits on a person's ability to move up or across the organization, conflicts with supervisors and work peers—the host of the show cited these as factors that prompt people to walk away from an otherwise good job. Midway through the program, an interesting shift began to happen: listeners were stating that the number one reason they had left a great job was that they no longer believed in either the work they were doing or the company that employed them.

One woman's comments stood out for me. "I had a high-paying job," she said. "There was a clear path for me to move up, my boss was supportive, but my job came into conflict with my values and I couldn't live with that anymore." Pressed by the host to explain further, the woman offered, "The company created products that offered no real benefit and mostly ended up in landfill sites around the world. I just couldn't be a part of that anymore."

This was the first time I had heard a personal account of a values-based approach to work. I must tell you honestly that I am still surprised by what I heard.

I made the decision many years ago to work for myself as a therapist. In doing so, I strived to create a life and a job that were twinned. Over the decades, I have often run into personal conflicts where my job or business collided with my values and I had to make a tough choice. Therapy is a business where people want to come and see their counsellor after their own work is finished—in the evenings or on the weekends. This means that most therapists and counsellors work evenings and weekends and are therefore not at home with their families or spouses. The irony of someone paying me, a counsellor who had little or no personal time, to help them with their work–life balance became too hard for me to ignore. I was missing time with my children and my marriage was under pressure because I rarely saw my spouse.

I knew I had to make some changes in the way I worked or else I couldn't be authentic. It was a hard decision, and I lost clients and revenue for a couple of years. I had to adapt, draw tight boundaries around my office hours and find new ways to work with clients. Eventually I became more of a specialist, which also made me a destination for clients—they adapted their schedules to see me when I was available. I reduced the number of evenings I worked in groups, and I moved my office into our neighbourhood so that I could walk our children to school and then walk to my office. The net effect of these changes was that they brought me closer to my views on work—that it should *support* my life, rather than *be* my life.

I learned that we always have this choice about our work and its relationship to our lives. We can always choose to have our careers and jobs align with who we are. We may make other sacrifices and compromises, but in the end, both our work and our life will benefit.

Maybe it's time to expose those stories you have about your work and ask yourself: Does it connect to who you are as a person? Does it build and support your soul, or does it take away from your well-being? What changes would you make—and what would you risk—to bring your work into alignment with your soul?

🌸 September 20

Tedium. Dullsville. Ho-hum. Boredom gets a bad name, but beautiful benefits. First, when we don't reach for our smart phones at the first sign of inactivity, we give the reward centres in our brain a much-needed break by preventing them from being flooded with dopamine. The cells of our brains' reward centres are constantly being stimulated by the flashing images and hilarious kitten videos that are so popular on our social media feeds. The same thing happens with those emails from work that you absolutely must read, or the ongoing thread of emoji bantering that accounts for much of our personal texting. We're suffering from a white line fever of dopamine.

When you're bored, it can feel as though you've died a mini-death. Your mind may race and panic, demanding that you get up and move or simply do anything other than just sit or lie in one place. Trust me: this too shall pass. This temporary state of stasis is the second benefit of boredom. Identifying boredom as a "meaning hangover," Norwegian author Lars Svendsen comments in *A Philosophy of Boredom*, "I think that if you wish to sort of find your way out of this boredom you really have to figure out what to care about. That's the essential question."

So to paraphrase Svendsen, boredom is a universal pause we all experience, and it helps to jolt us into a more meaningful thought, behaviour or endeavour. Meaning that the next time you get the urge to say out loud, "I'm bored!" try to stay with that tedium until it is more than unbearable, because it is likely that you are on the precipice of something more meaningful, more purposeful, more creative.

✿ September 21

Summer is giving way to autumn, and as the days get shorter and the temperature dips, I start to feel that familiar tightening in my stomach that is worry. This is when I start to think long and hard about winter.

Our farm is in a place that experiences big swings in temperature from summer to winter, and within a single day it's not unusual to see the mercury move forty degrees above and below zero. Our task is literally to keep our animals alive and not just comfortable. After a few years of this cycle, we've learned a great deal about what to do and when to do it. But regardless of the lessons we have learned and our efforts to be prepared, the worry never goes away. Life has taught us to expect emergencies and that there is only so much preparation that can be done. We can't stop the temperature from dropping. We can't control whether our power goes out or our heated water lines freeze. We can't force our animals to drink if they don't want to. And it is impossible to predict how many days will be marked by a heat wave, heavy rain and mud or, at the other end of the scale, whiteout snowstorms. We must just live with these things and do our best to stay focused on what's really important—and at times that focal point can change in minutes, if not seconds.

There's a calmness, if not a lightness, that comes with experiencing numerous 911-like emergencies, and with many of these under our belts it feels like we're becoming more resilient to panic. Or perhaps more truthfully, we don't panic anymore because, as we have found our way through each urgent situation, our confidence in ourselves and our abilities has grown.

But again, the worry never goes away. It remains a low-grade gnawing in our stomachs and a soft whirring in our heads as we review every decision we've made to ensure we have done all we can. We're learning to accept this reality and make friends with our worry.

September 22

We can do something kind for ourselves today. We can set aside time for ourselves—time to expand, to exhale, to release, to open to the most exquisite and surprising parts of our nature.

If we make this commitment, we will flourish! Listen for the whispers inside and you will hear lovely, surprising ideas and hopes and dreams. Take a theatre class. Learn to paint. Travel. Dance. Create. Be on the water. Build something. Raise chickens. This is our destiny whispering, and it *can* wait, but why should it? The suggestions it makes don't have to make sense or lead anywhere. They are beautiful in and of themselves, as are we.

More than a trip to the spa or a new purchase, this is time invested in learning and expanding, and we can make no mistakes. Everything is a good idea if it comes from inside of us. Choose the one that feels easiest or gentlest today and take a step towards it. This is an investment in our joy, our joie de vivre. This is a big part of what makes life worth living, and the next pieces of our journey come through these walkabouts. Everybody benefits when we beam rays of sunlight everywhere we go—especially us. Feel your sunshine coming through!

🌸 September 23

Work is a lot like family, isn't it? A random assortment of characters thrown together, sometimes for years to come, to spend the better part of their day with one another. How we behave in our place of work—which is where most of us spend most of our time—is a huge factor in our overall well-being. It's critical that we find lightness here.

A dear friend of mine has an awesome way of framing her work as her way of contributing to the world. Her faith that her life has purpose and meaning is rock solid, and her work journey exemplifies it perfectly. She is the most faith-filled person I know, and I admire her so much.

Consider the part you play in the work you do. Think about the gifts, strengths and talents you bring, and bear in mind that your impact extends well beyond the actual job. Your way of being, the way you "do" life, your personality—all of these affect the people around you. We have an incredible opportunity to value ourselves, our time and our contribution to others.

Thinking of work life as family life—with your co-workers as aunts, uncles, siblings, parents, grandparents and cousins—would you do anything differently? Maybe we can do lunch at work the way we do at home. For me, that would mean making something and sharing it with another. We can adorn our workspaces so that they feel like home. Bring in a lamp or a plant or pictures that make you smile—whatever will fit your workspace.

Be yourself at work and carry yourself as though you are at home. Clean the washroom when it needs to be cleaned. Cook a meal at the office if possible. Notice who comes forward to connect and be around you. Be seen, be embraced, be appreciated for who you are as a person.

Make work days be about relatedness and celebrate the gifts you bring, and in doing so, may you feel lightness and appreciation.

❀ September 24

We feel better when we go outside. Try to remember this as a way to stay light. Whether we're in a city of skyscrapers or in a factory lot, we can feel the breeze or rain or sun on our cheeks. We can look at the sky and imagine we are up there. We can look at the pigeons, the dogs or the pebbles. Breathing all the while, in and out, until we feel ourselves again. Spending a few minutes outdoors each day, in silence, as a conscious way to reconnect inside, allows us to get out of our heads and remember who we are.

❀ September 25

One of the many amazing gifts that comes from sharing our true selves is that we get to find and connect with like-hearted others. These lovely beings may be found inside of decade-long friendships, love affairs or neighbourly relations. They may also be brand new. We may not have much in common on the outside, and we may not even live in the same country. The connection lives on the inside.

To see and be seen, to accept and be accepted, to listen and be heard, is profoundly amazing! It really is all we need to make a magical connection.

I wonder how far this kind of soul-filled connection can go? Imagine collaborating with, living with, and pooling resources with people who are physically, emotionally and spiritually safe to make something beautiful happen. Sounds heavenly to me!

Are your heart people actively in your life? Do you create with, work with, live with, travel with, write with, play with them? The way we experience our lives—our freedom and joy, our creations, our courage to do things, our ability to grow exponentially—will be amplified in the safe company of like-hearted others.

Whether they have arrived yet or are on their way, let's ask for them, invite them into our lives, even when we don't know what that will look like. Ask for these people to come into our lives and then create something wonderful together. Our hearts will sing.

✹ September 26

Clutter represents delayed decisions or difficult choices yet to be made. So say professional organizers. We let things pile up around us because we're emotionally attached to them and we're just not ready to let go of what they mean to us. We don't want to make that choice just yet, so we put it off, waiting for "someday" to arrive. When it comes to our stuff, we have two big fears: a fear of being unprepared for the future, and a fear that we will forget the past.

We keep clothes that don't fit, hoping for the day we drop the weight; we have boxes of photos and papers to sort through; we fill our closets; we jam stuff under our beds; we stack boxes; and when we run out of space in our homes, we rent spaces in self-storage buildings to hold our overflow. As a good friend of mine shared with me recently, "The self-storage business is based entirely on guilt—people feel guilty about getting rid of stuff."

There's our stuff, our parents' stuff if they've passed, our children's stuff that we're saving for when grandchildren arrive, the stuff we've carted back and forth since university, the downsizing stuff we don't need in our apartment or condo but are saving because we may own a house again—lots and lots of *stuff*. Not because we need any of it, but because we have too hard a time letting go of it. And before you say,

"But we need our stuff," or "Our stuff is really important to us," let me tell you we have the same trouble making choices about our closets as we do with our email inboxes, the photo collections on our phones, our bookshelves, our desks and filing cabinets, and those handy storage compartments in our cars.

We just don't like making the decision to "edit" our stuff. If our external behaviour reflects our mental condition, then it stands to reason that many of us are walking around quite full and cluttered on the inside as well.

We have a few more months together to purge all the stuff that is weighing us down. I don't know about you, but I'm ready, with bags in hand, to get at it. I feel a purge coming on.

❋ September 27

With more than two million copies sold worldwide, *The Life-Changing Magic of Tidying Up* by Marie Kondo is a publishing phenomenon. Around the globe, fervent fans who call themselves "Konverts" follow Kondo's method of sorting through and parting with things based on whether they "spark joy" in the moment.

The KonMari Method is proving to be both popular and liberating. Diehard fans say their lives have been forever changed; no longer being surrounded by mounds of clutter has saved them time and made their homes feel more spacious. As an aside, numerous studies have revealed that human beings will work to fill any space in front of or around us, whether it's a dinner plate or a room, and the size of the space determines how much stuff we will heap in or on it. Want to eat less? Replace all your large dinner plates with smaller side plates. Want to have less stuff? Move into a much smaller space. It seems we have a comfort level with a certain amount of clutter, and we will always maintain it by adjusting our consumption to fit any change in our physical circumstances.

Kondo advises that, in a process that can take up to three months, we begin purging our clothing, then move on to our papers and documents, and finally to potentially more meaningful items, such as photos and mementos. Working steadily with the intent to sort, tidy and lighten each area of our lives, we gain practice in the method and reinforce our choice to live amongst only those things that spark joy in us.

It's late September, so many of us are transitioning from one season to another. Isn't this a perfect time to begin a purge? The change of seasons means our clothing will change anyway, so it seems to be a built-in signal to take a hard look at what we have, keep what sparks joy in us and donate what does not. We can do this for ourselves, for our own liberation and freedom. And we can do this today, right?

September 28

Why are we so shocked when someone we revere or admire is found to have shown poor judgment or acted on their baser instincts? To be clear, I'm not including the ones who deny their behaviour and try to maintain a sparkling veneer; I mean the people who make mistakes, doing or saying things that don't meet the high standards we've come to expect from them. Is it because we forget that we all have two selves within us that are often at odds? Or is it that we are deeply attached to an ideal of this person whom we have placed on a pedestal? Maybe it is a combination of both, as well as our dislike or abandonment of our lower, baser ways of being.

What if we accepted that we are capable of being jealous, greedy or selfish as well as benevolent, kind and caring? What if the real point of this journey is not to focus on being one way or the other, but to take stock of how often we make a conscious choice to be good or bad, as if we're all living with a moral balance sheet?

None of us is perfect—or really ever evenly balanced. Former US president Barack Obama admitted that he slept less than seven hours a night and "fell off of the wagon" many times when it came to quitting cigarettes. Cameron Diaz confessed she has a thing for cursing. Winston Churchill was reportedly a high-functioning alcoholic, and Martin Luther King Jr. allegedly had numerous extramarital affairs. That's why I like to read biographies and memoirs. Reading about someone else's struggles with their own nature—especially someone I admire—normalizes my own. What I've come to understand and accept is that I alone have the choice of how I want to behave in every moment of my life. There are times when I choose to be in my higher self, and moments when I want to be in my baser self. The latter is not about sinning in the religious sense but behaving in ways that are selfish rather than selfless.

The lightness for me comes when I exercise my conscious awareness and choose how to behave, and that includes taking responsibility, apologizing or making amends when I have done something that I know in my heart I could have done better.

There is lightness and empowerment in our choices, but only if we can accept that we are fundamentally living with two selves.

❀ September 29

I used to throw myself into the fire for the sake of having a breakthrough. I forced myself to do things that scared me, in hopes of feeling adventurous, successful or fulfilled. Not once did it build my confidence or self-esteem or stop the shaking inside.

Social norms are leaning towards simplicity and ease, avowing the benefits of mediocrity. While I appreciate the toning down of expectations, I don't aim for a life of mediocrity. Do you? I think we all want our hearts to sing, our spirits to soar, our will to float on air with the joy of being fully alive.

There is a midpoint, neither breakthrough nor mediocrity, that is gentle. Take the branch offered. Hold someone's hand.

Our inside voice that whispers softly is the one to listen to. It speaks the truth of our desire and points to a safe way forward. Truth never yells, insists, negotiates, minimizes or promises, nor does it dazzle. It doesn't need to. As we start to hear this voice, all there is to do is listen.

🌸 September 30

Do we trust ourselves?

Do we trust ourselves to create financial safety for ourselves and our families? Do we trust our relationship choices? Do we trust our instincts? Do we trust that we are good people—kind and generous? Do we trust our bodies to survive, to be strong, to endure, to physically express our true nature? Do we trust ourselves in an emergency to do right for ourselves and for others?

Our anxiety and stress come from a lack of trust in ourselves. Worries about work may stem from questioning our own value, feeling a lack of power to get another job or unable to do our best at the job we have. Worries about relationships may stem from questioning our worth, wondering whether we deserve a better partner.

Are we willing to learn to do for ourselves? The more knowledge we get for ourselves, the fewer our worries become. Think of the lion walking confidently, sleeping in the open, living unafraid.

Knowledge is power. It's available to all of us and there is lightness in the ability to walk the earth, confident in our abilities. Self-reliant, self-responsible. When we meet another, we can truly see them and love them for who they are, rather than for what we need from them, or what they need from us. Love based on respect and admiration and mutual understanding, shared interests, creating together, partnership.

It would take a shift in our approach and attitude, away from separating or distancing ourselves and in the direction of infusing ourselves with knowledge and ability. Let's invest time in learning, grooming ourselves, pursuing our interests and filling the gaps in our ability, so that we walk like lions.

October

🌸 October 1

I learned something about myself the other day. I apologized to someone, and they said thank you. Later I apologized to a second person,
and I didn't hear back from them. In both instances my reaction was to
feel indignant, panicked, ashamed and angry. This took me by surprise
at first, because both times I thought I was offering the apology from
a place of love. Yet my reaction shows otherwise. In the first case, I
apologized quickly because the other person had disagreed with me.
I was feeling shame for being different and wanted to quickly return
to sameness—false alignment. With the second person, I had judged
them as being wrong, so I apologized as a gentle way to secure the
expression of regret that I thought was due to me.

I sometimes say "I love you" because I want to hear it back. I know
this because when the other person says thank you and nothing more,
my mind revs up again, judging, pointing, objecting like a defence
attorney!

Validation from outside is a shaky foundation for my self-esteem
to be built upon. I am glad to recognize this in myself. It shows me
where I can spend time developing my own points of view and cali-
brating my own moral compass so that my apologies come when I
truly feel remorse for hurting another, and so that I reserve "I love you"
for magic moments when the words dance off my tongue, giving voice
to the delight in my heart.

"I am sorry" and "I love you" are two powerful personal statements. They carry our integrity, our honour, our compassion and our
humanity in their words. I save these precious phrases as moonlight
kisses to bestow freely and easily in times of truth.

October 2

When was the last time you went to the library?

For our quest to live lightly, the library is a wonderful resource. Touching the book covers, looking at the jacket designs, running our hands along the shelves and, of course, feeling the texture of the pages. These are the rituals of the library.

What a lovely place to find solitude amongst company. We can go with a friend or in a group, each meandering to our favourite sections, and we can meet with our treasures at the checkout counter, presenting our library cards. We can sit together during weekend afternoons or in the evenings, silently reading. This is a magical experience, to fill our minds with words and stories and imaginings together, in quiet.

Reading in the company of someone who is also reading makes for an amazing, unspoken, felt connection.

October 3

Out of the blue, our son decided to give up eating meat for a while. This is a person who adores eating meat. He is studying the body and wondering what the impact will be on him. And just like that, he is eating quinoa. Just like that.

Our dog passed away unexpectedly this month, and our tween daughter, who cried upon hearing the news, no longer shows signs of grief or sadness. I asked her how she was feeling about Hank, our dog, and she simply said, "I know he wants me to be happy, so I'm being happy."

Wow. That is lightness of being, so beautiful and generous and natural. It lives in all of us. Youth, when they are fortunate enough to have a loving childhood, have fewer layers of pain sitting atop their vulnerability. We adults need to dig a wee bit to uncover it, but it is there, that golden light in all of us.

We can change, choose differently, live in light.

What we practise—meditating, finding stillness and quiet, loving ourselves—helps us to feel our own lightness. Let's keep going.

❋ October 4

Over the past six weeks, we have been hosting family members. We have quite an extended family, and they come up to our farm, one day here and there, one or two members at a time. Being with family is a tough test of lightness, because it is the inner sanctum of our emotional development and healing.

Triggered at times, I pulled away, shut down, not being fully myself. I want to be light everywhere in my life, especially with family, so after the visits are over, aided by my partner's wonderful listening skills, I unpack what happened, with the goal of finding the parts that need healing. My family doesn't need to be involved as I search for my truth and try to recover. I start by remembering the details of my physical, mental and emotional states when I was upset.

On one occasion, I remember feeling a physical heaviness wash over me as if a dark cloth was being draped over my head and face. I was emotionally numb and my stomach felt very full. I know that the four feeling states are sad, mad, glad, and scared, and my symptoms did not indicate sadness, gladness or fear, which left anger. Hmmm. Anger can have an outer layer of resentment and jealousy. And that fit my situation accurately.

Please sit with someone who can witness and listen as you work this out—someone who won't succumb to their own family triggers. A professional is always a great choice.

I ask myself, "From what time in my childhood do these feelings originate?" Because I know the negative emotion I feel now is the result of unresolved childhood dynamics, with a bit of current behaviour and differences layered on top. There is an underlying hurt still to be healed. In this case, it was my resentment as a toddler that my parents' attention and love would have to be shared with a new baby. The inequalities I perceived between me and my sibling are no one's fault; they are universal and archetypal. And still, at fifty years of age, the hurt inside me is unhealed.

So where is the light in this? Well, I can lift the blame off my sibling and parents, which provides me some comfort. Realizing that I have unresolved resentment at being the oldest child in my family gives me hope, because once we become aware, we can heal. With my childhood hurt now moved to a separate, conscious part of my life, I can clear space to relate to my sibling.

Feel all the relief, the restored energy, the vibrancy of your natural self bubbling back up into your relationships when you find parts of yourself that still need healing.

October 5

It's a surprising thing to do if you're looking for a quick boost of lightness, because on the surface it sounds a bit counterintuitive: simply learn more.

Our brains will frequently get stuck in routines, schedules and repetitive tasks, and though all of this organization may be helpful, our minds can fall into a kind of dormancy with too much predictability. When it comes to learning something new, our minds get more stimulation if the skill or knowledge involves more than one area of our brains, like learning a language; if it is tactile, like working with our hands or doing crafts; or if it makes us more social, like taking a class or doing a workshop. There's no requirement that this new learning involve a lifelong passion or hobby either. Remember, you're looking for a short boost of lightness—something to shift your brain into more electric activity.

Long resistant to crosswords, I found myself at an office lunch table one day with a colleague who was passionately trying to solve the daily puzzle in a newspaper. I'd seen this person before, and despite being invited to join her, I would glance at what she was doing, say "No, thank you," and walk away. I told myself I had neither the time nor the interest to join her. Truthfully, I was more concerned about how I would look if I didn't prove to be good at solving the clues. This is true of most new things I want to try: I want to get past that resistance and anxiety about looking bad and being judged. It turns out this is the number one reason preventing people from learning something new.

On this day, I said "Sure" and sat down with my colleague. She patiently walked me through her strategies for working out the solutions. She was a great teacher, and as is the case with all who enjoy sharing, what she taught me was wrapped up in joy and excitement, which became contagious. I was hooked after one puzzle, and I've carried that enthusiasm with me for more than two decades.

I've learned that life offers many of these seemingly small and insignificant pastimes, things we can try to keep our minds active and our spirits light. It is when we are curious and open, or when we need these things most, that we discover a world of hidden treasures where whispers of "try me" are everywhere.

October 6

I watched Jerry Seinfeld talking with Jerry Lewis last night. They were both glorious in their love of laughter. Their faces told it all—they knew when a funny moment was coming; each trusted the other's gift for timing, for knowing when to pause to craft the perfectly delivered joke. To see their faces break into laughter, first in their eyes and then their open mouths, was heavenly to me. I smiled all the way through this and three more episodes of Seinfeld's series *Comedians in Cars Getting Coffee*. I very much appreciate people who love to laugh. We know that laughter is medicine, literally tipping our body to produce healthy oxytocin and reduce our heart rate and blood pressure—all good things. I went to bed with a smile on my face. Lovely.

Will you give yourself a laugh today? It can be easy. Watch a clip that is guaranteed to make you laugh. My brother watches videos of police dogs wearing booties for the first time, and he giggles every time. Try telling someone your favourite joke. Do whatever makes you laugh every single time.

Life is full and intense at times. We are engaging in deep self-exploration, so today might be a good day for a laugh. There is never a bad day to laugh and lighten up a little.

October 7

Can you envision the most restorative, relaxing, healing experience for you? What does it look like and feel like? What would you design to support all of your mind's and body's resources to heal you when you needed it most? These were a few of the questions that managers at the Oslo University Hospital in Norway asked themselves when they set about to design and build a new facility. Their early clues and extensive research brought them back to nature as a powerful counter-experience to today's sterile, technology-driven hospitals.

"There's a lot of evidence now that nature has an effect on us when it comes to stress regulation," says child psychologist Maren Østvold Lindheim. "We can see the body calms when it's in nature versus the built environment. This is especially true for children."

In a study published in 2015, researchers at Stanford University concluded that subjects who took a ninety-minute walk in a natural setting showed reduced symptoms of depression, and a 2018 study published in the journal *Behavioral Sciences* found that people who spent time in nature had lower psychological and physiological stress levels than those who visited an urban outdoor area and a gym.

In Oslo the evidence was conclusive and overwhelming. The result of the hospital's discovery process is a stunning, tree fort–like retreat for patients and their families, complete with pathways that accommodate a hospital bed and resources to connect with staff, all located about two hundred metres from the hospital.

What I find inspiring about this story is what we can achieve when we are willing to question the way things are always done and ask ourselves honestly: What would make us feel healthy? Another example of this kind of thinking is Maggie's Centres, a network of cancer treatment centres envisioned by writer and designer Maggie Keswick Jencks. In the 1990s Jencks was being treated for cancer— the last two years of her life were spent visiting a drab, windowless room for chemotherapy. That's when she was struck by the idea that cancer treatment environments and their outcomes could both be improved significantly through good, natural design. A story on the *Arch Daily* website summed up her rationale: "Wouldn't it be better to have a private, light-filled space in which to await the results of the next bout of tests, or from which to contemplate, in silence, the findings? If architecture could demoralize patients . . . could it not also prove restorative?"

You and I aren't likely to find ourselves designing large institutional environments for people seeking medical attention (although if you are, I hope you're pausing for some deep thought right now). For most of us, today's entry is about where we live and work and how close we feel to the natural world. And to be clear, I'm not talking about looking at a tree from a window—passive observation only creates longing and dissonance. To be healthy, to feel truly restored, we need to sit under or climb that tree, lie on the grass, sit near or dip our feet in free-flowing water and feel the wind and sun on our skin.

We are natural beings, and to be light we must be connected to nature.

❀ October 8

Even though gratitude is proven to have positive health effects that increase over time and last several months, part of me turns away at the thought of it. Thinking that I was a bad person and I should do something to change this, I reflected on my resistance to gratitude.

I believe that you and I are grateful when we are in the moment. Gratitude as a scheduled task, on the other hand, diminishes our natural feeling states, the ebb and flow of our emotions. I resist being grateful as a "should," if it comes with a mandate to pretend to be so all of the time. I resist pushing myself to feel positive and happy all of the time because that is neither humanly possible nor normal. What I aspire for myself and for you is freedom to be and to feel, because in the act of feeling there is relief and release—and space to move to the next moment. Denying and pretending is a suppression of our natural ups and downs, and it puts pressure on our bodies that builds up over time. An article from *Time* magazine in February 2018 explains it nicely:

> Emotions have energy that pushes up for expression, and to tamp them down, our minds and bodies use creative tactics—including muscular constriction and holding our breath. Symptoms like anxiety and depression, which are on the rise in the US, can stem from the way we deal with these underlying, automatic, hard-wired survival emotions, which are biological forces that should not be ignored. When the mind thwarts the flow of emotions because they are too overwhelming or too conflicting, it puts stress on the mind and the body, creating psychological distress and symptoms. Emotional stress, like that from blocked emotions, has not only been linked to mental ills, but also to physical problems like heart disease, intestinal problems, headaches, insomnia and autoimmune disorders.

We are naturally grateful beings. It is inherent in all of us. Let's trust ourselves about that. We need to express our feelings and acknowledge them, and as soon as we do, we need to trust that they will be released and the energy will disperse. We need to be real. This is so important to our well-being and to living lightly—which is also about moving through darkness and feeling heavy at times; it is the only way to live in lasting states of gratitude and grace.

❋ October 9

Lately our eleven-year-old daughter has taken to kissing me goodnight. With a small peck on the mouth and a tender "good night," she connects with me and then makes her way up the stairs to prepare to go to bed. It's been about two months since she added the kiss; before that, she preferred to yell out "good night" from some part of the house, with no particular tenderness.

I know too much about human behaviour to believe that this change is a random act on her part. I know that, in her mind, something has shifted—but what? I'd love to know what she is thinking, what she now believes, what has become important to her.

To be honest, it's sometimes challenging for me to accept this kind of unconditional affection because I didn't grow up with it. Later, in many of my adult relationships, affection was still conditional, even political. I learned to shy away from it, stiffening and freezing when someone kissed me or tried to hug me, the message "Not safe!" flashing across my mind like a highway billboard. The clinical diagnosis would be that I have an attachment disorder. Having never experienced safe bonding with either of my parents, I long for, and yet am fearful of, emotional intimacy. As a result, love is work for me and it is never light or euphoric. It can actually be terrifying for me.

And so I find myself now, as a parent, being loved unconditionally and experiencing affection that is unfettered. A small battle wages on inside me each night as I anticipate her goodnight ritual. Will I accept and be open to her, or will I reach an unknown or unseen limit and try to diminish or invalidate her gesture? Will I make a joke, turn my head to the side, or make a raspberry—all defences against her closeness?

Last night, I accepted her kiss and "good night," and I melted, and a part of me even felt bubbly and light.

One day at a time.

October 10

Follow the light.
In people and in everywhere we go.
We can feel light in a person, in an invitation, in a place.
When logical, well-thought-out plans unravel, there will be light in
*   the cracks.*
That makes life better than we imagined.
A conversation with another that is "nice" and "fine"
Leaves a weight and a wait.
A conversation bathed in light lifts us up, pulls us forward, Energy
*   moving up, up, up.*
Hold out for the light.
Look for it to shine through space in the cracks of a well-thought-out plan.

October 11

John Bradshaw, in his 1988 book *Bradshaw On: The Family*, reveals a secret that most people never discover: a family is much more than the sum of the individuals who make up the group; it is a system that is the beginning for our own mental and emotional health. Bradshaw goes further, demonstrating that many adults never fully mature out of their own family system, and they therefore model and repeat those dynamics with their own children. This is how family dysfunction persists through the generations.

When I read this book years ago as part of my training, I remember being shocked by the information—and shocked that no one had ever shared this revelation with me before. I wondered why it wasn't included in our basic health education in senior elementary or high school and why it wasn't a mainstay of discussion on news programs and radio talk shows. If the family was the root of all that we understood about ourselves, why weren't we taking a really hard look at our families to better understand what we had inherited and how we had been raised?

I was younger then, and full of fire and possibility. Years later, time has revealed to me that it takes a combination of courage and willingness for a family to rewrite itself—which is why so few families actually try, let alone succeed. Instead, the more courageous members of that family—the psychological outliers—are the ones who lead the change for themselves. It is the individual who decides they want a better quality of life and deeper intimacy, and who wants to become more conscious, that starts the ball rolling.

Is that you? Are you that person? Have you arrived at a point in your life where you have more questions than answers about who you are? What is it that you're trying to discover about yourself? Here are the questions that began my journey to better know myself:

- Why am I so intense?
- Where did I learn that love is painful?
- Why do I hurt myself?
- How is it that I feel safer when I am by myself?
- Why do I need to feel necessary, yet don't want to be depended on?
- How did I learn to listen so well?

I don't believe it matters which question we begin with—all honest questioning leads to an unravelling and unfolding, and ultimately to the truth and lightness. I wish for you a journey rich in questions.

🌸 October 12

For some reason I am at my best in the role of parent. It is the one area of my life where I have surrendered to not knowing and focused on giving my best, willing to be open and flexible. My wish for our children—actually, for all beings—is that they be healthy, happy and safe. I am rewarded with a beautiful, reciprocal love that expands and changes, challenges and nourishes my soul.

What role brings out your true self in this way?

We play many roles in life—neighbour, parent, spouse, sibling, son or daughter, friend, partner, employee—though we are likely to be our true selves in only one domain. I yearn to expand this satisfaction elsewhere in my life.

If I look at who and how I am when I am parenting, I see that I have found comfort and balance between dependence, independence and interdependence. This balance can set us free, in all domains and all of our relationships.

I trust my children are innocent and good and safe for me to love. While I feel safe in their vulnerability, my job is to teach them how to feel secure in themselves, through building their self-esteem, self-confidence and self-responsibility so that their vulnerability grows into ability and assuredness. In the face of their new independence, my defences may rise. The less they need me, the more my insecurities may surface. I need to teach and stretch myself to continue loving them wildly and openly, even though they are now independent. I must show them that our love can and will survive hurt, disappointment, distance and disagreement.

It is a critical milestone when children move from being dependent to independent. If we stop growing as parents at this point, our children may be happy, safe and healthy, but distant. We have the opportunity at this point to model interdependence—the dependence of two or more people on each other. If I am willing to respect, trust and be vulnerable, then as our children mature our relationship will expand into interdependence—a beautiful dance of equals, if we are willing to make them our partners. Let them fly, ask them to teach us, ask them for help, create experiences together, experience life together.

Being in relationships with our children offers a beautiful opportunity to learn interdependence, bringing us a deep sense of closeness and security.

🌸 October 13

I've missed more than nine thousand shots in my career. I've lost almost three hundred games. Twenty-six times, I've been trusted to take the game-winning shot and missed. I've failed over and over and over again in my life. And that is why I succeed.
—Michael Jordan

I'm placing this quote here today probably more for me than for you. I just needed a reminder that an "L" is as important as a "W" in life. I've been paused for a while, stuck slightly, because I'm worried whether I'm doing the right thing. More truthfully, I'm worried whether my thoughts—and what I create out of that thinking—are good and valuable, or something that others may regard as a waste of time. I don't have as much of an issue with failing as I do with looking bad to others while failing. I can take a loss as easily as a win any day; I learn from losses and mistakes, using them as teaching experiences. But what I still have an issue with is looking bad or being humiliated by others for losing.

This is something that dogged me when I played competitive team sports, and it's the reason I gave them up in favour of such solo athletic pursuits as rock climbing. It seems today it is still lingering with me. I know I need to come through this because this fear or worry limits my risk-taking and creativity—both of which are necessary for my full enjoyment of life. I envision a day when I'm walking a knife edge of full-out creative expression with humiliation on one side and fulfillment on the other, and I'm deliberately placing one foot in front of the other going forward always, always forward.

So today this is a reminder to me—and to you, if you need it as well. Let's be willing to really lose, and more importantly, let's be intimately familiar with feeling loss, judgment and humiliation without taking a single step back.

🌸 October 14

Being a human who is trying to awaken in a world that wants us to stay asleep and unconscious is not easy. Bumping into our blind spots, orchestrating support for ourselves, having the courage to open when it is so much easier to close—these are not easy! But we both know it is worth it. That light feels so darned good—being at peace, being filled up on the inside, having grace, being a good person, connecting from a place of love. There is no greater, more exhilarating joy. It's worth it and you are worth it.

I appreciate your courage, your heart and spirit. If you feel tired today, find rest. If you need to be taken care of today, ask. If you need to pause, do so. Because lightness finds us there too.

🌸 October 15

Difficult people are ... well, difficult. And stressful. They add unnecessary drama to our lives, and we spend far too much time and energy trying to figure out how to deal with them effectively.

I'm not so sure it helps us to label their difficulty either—knowing whether a person is a narcissist doesn't help us steer clear of their rude or self-absorbed ways. Nor am I positive that trying to uphold a social convention regarding politeness, fairness or respect works that well, since there are so many different cultural norms around our globe. To say "our" way is better than yours really isn't helpful.

In my view, the best way to handle a difficult person is to be honest and direct about what works for you as an individual—in other words, lay out your interpersonal boundaries. How do you like to be spoken to? How do you like to be treated in a relationship or a friendship? What boundary lines about your person, your body, your values or your principles have you established to make you feel safe?

Knowing our interpersonal boundaries gives us a sense of solidness and confidence that tends to radiate out into the world. Think of Robert Mueller, the special counsel tasked with investigating alleged Russian interference in the 2016 US presidential election and suspicious ties between President Trump's associates and Russian officials. He just gives off a sense that one shouldn't mess with him—not because he's deeply insecure and putting up a tough front; quite the opposite, in fact. Someone like him is so secure in himself that there's no point in trying to tip him off balance. Just as an aside, have you noticed that Trump didn't come up with a derogatory nickname for Mueller the way he has done with almost everyone else? What quality is it that rendered Mueller untouchable in Trump's estimation? Right: his strong sense of self.

Getting back to dealing with difficult people, the best approach I've found is to use honest, direct statements like "I don't like the way you're speaking to me," "I don't like (or will not accept) the way you are treating me," "I'm not serving you if you continue to speak to me in this way" or "I don't accept being lied to in a friendship." These are all simple to understand, and they tell the other person, "Hey, you've hit a boundary—you'd better back up."

Difficult people thrive in social situations where interpersonal boundaries are soft and vague. Deep down, they count on others to be too afraid or too constrained by convention to push back, so they keep testing and testing until they hit a hard line.

Let's be hard-liners today—I think you'll like how it feels to be your own advocate.

🌸 October 16

"I've just been diagnosed with stage 4 prostate cancer," he said as he sat in the chair opposite me and straightened his shirt. "My wife and I are separating after twenty-seven years of marriage and two kids, we have to sell our house and I'll have to start over, and just last week I found out our whole shop floor is being laid off in six months."

Taking a quick, tight breath, he added, "Oh, and to top it all off, my mother, who is an alcoholic, can't stay in her apartment, and I have to find a place for her to live by the end of the month."

"That's a lot," I said. Then I took a big breath and let it out. "That's a lot to carry around."

He looked me in the eyes, waiting for me to say something else, and when I didn't, his eyes started to blink in disbelief, then eventually tear up, and finally he broke down sobbing.

"It's too much," he said in between deep breaths. "I just can't do it anymore."

After sixteen years of counselling and interviewing close to a thousand people on *Hello Goodbye*, I'm no longer surprised or shocked at how much emotional weight people carry around with them every single day. It's been my experience that we all carry too much—much more than we can really deal with, process or accept. Many of us, myself included, further complicate our lives by holding on to worry, angst, stress or anger longer than we should, as if they were foods we needed to digest rather than feelings we should release.

The net effect is that we're full to capacity and walking around disengaged or distracted from reality because to be present, truly present, even for a moment would uncork a waterfall of emotion. And don't talk to me about resilience, because unless you practise processing what you feel, it's likely not resilience you're building, but dissonance.

We are not built to hold on to everything life sends our way. We are meant to feel, process and accept. That's the way our design works best.

Feel, process, accept. This is our path.

October 17

After a phone call with someone who had bad health news to share about another, I hung up the phone and felt unsettled. It was the third time this month I had felt this way—someone had shared difficult news, after which I felt like I hadn't really absorbed what they were saying or I hadn't really listened, and so I had missed the opportunity to empathize, console, support or connect.

Then it hit me: I had bumped right into my Shadow. Have you met your Shadow yet? It's the unconscious or subconscious part of ourselves that we are unaware of but that is our primary way of protecting our psyche—by hiding away or disguising parts of ourselves, beginning when we are children, in order to be loved and accepted. These hidden parts are our richest gifts, strengths that make the exquisite process of exploration and excavation worthwhile. Trying to do shadow work alone might make you feel worse about your self, so I strongly recommend finding a professional, a retreat or a workshop.

As we are together now, and as we seek lightness, we are all likely to bump into our Shadows. By focusing on light, we are illuminating our Shadows. This is a good thing. It can change our life and our experience of life.

I am learning that my Shadow gets activated as a cover-up when I feel sad or fearful. One aspect of my Shadow is like a badly behaved eighteen-year-old from a 1980s movie. I picture it as spoiled, self-absorbed, mean and spiteful. I also imagine that it is brave, articulate, fit, smart and spirited. When it is leading in my life, I may act insensitively to cover up my insecurity. My Shadow fools me as well, and for years I have thought it is who I truly am. I have judged myself as insensitive and selfish. I am learning now that, while I may act this way, it isn't my true nature. Learning about my Shadow and being able to picture it give me a choice of how I want to be.

I share this in case you are noticing a desire to act out or behave badly (however you might define that). This could be your Shadow showing itself to you. I urge you to find a therapist if you are interested in knowing your Shadow. And if you are not interested in going any further, that is perfectly fine. Please know that your Shadow is a necessary and valuable part of you and wants only to protect you. Every person has one.

Lightness comes as we acknowledge the presence of our Shadows. I am learning, in the safety of my home, to show my fear and my sadness. I am astounded at how often life and the world produce fear and sadness in me. I'm not sure where this is leading, yet I trust that being open and vulnerable and accepting of myself is a good path to follow.

Blessings to us all as we acknowledge our Shadows.

✽ October 18

What does living lightly mean? I'm thinking about this today, mulling over all that we've talked about so far and wondering if a kind of manifesto is possible—a template that could outline the basics of what a life of lightness really involves. For me, it means not getting overly attached to life going one way—or my way—but to be flexible and adaptable to how quickly or profoundly life can change. To be light implies that

I work to strengthen my mind and tame my ego. I am more conscious of my thoughts and behaviours and clear that what I do and say are aligned. Along with my words and actions, my principles, values and morals make up my character, of which I am the only author. It is crystal clear that I can have an impact on others, but any thoughts I may have that others are personally against me are false. I realize that what people do is a reflection of them, not of me.

Living lightly means I travel light when it comes to emotions. I unpack any baggage from the past or triggers in the present and make sure I process what I feel instead of letting emotions build up and fester inside of me. Being light is about putting more effort into knowing myself than trying to explain and understand what motivates other people. Lightness is being health-centred and movement-focused and understanding that my physical, mental and emotional health are all connected and need my attention and effort.

I suppose that, most of all, living lightly is about feeling a certainty in my body that I am in a relationship with everything around me—and each of those connections is a doorway to better understanding myself, to loving myself and to giving of myself. This is what I have so far, but I'm certain more learning is on the way.

❀ October 19

Is it possible today to come out of our plan? Are the people who depend upon us taken care of today? Do our partners perhaps have plans of their own? Could our work use a day to percolate? Many times I assume the day needs me, when most of the time it is the other way around.

What do we need today? What will nourish us?

Our intuition will flash an idea of what we need—"we can have an hour here" or "we could walk there today." One word might pop to mind—quiet, sleep, rest, water, air, book, trees, laugh, stretch. We can trust these messages. They are real; they are for the highest good.

Intuiting means working things out by instinct. It happens fast and involves a subtle "gut" sense. Go with your first feeling; surrender to the thought that this is the intuited choice. Notice a return to vibrancy simply from being willing to engage your intuition.

Try intuiting what will nourish you today.

October 20

It's okay not to know—to be without a clue or to have no idea about what is going to happen in the near future, even tomorrow. Sitting with the tension of empty doubt for even a few moments can feel like an eternity. Sit with it for days, even months, and most of us would slip into a deep despair. I know: I've had periods in my life—months, even years—when I had no vision for my future. Honestly, when I look back on that time, it seems as though all of the days blended into one another in an endless sludge of time.

I think what I was searching for was my purpose, which at the time looked like a career or a profession. That was the expectation I had for my life. The tension inside of me as I hoped to find that profession was unbearable at times; I went through giant swings of anger, sadness and fear. And in the end, I never happened upon that career.

But you know what was interesting? While I was looking for that one answer and experiencing all that feeling, I was also learning how to live with doubt. Day after day I made myself do the things that ensured my basic needs were met—I always had a job, I stayed connected to my friends and family, I took some courses and got involved in community teams and organizations, I fell in love a few times, and I took to journaling to connect with my longing and discover my soul.

I discovered that the answer to coming through doubt and unbearable tension is not to double down and work harder to figure it out, but to be with it, place it on a back burner in your mind, let it simmer, and do all the small things every day that make you feel good and keep you alive. Ensuring our quality of life is as important as discovering our purpose in life. In fact, we may never discover our purpose for being alive—tough as that may be to believe or accept—but we are always in control of each moment and the richness of being alive.

October 21

Lifestyle mentor Rachel Fearnley talks about joy as coming from inside of us, whereas happiness is sourced from outside of us. She says joy comes when you make peace with who you are, why you are and how you are.

I think of a child, a puppy, a kitten—any baby bundle of human or animal cuteness—as a great expression of joy. Their joy is in them everywhere they go; it's universal, meaning everyone is invited to enjoy it.

When I look myself in the eyes in the mirror, I see joy in there. It is a bit confusing—by which I mean I could be sad or mad, yet joy is still there. I think this process of self-exploration and letting go is building joy inside of me. We might be the last to know!

I am grateful for my joy.

Let's reflect on joy today; look for joy around us and inside of us. Let's move in closer, snuggle up right beside her and get to know her better.

October 22

Children singing. Reunions at airports. Witnessing kindness. An acceptance speech. Anyone's wedding.

These events always move me to tears. Human vulnerability and joy reach right into my heart and I am moved beyond belief, to tears of inspiration and appreciation and love.

Alan Page Fiske, an anthropologist at UCLA, calls this feeling "kama muta," which is Sanskrit for "moved by love." As a 2018 CNN story reported, with kama muta we "feel flushed or get goose bumps and want to be kind and loving, whether that means calling our grandmother or helping a friend." We feel "moved, touched, stirred or smitten."

I believe kama muta happens when we feel our own holiness, and I believe that living lightly could be a form of kama muta.

Recall a memory that you know will put you in a state of kama muta. This is what it feels like to be filled with grace. Revisit that memory often or find new ones that enable you to conjure up the same sensations, emotions and thoughts, and you will have found lightness. You will be living lightly.

🌸 October 23

Reading an article the other day on how younger professionals are abandoning the idea of living and working in cities and are relocating to smaller rural communities, I was amazed and inspired by their willingness to spurn the environment they grew up in. These people took a hard look at their lifestyle and saw that the dream they were pursuing was really an illusion. It brought me right back to that moment in the film *The Matrix* when we understand that all the different life scenarios created by the machines are being dreamed by humans who lie in stasis in pods—each human living in their own illusion.

Busting an illusion is simple, though not easy, which is why only a few of us are really willing to attempt it. We have to begin by being curious and asking deeper questions of ourselves, and then, most importantly, answering those questions with radical honesty. I say "radical honesty" because unless we think outside of our norms or comfort zone, new answers won't surface. So rather than asking "What makes me happy?" or "How much money do I need to be happy?" it may be better to ask "When were my happiest moments?" or "If I made $50,000, where could I have the best life I can imagine?"

It's questions like these, and the truthful answers that appear, that have led people to change the nature of their work or even the way their existing work is done—for example, telecommuting or choosing variable work hours. More and more people have decided that space and peace, nature and community are more important to them than salary or status. And all of this is evidence that they are willing to do some hard work to bust an illusion for themselves and rewrite or edit the direction and plot line of their life.

Maybe there's an illusion you live inside of today that you have yet to question. It could be a part of your everyday life or an aspect of your identity. It feels real and true, but if you take the risk and scratch at it, you can see that it has cracks. Keep scratching. Be curious. Change is coming!

October 24

But why would someone choose not to think deeply? Why would someone choose to think only simplistically, superficially, and reflexively? The answer, again, is that, despite our consciousness, what we have in common with the other creatures is a preference for avoiding pain. Thinking deeply is often more painful than thinking shallowly.
—M. Scott Peck, *The Road Less Travelled and Beyond*

The deepest thinkers I know share a powerful aura of lightness in their being that comes from their willingness and commitment to experience truth's pain and discomfort. Meanwhile the people I have met and know who tend to suffer in life share a powerful aversion to exploring anything deeply.

The former group ignores distraction, while the latter craves it.

The deep thinkers value being present in the moment and pursue simple contentment, while the shallow thinkers value possessions and pursue layers of stimulation, exhilaration and sustained happiness.

One group is calm, even creative during the tension of boredom; the other experiences being bored as if ants are crawling all over their skin.

One group is a universe unto itself while the other is separate, alone and deeply fearful of a universe different from its own.

Some are deep and light; others are shallow and heavy.

For some, pain is about suffering and is to be avoided; for others, pain is liberating.

I humbly invite you today to dive deeply into yourself.

October 25

How tightly do we cling to those we love? I would protest that I will never let go of those I love—that is how tightly I am hanging on! I prefer to think that attachment itself is what I release, and that my love remains free to be expressed and expanded.

Let me try to explain. Children going away, breakups, best friends moving, illness, accidents and, of course, death are some of our most heart-wrenching moments, when life creates change. But the idea that change is necessarily loss is, I suspect, the grief. The attachment to wanting things to remain forever unchanged is the pain.

Am I willing to consider love in other forms? Am I willing to consider belief in the unseen?

When death has come for one I loved, I have experienced their energy around me years later. There have been days when I have felt my grandmother nearby; my mother, in a different city, has said that she felt her presence too, on the same day. It comforts me to feel that energy and to believe life is bigger than what I can see, more complex than what I already know. This is an ongoing inquiry for me, and I'm not totally there—I still grieve the loss of their physical form and the loss of our interactions in the physical realm. Yet so much of our human development and study of energetics is about the non-physical realm—that which we cannot see. Learning how to connect with those who have passed, in energetic form, will allow me to release my pain by releasing my love again.

Am I willing to consider the other to whom I cling?

When our son left for university, it was devastating to me, but when I looked into his eyes, I saw hope and happiness. I saw that he was ready to have his freedom. Loving him, I turned his move to university into a new focus for how to give my love and support, which made letting go much easier and lighter. It became a change rather than a loss.

Am I willing to consider changing forms of love?

When my first marriage ended I was taken completely by surprise and was devastated. My attachment to being together forever was so deep that I had become unconscious. I was shaken awake, forced to reimagine so many aspects of life, and it empowered me. I became aware of my stuckness and then became grateful to the other for waking me up. I realize my love has changed into gratitude and empathy, compassion and appreciation, feelings that would be there if ever we were to see each other again.

I am constantly letting go of my resistance to change and holding on to love.

🌸 October 26

I love words and their meanings. A few years ago, after hearing the word "inspire" frequently in conversation, I decided to look it up to better understand what it really meant:

inspire   a. archaic : to breathe or blow into or upon
            b. archaic : to infuse (something, such as life) by breathing

These are two of the four meanings for the word "inspire" in the *Merriam-Webster Dictionary*, and what catches my eye is the suggestion that to inspire is, in a way, an action we can be personally responsible for. In our modern age I typically hear the word in the past tense as an experience people receive from others. Rarely, if ever, have I heard someone say, "I aim to inspire," or "I will inspire." Perhaps ego, modesty, some type of humility, or fear of the tall poppy syndrome is to blame. Regardless, I think we are the lesser for it.

Imagine putting "INSPIRE" on a T-shirt and wearing that shirt every time you go to work. What would happen to you (or for you)? Is it possible that your manner and method of work might be influenced in some way by the mantra on your chest? What if you shared a few of these T-shirts with your colleagues and peers and invited them to live with and within the message? What kind of impact could you foresee it having on the world? Imagine further individuals in a community, each wearing an *Inspire* shirt, are active and engaged with one another, supporting one another, helping one another to learn, grow and heal. Picture a newsletter titled *Inspire* that reaches out to that community, bringing the members together in a dialogue about, and for, change.

On a cold day in October 2006, I looked up the word "inspire" in the dictionary, and over the next nine years all of this happened. I and my friends and peers built a community of people, all in group therapy, and our work changed not only each person but also the people in their lives. Many of us are still connected today, forever changed by our experience.

This is what can happen when you love something so much that you want more of it in your life.

October 27

What was your last new beginning?

What I mean is: When was the last time you put yourself out there for a first-time experience? Do you remember that sense of aliveness—that thrill with a touch of terror? And the feeling of absorbing, of soaking up the people and the information until you were full? If we can keep our minds at bay, it can be exhilarating to experience a new dimension of ourselves—a newly discovered talent, an angle we thought was flat.

Being a beginner can be a physical, mental, emotional and spiritual experience. It can entail a change of perspective—for example, making the transition from worker to manager, employer to student, child to parent.

A good place to find our next new beginning is to take the phrases "I will never" and "I always," and then consider the opposite.

The newness is where the magic is, not in the size of the feat. Changing a tire can bring an exhilarating self-esteem boost that is beyond belief. The idea is to crash through the stories and limits we have placed upon ourselves, consciously or not.

Expansion is best done in a gentle, supportive way. Remember, if we terrify ourselves, our brain starts producing cortisol (the "fight or flight" hormone) and our capacity to learn and change disappears. So if you get a sense that a new beginning is calling you, look around for someone with experience in that realm, or consider joining a related community. Remember, this is not a breakthrough; this is more like an expansion—like rolling lovely wild-yeasted dough to bring up its springiness, resilience and complexity as it rises.

Think of the people you will meet and the places you will go! I am smiling at the thought of all of us launching ourselves as newbies into the world. How wonderful!

October 28

You are a minute of quiet in a loud, shouting world
You are a mirror of love in a critical, judging world
You are an instant of courage in an anxious, doubtful world
You are a hug of caring in a detached, indifferent world
You are a spark of presence in a numbed-out, distracted world
You are unstoppable life in a concrete, paved world
You are a shoulder of friendship in a superficial, conditional world
You are a bubble of lightness in an absorbed, conflicted world
You are an everyday hero in a world looking for salvation

October 29

I'm on the phone with my best friend, listening as she talks about being with her father in his final days. She begins with small talk, and then offers surface information about nice nurses and cold weather. She moves on to asking questions out loud, unveiling another layer of her feelings and thoughts. She strings together new awareness in hearing herself speak. She says "anyway" to move us on, to change the subject and get us out of the discomfort.

I hear the tears come, and the sniffles, as she searches for meaning, fighting for her own clarity. She speaks of feeling anger coming, now reaching another level of awareness, sharing the injustice, the wrongness. She laughs, describing a comedy show she watches at night, launching into the relief of laughter and sadness as one. She declares what she will and will not take as her own, picking through all that she cannot control. I hear strength and resolve. I hear her deliberate not only for herself, but for each of her daughters, who also grieve. She decides for and holds space for three—four, including her father. She tells me she is living through the many layers of letting go, and that it feels a lot like winter: quiet and still, peaceful, beautiful.

Hold space for another to travel through the depths of their own experience and watch them float back up to the surface in their own way. It is a blessing.

❁ October 30

Do you ever play with your name, going by the shortened—or lengthened—version, or your middle name? Have you ever invented a name to use when making a takeout order?

I ask because a name is a very powerful draw on our psyche. The stories and attachments associated with our name can be limiting or expansive. Changing the name we use, even temporarily, can provide a completely new experience.

Pick a name that expresses a character trait you want to use more often. I can always benefit from more time with my feminine side, so I like a French name like Véronique or Annette. I can feel my being respond even as I type this—shifting into my feminine side and feeling more in my body. Sometimes I use my full first and middle names and notice a change in my demeanour to one of elegance and grace.

We might call out our vulnerability or courage, humour or intellect. There is nothing more to do than to take on the name and feel what happens. It is amazing to me that the suggestion itself is enough for our psyche to grab hold and embody.

The same is true of colours. In chakra work, wearing, eating and noticing the colour assigned to a chakra can be a very powerful way to clear and strengthen it. For example, the essence of the solar plexus—the third, or "I" chakra, found in our core—has yellow assigned to it. Wearing yellow, eating yellow foods, noticing yellow items, being in the vibration of yellow are fun and potent ways to experience the energy.

We can have fun with names and colour, all the while feeling expansion and energy. What wonderfully attuned beings we are!

October 31

The dictionary tells me the word "allow" is defined as "to give permission to" and "to give the necessary time or opportunity for." That definition feels so good, I read it over three times.

It begs us to take a pause, doesn't it? Let's press pause in this moment. Have we given ourselves permission to live and have and be the way we know our heart desires?

Let's give ourselves permission to have joy, love, freedom, health and all the dreams that are ours. Give ourselves permission, affirming, "I am allowing joy, love, freedom and health to flow into my life, greater every moment, for my highest good and the good of all." You can use this affirmation or create your own—most importantly, using "I am" (not "I will"). Say it often—out loud, in your head, to the mirror. Write it down if you find it helpful—whatever it takes to *feel* it.

This is where I struggle at times. Am I present in the moment, to changes happening, to the growth and the good that are already flowing? Will I trust and move ahead, knowing that all is good, simply because we asked, and we deserve it? I keep myself in the present moment . . . and I breathe, I breathe, I breathe.

There is nothing wrong or missing, ever, in the present moment. The true gift is right here, together, in this moment.

November

❈ November 1

Have you heard the saying, "Build a life you don't need a vacation from"?

Think of the vacation you would enjoy most, even if it is only a dream. Where are you? What are you doing and who is with you? Imagine your "happy place." Be mindful of the distinction between thinking of a beautiful getaway and feeling fulfilled by a place.

I usually think of escaping to warmer climates, especially during a long, cold winter. But I have learned that the vacations I truly enjoyed most were spent *in* the winter—outdoors in the cold, cross-country skiing and spending time in a quiet winter forest, followed by a hot tub, a good book and a cozy glass of wine in the chalet. Quiet time with my partner and our animals, and loud family time with the kids. Laughing, loving, connecting, playing—*ahhhhh*, it makes me warm inside just to think of it. In that environment, I am deeply content, calm, satisfied, smiling, slow and grounded.

I love to travel, whether it entails days of doing nothing but swimming or days jam-packed with sightseeing. These are adventures, and I hope my life always includes the ability to travel. But when I think about where my heart wants to be, it now wants to be home. We took a chance to make a big change, moving out of the city to a property that resembles the winter cottage we loved to book yearly. Our home has tons and tons of snow in winter. We have a hot tub outside, surrounded by trees and a big, wide-open sky to look at, a fireplace, backcountry skis, snow pants and wineskins.

When I think of a vacation and a break now, my mind still says to go south, but my heart whispers, "Farther north." I'm not sure why images of seals and glaciers and the aurora borealis pull at my core, but they generate that familiar feeling of longing when I get the sense it's time to add a piece to my life. One day I hope to be able to see the image of these puzzle pieces fitted together!

I highly recommend reflecting upon what your heart longs for when you imagine vacationing and serenity. Adjusting your lifestyle into that heart picture will not be a big stretch—life has a magical way of lining up so that the shifts are gentle and achievable, more like a lateral move. It will be as though life is helping you.

In the words of that old saying: "Build a life you don't need a vacation from."

🌸 November 2

A cup of tea changed my mood today. I was shuffling around this morning, not aware of what was happening around me and lost in thoughts and plans inside my head. I decided to make myself a cup of tea, and out of habit I reached up into the cupboard, grabbed two cups and, without asking, made my partner a cup of their favourite tea as well. Our tea of choice is always peppermint, so as I poured the boiling water into the cups, the essence of the mint floated up into the air and inside my nose.

I was quickly aware that I was becoming more and more awake and the cobwebs that had clung to my thinking were clearing. Literally in seconds, I felt my eyes widen and my shoulders come back, and I took in a deep breath, bringing more of the peppermint into my nasal passages and lungs. My mood, which until that moment would have been best described as "meh," lifted and vapourized and I began to feel much, much lighter.

"What is in this stuff?" I asked myself. It turns out that peppermint is a powerful stimulant for the olfactory system and the hypothalamus. It helps elevate our emotions if we are depressed and calm us if we are anxious, and also triggers strong associative memories from deep within our minds. The ancient Greeks were well aware of mint's properties as a digestive aid and used it extensively as a decorative digestif on their tables. Peppermint, which is a hybrid of water mint and spearmint, is so rich in mentha oil that it has become a highly prized additive for foods, gum and, of course, candy (*strong* associative memories from childhood!).

But this really isn't about peppermint or the rich mood-elevating properties of peppermint tea. The real mood boost happened for me when I delivered the steaming-hot cup of tea to my partner. I was greeted with a wide-eyed look of surprise and gratitude, a warm smile and genuine appreciation for the gift of the cup of tea; it was enough to shift me from the deep, groggy, navel-gazing, woe-is-me place I had been living in. I became aware of something much greater than myself, something that re-sorted my life and helped to put it back in a more balanced perspective.

A simple, refreshing cup of tea, given to my partner unprompted, had provided me with connection.

❄ November 3

When it comes to being a drain on our personal energy, I don't think there's anything greater than an incomplete task. I have lots of what I judge to be small incompletions that hang on to me and follow me around everywhere—bills to be paid, paperwork to be filed, small objects to be repaired, projects to be finished. These are the kinds of things that need my full attention, but I delay offering it, and so they live on the shoulders of my everyday life.

Years ago I used to have big incompletions such as filing my taxes, renewing my passport or finalizing my divorce—all of which became much larger emotional weights until I did two important things. The first was to ask for and really receive the support I needed to work through them; the second was to allow myself to feel the emotions that had been holding me back.

I'd been separated for about five years, living as a single parent and doing my best to convince myself and rationalize to others that I really had no need to "be divorced," since I was already living as if that were so. This was not the truth, however. It should come as no surprise that in the relationships that followed, I held back and resisted letting them deepen. I was out of the marriage physically, but still very much in it mentally and emotionally.

A good friend at the time challenged me in a firm yet gentle way to complete my divorce within six months. He offered to support me along the way, helping me file the paperwork and travelling with me to the court where I would receive my final stamp of approval. I remember that exact moment vividly. We were both standing in front of the registrar, and as the rubber stamp came down to hit the paper, I froze in a moment of panic. "Approved" suddenly appeared in bright red ink on the corner of my divorce application and I blinked . . . then blinked again, took a deep breath and cried. My good friend put his arm on my shoulder and said simply, "You did it. Now just let it go." The release and relief in that moment made me feel like I had shed half of my body weight. I felt light as a feather, as if filled with helium. To be truthful, I was sad, but what I now know was melancholy and fear had evaporated with my tears.

This is what it felt like to be free of that incompletion. I wish for this vapourizing of heaviness for you too. I imagine that, like me, you may have one or two big incompletions lurking in your life. There's always time to free yourself from them—it just takes two things: support and the willingness to feel what's been holding you back.

❋ November 4

What are we willing to do for another?

As we reflect upon togetherness, abundance and joy together, it leads me to wonder where the limits of my generosity lie. Certainly, I can feel there are conditions.

I say yes unconditionally to any needs my children have. I don't always know how, so I say yes and then we work together on how to make it happen.

I realize I have conditions on my generosity for everyone else. I say yes *conditionally* to my partner, though it often involves challenges and conflict.

Mainly, I need to be in the mood and prepared to say yes (no surprises). I wish I were different, but the truth is I tend to say yes on my terms.

Every now and then I say yes because I want to be a yes—for instance, if I get an unexpected phone call from a charity. Spontaneous and in the moment, my true self is always a yes. It's my ego that adds the conditions on top.

I have not had people in my life ask much of me, and it may well be because I haven't been open until now. Do people in your life come to you for help? Are you approached as an open door? Are you able to say yes unconditionally? If so, what a gift you are! I admire you and hope you are embracing your generous heart.

For the rest of us, what are we afraid of, deep down? What is it that we think a spontaneous, free, unconditional yes will do to hurt us?

As we connect to our own spirits more and more, whereever we stand on generosity is absolutely okay. As with everything else, awareness is powerful.

The bottom line is, we give as we give to ourselves. Please let's reflect on this today.

❊ November 5

By now I hope you've understood that our journey towards living lightly involves two elements: action and perspective. We need both, and they feed into each other and support one another in important ways. They are the keys to winning back a more meaningful, contented and conscious way of living. Some people believe one or the other is enough to turn our lives around, and on the surface this seems true. But I believe this approach can only result in short lifts of mood. I don't believe it is sustainable.

There are simply no hacks or workarounds to help you level up, no quick fixes that will have you suddenly living lightly. This journey we are on isn't about relieving temporary pain—or relieving pain temporarily—but about forever changing ourselves on the inside. Deep tectonic shifts only come from applying consistent effort—small steps taken every day—and allowing the impact of those steps to sink in and resonate within us, shifting our minds out of their comfort zone. We restore our balance with nature not in one walk through a forest, but by being present to that forest in some manner every day for years. So too we become generous people by offering small acts of random kindness to everyone we meet and being open to our impact on others.

Everything we have offered so far and will continue to offer is an invitation, a doorway for you to enter as we have, so you can experience yourself in a new way. This is the path of a more purposeful life, and we are walking each step with you.

❊ November 6

I love it when a book pulls me forward. I recently told a friend that I first went to Africa because of a book—one I received from my uncle as a gift when I was seven or eight years old. To this day I have no idea why he chose it for me. It was a thick hardcover book with a magnificent picture of a Maasai warrior on the cover. I don't remember talking about it and I don't even remember reading it, but the book planted a seed in me to visit the continent.

Years later, in my late twenties, I would go on safari alone. Then I went on to work and try out love in South Africa. I didn't find the life chapter or the answer I thought I would—there was no denouement for me, no big reveal—but I thoroughly enjoyed Africa's wildlife. Then, realizing how much I love Canada, I came home, heartbroken (again), but this time in the neighbourhood and the heart space to meet my forever love.

Our lives likely aren't affected by a book because it was a favourite read, but because it grabbed our attention in some way. Maybe the book is attached to a person, a place or a theme that has played out in our life. Maybe the physical book is the thread to the person or place it came from and what it meant.

When I think about how a book has played an unexpected part in our story, I sometimes wonder whether destiny is involved.

November 7

If there is a meaning in life it must be centred upon a person, she thought, nothing else. It had to be a person.
—Henning Mankell, *Kennedy's Brain*

Human beings can form strong emotional attachments to other people and to all manner of things. Attachment generally helps us to feel more psychologically secure, especially if the bond provides a safe and loving connection. But bonds don't have to be beneficial for us to feel their pull—we will long for connection and belonging even if those ties are painful and traumatic. Perhaps this explains why many people would rather bond with things than with other people. (By "things" I mean material possessions as well as the pursuits and passions we believe will lend meaning and purpose to our lives.) Things are incapable of letting us down or betraying us.

We can be committed to important work, passionate about our accomplishments and keen to leave a legacy—but none of these things provide real meaning or purpose in our lives. In my opinion, no thing can ever be a meaningful reflection of our humanness. Only other people can help us feel purposeful.

A friend of mine shared a story with me a couple of years ago about the moment he realized he had to turn his life around. "She was seven, my daughter, and we were laughing at a joke I had just told her. I was home for the weekend and packing to get back on the road for a busy week of meetings. 'I think it's sad,' she said, 'that I'm seven and I'm only now figuring out that my dad is funny.'

"Her words really hit me," he said. "It was like a slap in the face. Here I was, travelling fifty weeks a year and working crazy hours to build this business, and my daughter had no idea who I really was. This was the moment I knew I was going after the wrong thing. That's when I decided to wrap it all up."

And he did wrap it up. He exited a highly successful, profitable partnership to be at home and make sure he and his daughter got to know each other. I know this isn't possible for everyone—we can't all just drop everything to make this kind of life change. But what we can do, what is certainly within our power, is to develop a close connection to someone like a partner, a friend, a family member, a neighbour or a colleague—a connection that is deep and meaningful and gives us a sense that we matter and that we have a purpose.

November 8

I love snacking. Consuming morsels of food, reading a few pages of a book or an online article, listening to a few songs on a playlist, taking a short walk through our forest, taking a break from work and having a brief catch-up chat with a friend—this is how I enjoy my day. Snacking is a sort of life philosophy for me, and it helps me to find contentment and enjoyment frequently in bite-sized moments.

It seems that researchers at McMaster University agree with my life ethos. Calling their findings "surprising," they have discovered that short bursts of exercise throughout the day, every day, are as effective as workouts of longer duration a couple of times a week. "Exercise snacks" like walking up a flight of stairs, taking a brisk walk around the office or out on a break, or even a few old-style calisthenic exercises like push-ups or burpees can provide us with the same physiological benefits—including increased cardiovascular health, muscle strength and stamina—that our typical "go to the gym three times a week" routine delivers. "The findings make it even easier for people to incorporate exercise snacks into their day," says study co-author Martin Gibala.

I believe the message for us is clear: we are beings that need to move to be healthy and content. Being sedentary in any way—physically, mentally or emotionally—is counterintuitive. We are all about the flow.

November 9

I can count on one hand the number of arguments I have had with friends. I tiptoe around disagreements and usually don't say anything if I feel hurt. I'm scared to fight because, growing up, I saw my family's way of fighting was to leave. And I don't want to lose my friends. Consequently, a bit of distance and defence get created each time.

Recently I invited two very close friends and their families to our farm for the weekend. One week before they were to arrive, I cancelled. I felt relieved, trusting that my friends would understand. A few weeks later, though, I received a text from one of them, saying we would need to clear the air about the cancelled visit. I sent a cautious note and a voice mail in response, and hearing nothing back, I started to tiptoe and worry.

Stories and assumptions whirled inside me. I felt fear and shame as my body prepared for defence. But then I thought, "What a perfect time to be different." I decided I would try to fight lightly. Rather than pretend all was okay or allow distance and hurt feelings to grow between us, I decided to trust that the relationship would hold, with both of us being ourselves, with our feelings and imperfect behaviours, as we worked towards a deeper truth.

To fight lightly, I think, is to treat the friendship as though it will last forever. And in the context of a forever friendship, what difference does a disagreement or two make? Not a big deal, in the big picture.

I texted my friend to ask if she was ignoring me, and I dared her to wrestle me about the cancelled visit. "This could be our first fight!" I enthused. She texted back immediately, saying she was hurt that our annual family time didn't happen because it was important to her, and that she would have preferred that we come together to make it work. She said she wasn't angry but was open to a wrestle.

I felt buoyed and bubbly, so appreciative of her truth and her love for me and our friendship. I felt unafraid, for the first time in our friendship, to speak my truth. We played and jousted, signalling our hurt while still dancing together.

I could have avoided unresolved endings in my past friendships by fighting lightly, coming from love rather than fear. Most of the available information about solving conflict with friends focuses on lists of what to do and not to do—back to tiptoeing, in my opinion. When we go beyond stories and defences and commit to a forever friendship, we will always speak from love—no tiptoeing needed, ever.

Consider learning how to fight lightly to deepen your friendships and be your true self in more parts of life. Think of it as a wonderful new garden of friendship.

✹ November 10

Fear is a powerful emotion, one that can be very tricky to know and understand, yet immense relief can be found when we do recognize it. For those who suffer from trauma or fear for their safety, I am praying for you and acknowledge that for you, fear is all too clear as a feeling. The rest of us can be unaware of when fear is present, believing instead that we are angry, sad or even glad. Left unattended, fear can turn chronic and become anxiety—unease over what might happen.

I am surprised by how often I feel fear. Regardless of the situation, there seems just one level of intensity: all-out, "code red" emergency fear. I believe I cover the fear with anger to justify the terror and panic I feel, and in order to function. It's so exhausting to contain and push down this level of energy on a daily basis!

I feel afraid of change. I feel afraid of conflict, of hosting people, of being wrong, embarrassed or ashamed. I feel afraid of bad things happening to people and animals I love. I feel afraid of trying new things and of both failure and success. I do not feel afraid to sleep, drink, eat, watch TV, do yoga or pet large animals.

Making a list of all that I do and do not fear is helpful—it builds awareness. Now, whenever something from my fear list occurs, I tell myself I feel afraid. Being able to tell ourselves when we feel fear opens us up to be gentle with ourselves, comfort ourselves, find a friend, pause or step back to ease the fear for a moment. How lovely. It also stops anger or another artificial feeling from layering itself on top of the fear. We can function in the world while we're afraid. We may need a little practice and have to go slowly, yet we can do things and feel afraid. Once we trust that, we will endear people to us because we are being real. We will be able to do things we want to do, because fear that is felt and acknowledged becomes courage.

Let's start gently with a list in our minds of what we are afraid of, then notice when those things happen. The rest will occur on its own.

We are wonderful for being willing to know fear and for letting it be so that it can transform itself. We are butterflies emerging.

🌼 November 11

Years ago while I was looking for a group process that would help people begin the dive into issues, concerns or questions that recirculated often in their lives, I stumbled upon something interesting from the Quaker community called a "clearness committee." The thinking behind it is brilliant: an individual with a question or concern asks a small handful of friends or acquaintances to sit with them in committee. After they outline what their issue or question is, in the greatest and most relevant detail possible, it is then up to the committee to ask questions that may enlighten the person. The committee cannot offer advice or make suggestions; they may only ask questions that are meant to help the person expand or deepen their knowledge of the issue. The entire process is conducted by a moderator whose job is to ensure that the committee stays within their mandate.

I tried it myself and asked my committee to help me understand why I had never completed many of the important goals in my life—what was getting in my way? The genius of the clearness committee is that there are many minds at work, and with no question being off-limits, truly amazing results are possible.

One friend asked me, "If you were to complete these things, what would that make you in your mind?"

"Legitimate," I answered. "I would be legitimate."

Another friend asked, "Tell me, have you ever felt legitimate? What's your earliest memory of feeling this way?" I thought back over my life and searched through my memories. I had felt loved, worthy, respected, understood, welcome—many things, but never legitimate. "I have no memory of feeling legitimate," I answered. "I have always carried with me that I was an interruption. I was loved by my parents and extended family, but my birth was an interruption in everyone's life." A few moments later, I added, "I wasn't expected."

An uncomfortable silence crept into the room. Then a neighbour I had invited asked, "Is it possible that being incomplete is your way of affirming that feeling—that there's nothing to be expected of you or by you?"

I paused. "Yes," I said, "that's it. No one has ever expected anything of me other than to be responsible." No one held a dream of mine out for me and said, "Keep going. You can do this. I believe in you."

Then a dear friend asked, "Then why would you ever complete anything?"

I finally had an answer to the pattern that, up to that point, had defined my life. Thankfully, I was able to deduce that completion on its own is a powerful way of affirming our self-esteem and self-confidence. And I am forever grateful to that committee of friends who loved me enough to help me get there.

November 12

According to Wikipedia, "Spectrums are a way to classify something, in terms of its position on a scale between two extreme or opposite points." When they are used to highlight differences, spectrums create separation. Most aspects of ourselves now sit on a spectrum in society, with labels and bias and an artificial "normal" point—gender identification, religious affiliation, spiritual beliefs, ethnicity, sexual orientation, political ideologies, language, marital status, weight, height, hair colour ... the list goes on and on. We can feel the separation, judgment and creation of hierarchies.

Spectrums can also be used to highlight uniqueness or distinctions among individuals, which creates togetherness. Have you ever been a part of a continuum line in a class or an exercise? That's where individuals self-identify by standing in a group—sometimes in a line—if they answer yes to a question. Continuum lines illustrate shared experiences within a group or the range of experience in a group.

It can be very freeing to let go of the spectrum entirely. For instance, the incredible transformation that is taking place thanks to courageous individuals advocating for gender rights is erasing the gender spectrum. They are showing us how to live without a gender label.

Imagine allowing ourselves to be attracted to someone based on their soul, not their gender. Imagine the masculine and feminine inside each of us being allowed to live in harmony, expressed individually from moment to moment.

The same is true of mental health. Society uses a spectrum with an artificial normal point that forces judgment and bias, when the truth is that we will all have mental health challenges during life and there is no normal. Imagine society offering mental health care for all—not if we need it, but when we need it.

We can choose, as we become aware, to take ourselves off of spectrums enforced by society by refusing to label ourselves—refusing to judge ourselves. Let's start with ourselves, trusting that our own freedom will benefit others. We will exude joy and light in our found freedom, others will show their light too, and in this way we will have helped one another.

Today let's take ourselves off spectrums and feel what it is like to live without any labels or comparisons or self-identification; let each of us be an individual to be discovered.

November 13

There is a children's song from the 1970s called "Three Is a Magic Number." And that's so true. If we have three people we feel close to, whom we can count on and with whom we are willing to maintain frequent and meaningful contact, we'll likely live longer. Social connection is the greatest predictor of life expectancy—so say the scientists—which is one reason why women tend to live longer than men. Throughout their lives, women are more likely to connect with and maintain close friendships with at least three people. Men, it seems, not so much. As men age, they lean towards being more isolated and alone.

I've felt my friendships become thinner as the years have gone by. In our teens and twenties, and even into our thirties, a few of us managed to stay relatively close by talking on the phone or getting together weekly or monthly for nights out. But as we all slipped into our forties and now our fifties, it seems that distance and a type of tiredness have settled in. We talk more about getting together than being together, and when we are together we spend more time reminiscing about past adventures than being present with each other to build new ones.

This thinning of connection is not something any of us ever talk about either. In truth, despite longing to connect with every close friend I have, there's only one friendship I can think of where we both feel comfortable saying "I miss you" to each other. With every other friend, I tuck that longing away, thus obeying the unspoken social code of not rocking the boat. Perhaps this unrealized longing for connection is the reason we tend to overattach and make our work or our life achievements grandiose.

All I know is that if someone had given me a handbook that revealed the key to living a longer, healthier life—having three close friends—I would have followed it.

❀ November 14

Trade a story today.
One about ourselves, for one from another,
Over lunch or tea or to start a meeting.
Places we have seen, homes we loved living in, first job, first love.

We have lived several chapters now—
So many stories, layered into a rich concerto
Or a textured, colourful, handwoven fabric, so intricate in detail.
Life is most fascinating in the telling of the story.
Share a chapter of life today.

November 15

I've never really understood why some people discount or disregard the views of others who are different from them, or go to great lengths to foist their views on others. What I really mean is that, while I understand it logically or cognitively, it has never seemed to me to be a sound strategy for learning and living. To my mind, thinking this way seems limiting, self-reinforcing and more than a little egotistical. Walk into any bookstore or public library and take in all that has been written to date, and then imagine that, as you are standing there, even more people are living, learning and writing about experiences in books yet to be published. It is truly humbling to understand that in my lifetime—or anyone's lifetime—we can't possibly know all that is known.

I love being a listener and holding space for people to share what they think and believe. I have met people only to realize we had opposite views, yet they still have had experiences and wisdom that helped me to grow. I listen, I ask questions to help me dig deeper into their rationale, and I build that wisdom into my own understanding of being alive.

I think we could all stand to be warier of our tendency to build boxes or fences around ourselves. Shutting out the world and protecting ourselves behind the walls and barriers of our beliefs is a symptom of our fragility, not our strength. We are designed and destined for a life of movement, fluidity and enlightenment.

✺ November 16

Christiane Amanpour, the well-regarded journalist currently with CNN, has a series on Netflix called *Sex and Love around the World*. Travelling around the world to explore the practices and realities of relationships, sex, love and intimacy among the young and old alike, Amanpour delivers an intriguing look at how people express their sexuality and love for one another.

What I found interesting was my own reaction to some of the more poignant and tender scenes of love. As a Japanese couple hesitated and tentatively approached giving a kiss on the cheek in front of the camera, my response was "That's silly—it's just a kiss!" When a couple from Delhi described how unsafe their intercaste relationship was for them, my mind screamed, "This is unjust!" And as women in Beirut share that their city is too confining and unaccepting of their openness and sexual liberation, again my mind is aghast. "What is there to be so fearful of?"

But it's not for me to judge, is it? Who am I to believe that my personal value system—or that of our society—is the best or the only way to live? From the comfort of my own box of self-justification, it is all too easy to draw boxes around other people and their cultures and decry them as being too different. Boxes of self-justification have become the immediate, reactive way many of us deal with our experiences of others. And with these boxes in place, our world appears to be populated with nations, neighbourhoods and houses of aliens who are different from us—so different, in fact, that we need to be wary of them. With these boxes in place, we are deceiving ourselves.

We must work a bit harder to break out of our natural tendency to draw these boxes and feel justified in our differences. There is no one way of being, there has never been one way of being, and we need to stop pretending or behaving as though there is. I believe our only responsibility is to accept difference and to have empathy and understanding. A former colleague shared their definition of intimacy with me as "the willingness of one person to have their perspective shifted by the experience of another." Watching *Sex and Love around the World*, I reminded myself of this meaning of intimacy and took a deep breath in. As I exhaled, I realized that love is love, and one person's experience of love is not greater than another's.

🌸 November 17

Driving on the highway one day, the four of us as a family, I remember that the vibe in the car was palpable, each of us in our own state of anger and frustration, though I don't remember why. Things started to escalate quickly as we rubbed against each other, so we all agreed to roll the windows down and yelled as loudly as we could into the wind. We rolled the windows back up, laughing and hooting, so impressed with ourselves and completely rebalanced. The energy was transformed as the anger and frustration were released and we returned to a state of peace and joy.

Anger is the emotion I call the "signpost," because its job is to alert us to boundaries crossed. Its job is to signal NO, and our body responds with a wave of energy to repel the intrusion. The anger energy is released, the boundary is protected and our bodies return to neutral. Within the support of group therapy, I have pushed, yelled, shaken, taken a bat and my fists to a bag—safely, using a supervised technique. I have looked another in the eyes and let them see my anger, my rage, while I released it safely into the bag.

Sometimes I have felt light and joyful immediately after an anger release, when the true feelings underneath are revealed. I have also felt deep sadness. Anger is a protective layer over the top of these other emotions, and releasing it is the only way we can reach that next layer down and relieve the hurt, fear, sadness, grief and shame. This is how healthy anger release happens, and it illustrates how anger is a good, beautiful friend.

Society conditions us to hide, repress and deny our feelings. So many of us walk around anxious, stressed, sarcastic, bitter, resentful or fatigued because we are trying to keep the lid on powerful waves of anger—an effort not unlike trying to control and contain the ocean tides. Repressing anger is exhausting. Releasing it is exhilarating.

Writing letters, exercising, breathing and talking to a friend are good bracketing techniques—ways to contain our anger until we reach a safe time and place to process our feelings. But bracketing is not intended to be done forever. I urge you to find a therapist or counsellor who does emotional-process work. Our friend Susan Aaron specializes in dealing with anger, fear and sadness using a methodology devoted to the healthy release of feelings and trauma. There are many such professionals who can help us. Learning how to be with our feelings is the key to our freedom!

I pray we all choose to move beyond our social rules, for the sake of our freedom, our health, our relationships and the promise of who we are underneath. I promise it is worth it.

✺ November 18

In the 2015 Pixar movie *Inside Out*, sadness is one of the emotions living inside of young Riley, the protagonist, and we are taken on a journey into her mind to see how her feelings interact—in particular, the power struggle between joy and sadness. I think it is such a lovely and accurate portrayal of our emotional responses to life events—in this case, Riley processing her family's move halfway across the country. Sadness, as a character, is described as "intelligent and in her slowness, she is more thoughtful. She has deep empathy and compassion for others and their troubles and can bring people in need together." A perfect description of the value sadness offers to all of us.

As is true of our other feelings, sadness can be deployed as a protective surface layer, shielding a deeper feeling underneath. For instance, many women express tears and sadness that cover deeper anger, because sadness is seen as a more socially acceptable response for women. The opposite is true of men, who are socially pressured to cover their sadness with anger.

Sadness gives life poignancy, showing us what we care about and what matters to us. And as with all feelings, if it isn't expressed, it is stored in the body. I find that sadness usually resides in my belly, and if I place my hand gently on the top or bottom of my stomach, the tears will come. Sounds have come, all on their own, when I have released sadness, my crying turning into high-pitched keening. Expressing sadness feels to me like surfing—I'm pulled out into deep water, where I wait for the wave, climb up and allow it to bring me gently back to shore.

Being witnessed by a trained professional is key to feeling safe and honoured when releasing sadness—and all other emotions.

Whereas sadness is a feeling, grief is a state of loss in which many if not all of the feeling states occur over a period of time. The five stages of grief, developed by Elisabeth Kübler-Ross and introduced in her book *On Death and Dying*, are the foundation of grief recovery work. The five stages are denial, anger, bargaining, depression and acceptance, occurring in no set order or duration. Grief is as unique as the person going through it. If you are grieving, my heart goes out to you and I am sorry for your loss.

To feel fully alive, we must be open to all our feelings. There is no middle ground. To know ourselves, we must know our sadness—where it lives in our body, what we sound like when we are sad—and we must know that releasing sadness, like our other feelings, puts us into a precious vulnerability in which we can feel love. That is what makes it all worth it.

Our sadness is a beautiful part of us, one that I hope you will get to love.

❋ November 19

We have been told so often, and on such tremendous author-ity—that of Plato and of Kant—as to take it for granted, that the *Ding an sich*, the essence of things, the inner reality, must remain forever hidden from us, that we stand outside our uni-verse like children before a shop window with their noses pressed against the glass, able to look in but unable to enter. It isn't so. We see our universe not from outside, but from inside. We are one with it: its substance, our substance; its history, our history. From that realization, I think we can take some assurance that what we see is real.
—George Wald, *Therefore Choose Life*

I believe a correction is happening in our world, one driven by our hav-ing enormous amounts of information at our fingertips and realizing that we, the clear majority of us, are more responsible for our well-being than those who have been chosen to represent us. We are choosing life. I see and hear it every day. Young and old people are taking it upon themselves to be stewards of their lives and of our planet. These are people who relish walking barefoot on the grass, cherish breathing fresh air, feel at peace in deep nature and get, in their bones, that we and our world are one. These are paradigm shifters who see that our world is not a buffet for us to fill our plates from, consuming and discarding in a mindless cycle, but it is us—our body en masse that we must have a personal, intimate relationship with.

Our world is on the verge of an enlightenment—a type of holis-tic opening that is contrary to the forces of protectionism, nationalism and fear. "But," you say, "we're seeing nationalism and consumerism on the rise in this place and in that place." And you would be right. The opening I am speaking of is growing, having been embraced by baby boomers, Gen Xers, millennials and now Generation Z, and it is expanding to the edges of our cultures, squeezing out all that would resist it. The pushback is coming from those who are afraid of losing the way of life they have come to expect and who are attached to living with an unchecked, unchanged identity.

But lightness and acceptance are happening regardless. It will take a while, and we will stumble and teeter, unsure of the strength of our own legs to bear our weight and carry us forward, but a few will keep the many taking the necessary steps. A lightness is radiating in our world as, collectively, we lift our heads from the distraction, chaos and blue din of our wired existence to stare up at the sky or out on the horizon and see that we are life. Our world is life. We must choose life.

🌸 November 20

Let's begin this day with a few moments of mind travel. Bring a pad of paper and a pencil or a pen and find a comfortable place to sit, either in your favourite chair or bench or a nice sunny spot on the floor. When you feel you are settled in, take three steady, slow, deep breaths. Bring the oxygen in through your nose and out through your mouth with a slight delay at the peak of the inhalation, imagining that it is the crest of a wave, and when you feel that wave begin to roll down, exhale. Three of these rolling, deep wave–like breaths. Relax your neck and shoulders. Gently roll your shoulders forward and backward in slow, widening circles, trying to bring the top of your shoulders to the bottom of your ears.

And when you are settled, look at your pad of paper and write the word "horse." Now, as you look at that word, I'd like you to imagine a horse—then close your eyes and place that horse into a setting. What do you see? What do you hear? What do you smell? Is there a taste you sense? What can you touch? Drop yourself into the setting where your imagined horse exists and picture yourself there. Breathe, breathe, breathe.

Open your eyes, and beside "horse," write down a couple of words that best capture your horse and where you saw it.

Now write the word "balloon." Look at the word you have written, and when you feel you can, close your eyes and imagine your balloon. Where is it? What is it doing? Where are you? What can you see? What sounds can you hear? What smells are being carried in the air or on the ground? What can you touch with your hands and feet, and what can you feel on your skin? Imagine everything you can about your balloon in this moment. Breathe, breathe, breathe.

Open your eyes, and beside "balloon," write down a few words that capture that moment involving you and your balloon. Take three long, steady breaths—in through your nose and out through your mouth. And now one more, with a big sigh on your exhale.

You are complete.

✳ November 21

We have been visiting core emotions because we are far along enough on our journey to be bumping into unfamiliar feelings, as well as people who seem "heavy" or with whom we find it difficult to stay light. Our natural instinct will be to deny, distract, repress and run away. Or we may react with anger, pulling ourselves out of our peaceful place. Take a deep breath. This is awareness and an important opportunity to integrate our inside and outside lives. It is time to find a bridge.

The bridge lies in feeling the feelings, going right into them, supported by a professional as we talk about them. Our feelings tell us what we need to heal. Continuing to separate into a bubble of spiritual friends or feel-good classes, or striving to transcend at the expense of daily living, is called spiritual bypass, and it can further repress the very parts of ourselves we want to befriend.

Please take a breath and face the unknown parts of yourself that light is making newly visible. We are meeting our unknown aspects, our deeper truths, our hurts, our longings, our feelings—which are as much a part of who we truly are as what is visible, and are perhaps even more precious because they have not been tampered with or eroded from exposure. Think of this as deep, rich humus that has absorbed and breathed in life, forming the uniquely personal aspects of ourselves.

Being whole is the goal.

My former therapist, who is now retired, will smile as she reads this, as I resisted for many years her guidance to "be a carrot." By this, she meant to plant myself into the ground and stop running; set down roots and grow, day after day, and live life as a beautiful carrot. I still struggle, at times trying to add wings to my carrot, but the parts of my life I cherish most are at the roots.

Each of us is a unique art piece, adorned with lines, crevices and indentations, with curves and edges, some smooth and visible, some dark and deep, some in between.

November 22

Maybe today we can tune into what the universe is trying to tell us. It may come from subtle hints offered in the quotations at the beginning of a book we are reading, or from a message printed on a T-shirt we see someone wearing. We may find a slogan on a billboard that catches our eye, or it could be a licence plate we suddenly see or a meme we catch while scanning our social feeds. Look for these messages today—let them pop through your consciousness so that you can take them in.

So far today, I have seen this one, courtesy of Winston Churchill: "There is something about the outside of a horse that is good for the inside of a man."

Which words will speak to you today? What will you find?

✳ November 23

Here on our little farm, we have ten pigs: Phoebe, April, Fatty, Fatty Jr., LP, Goldie, Cowie, Ringnose, Pinkie and Lucky. They weigh an average of 225 pounds, and they come running when we call them, rolling onto their sides to enjoy a belly rub. They are an absolute delight to love and raise.

One of my favourite times with them is when they eat. They are the epitome of gratitude and joy when they are eating. Imagine the sounds from over one tonne of animals—lip smacking, open-mouthed chewing, slurping, grunts and crunches. Juice running down their faces, lips turned pink from fresh beets. They race from bucket to bucket to be the first to find the treats, and when they do, they dive upon them with abandon, face first!

Several years ago, the David Suzuki series *The Nature of Things* featured an episode called "Fruit Hunters," about a pair of seed curators on the hunt to discover new, undiscovered types of mango. Until then, I never knew that there are over six hundred different kinds of mango! The program also showed researchers and farmers painting flower stamens by hand to pollinate banana flowers, the way bees do, so that a disease-resistant banana can be created and grown. The way they revere this fruit is inspiring.

Dr. Masaru Emoto showed the world that human consciousness has an effect on the molecular structure of water. He exposed water molecules to words, music and pictures, and then photographed them in an attempt to show how they were affected by each.

These three stories speak of celebrating the sacred aliveness of food and water. The more we awaken to our relationship with food, the healthier we can become, right down to infusing joy and well-being into food's molecular structure by speaking kindly to it—blessing it, as Dr. Emoto showed us. How incredible.

The most direct way I know of repairing our relationship with food is to listen to our bodies responding to it and connect with the animals, plants or vegetables themselves as much as possible.

I like eating salty chips on Sundays, yet I notice it is my mind that enjoys them while my tummy merely tolerates them. On the other hand, when I eat kale, my body gets very excited and my energy increases.

I've learned that raising food by hand puts me in a direct relationship with what and how I eat. We can have a chicken or two in the backyard, grow herbs indoors, and buy a whole animal or fish. The more we can appreciate qualitatively the whole life of the plant or animal, the more the experience becomes a celebration and a sacred exchange, and the better the food tastes.

Some of us live with eating disorders, allergies, intolerances and emotional traumas connected to food. I am sending you light and love as you lead us all in your need to establish harmony in our relationship with food. To worship food this way—to celebrate its beauty, diversity and sacrifice—is a magical illumination of how we care for and celebrate ourselves.

November 24

Let's come outside of ourselves today, to acknowledge the positive impact we have on others. Count the number of times we say thank you, look into another's eyes, shake hands, hug, wave or smile. Count the kind words we speak, the times we share, the minutes we listen.

These are very important things we have done today. We set love in motion today.

✳ November 25

Our well-being can be a difficult concept to understand. Most of us would chalk it up to whether we feel happy, content, healthy or grounded—maybe even light. Despite the word we choose to describe our well-being, it's clear that what we're really trying to describe is a moment or a general sense of being that is a combination of optimal experience and prime functioning.

Present-day scientific research on well-being (scientists are trying to crack the code of what makes us feel our best!) tends to look at two "schools" of well-being: one espousing the hedonic approach, which highlights happiness and defines well-being in terms of seeking pleasure and avoiding pain; and the other supporting the eudaemonic approach, which stresses meaning and self-realization and defines well-being based on the degree to which a person is functioning.

Take a quick glance at the outside world and it's not hard to see that the hedonists, or the pursuit of hedonism, are alive and well. There is no shortage of distractions, pleasures, mood lifts, substances or alternate realities. But I think the same is also true for the eudaemonists; we have many portals today for people to give to others, explore their authentic core and live in holistic health. I'm not here to prescribe one approach over the other; moreover, I believe most of us use both approaches— albeit not in a 50/50 ratio—as part of our way of being.

What I do believe is important is a question that has to do with pain: How do you deal with pain—especially mental and emotional pain? Because the way you answer this question—assuming you do it honestly—reveals something interesting and curious about you. You see, hedonists avoid pain, while eudaemonists explore, process and learn from pain. For the former, pain is about suffering; for the latter, it is a teacher.

Maybe that is enough to make you go "hmmm" today.

✳ November 26

We can learn a great deal about living from those who know they are running out of time—those who have an appreciation for how time is misunderstood and how moments of life are unconsciously squandered. Bronnie Ware is one of these people. Her years as a palliative caregiver revealed to her that time is precious and that so many people seek at the end of their lives to pass without any regrets. Her work with her patients in the last three to twelve weeks of their lives became the basis for her widely read online article "The Regrets of the Dying" in 2009 and her bestselling book *The Five Top Regrets of the Dying*, published in 2011 and now available in thirty languages worldwide. Later on I'll share more about those five top regrets and the lessons we can learn from them.

For now, I believe Bronnie Ware would agree with me when I say that most of us see time as a very important, scarce commodity. But what I believe we all lack is a deep understanding of how truly precious time is. It doesn't really exist—not in the way we human beings measure it and relate to it. Time is really more like the air we breathe: it is all around us, within us and freely offered and exchanged by all life on our planet.

For much of the history of civilization, we have conflated two concepts that really should never have come together: decision making and time. Because of our brains' ability for executive functioning, we are capable of making decisions immediately or putting them off to some future time. We tend to do the latter with choices that are difficult, uncomfortable or even painful. We sell ourselves on the idea that another, more convenient or better time exists to make the decision.

For today, let's grasp this simple truth: a better time is not going to happen. It never has and it never will. There is only now.

❄ November 27

Ahh, November. Where we live, it is grey, wet and cold. What is it like where you are? And how is the weather picture inside of you right now? Are the two climates the same?

I'm thinking it's a good time for a self-love song. One of my favourites is Corinne Bailey Rae's "Put Your Records On," because if *this* is one of *those* days, then putting on your own music is a beautiful way to come through it.

❄ November 28

Many times, my feelings take me by surprise. A wonderful rearrangement must be under way, and I may never know what the tears are for. Does it matter? Our feelings are real, even when we don't know what has caused them.

Be gentle on them. Maybe they've come a long way to be greeted. And when they release—and they will release—imagine that the particles left will fall and become part of the next wave.

Wherever you are at emotionally, I greet you today. All that you feel is welcome.

Today I am reminded of Rumi's quintessential poem about unexpected feelings, "The Guest House":

This being human is a guest house.
Every morning a new arrival.

A joy, a depression, a meanness,
some momentary awareness comes
as an unexpected visitor.

Welcome and entertain them all!
Even if they are a crowd of sorrows,

who violently sweep your house
empty of its furniture,
still, treat each guest honourably.
He may be clearing you out
for some new delight.

The dark thought, the shame, the malice,
meet them at the door laughing and invite them in.

Be grateful for whatever comes,
because each has been sent
as a guide from beyond.

November 29

I was asked a question last week that has stayed with me, bubbling around in the back of my mind: "What is the difference between devotion and attachment?"

On the surface, it would seem that the two words and concepts are quite similar. I know people use these words interchangeably to describe the nature of their love for someone else. But I think they are quite different, and if we're not careful, misusing them could lead us into an unhealthy emotional place.

Attachment is something we human beings need. As a former colleague was fond of saying, "Humans are a pair-bonded species," and over the years his words have been borne out as I've come to realize that our attraction to others is deeply rooted in our physical, mental and emotional need to survive. Attachment is also at the root of the way we see ourselves when we're willing to do the work of figuring out how we attach and who we are compelled to bond with; all partnerships—familial, platonic and romantic—act as mirrors reflecting ourselves back to us.

Attachment can make us crave or feel hungry for someone or something. It can be like a deep itch we need to scratch so as to feel complete and whole, secure and safe. On the dysfunctional end of the attachment spectrum, we can feel as though we will lose ourselves if we do not bond; similarly, we can lose ourselves in the connection.

Devotion is the result of a conscious choice we make, and it is typically directed towards something higher than ourselves. It is a spiritual connection that we seek—not to any one person, race, culture or religion, but to the largest possible collective: life. In devotion, we begin from the place of being a whole person, confident in ourselves, and our aspiration is to move upwards and outwards because we want to connect with the forces of love and life. We are devoted to the whole not out of a desperate need to be a part of it, but because we clearly see our place within it.

We can be devotees of so much that is higher than ourselves, and such bonds would bring us a lifetime of purpose and meaning. But in being attached to others like ourselves, we find solace from the discomfort of loneliness.

November 30

I want to be with what is true today. My outside is messy and unsure. I am sure of my unsureness. I'm certain there is beauty in the truth of who we are. Not everyone will like us or agree, but from those who put out perfection, is there anything left for us to glean? Perfection is unreal.

There is a vast amount to be learned from those who show us their insides while they are exploring their selves, before they have anything figured out.

We are on a good path, to love ourselves and share what we find as we go.

December

✿ December 1

If you and I are alike, then you have been able to put some things in place in your life, making changes to lighten up. Maybe you have also dug down into your soul and looked at one or two beliefs or ways of being and, now that you're aware of what is happening, made the choice to change. It has been tough work, and you've skinned your knees or grazed your elbows metaphorically, but you know this is for the best. It is what you really want for your life.

And now, I wonder if there is something that has been simmering inside of you for a while that needs a concerted effort to bring to fruition and make manifest. A thing or a part of you that, with thirty days of conscious, loving attention, you know would change.

Could you quit smoking? Could you make a new friend or make amends and repair a friendship? Could you sign up for that course or program that you know wholeheartedly will take your life in a new, desired direction? Would you start walking more? Is there a letter you would write, a phone call you would make? A caring self-practice you would begin or a job you would leave?

What is the change you want to make so that, when you look back in hindsight, you will feel thankful and appreciative for taking action? Yesterday a friend shared with me that he had called a business colleague to talk about a project they were working on together. The phone rang three times, and then a recorded message began: "Hi, this is John. If you're hearing this, then I need to tell you that I've just been diagnosed with stage 4 brain cancer and I have less than a month to live. So you can leave a message if you want—but I won't be answering this voice mail. I've left town—in fact, I've left the country. I have a lot to do in the next thirty days and I can't waste any time. No hard feelings. Nothing personal."

There was a pause, then two short beeps.

Thirty days.

🌸 December 2

Is there a person whose voice lifts your spirits every time you hear them speak? Imagine hearing their voice now. For me, when Deepak Chopra speaks, my whole body relaxes as if I have come home. His tone, his accent, his pacing and pauses—I love everything about his voice. Whose voice does your being respond to fully?

On days like today I remember how powerful sound is as a healing pathway. In *The Magic of Quantum*, Phyllis Kirk puts it in the simplest terms I can find: "Everything is energy" and "Energy vibrates."

In a sound-healing course, we walked through a "sound forest" with our eyes closed as the sounds of different instruments washed over us, and I could feel the vibration of each in a different part of my body. As I reached the end of the "forest," I had a very clear vision of standing in front of a dark horse. When I opened my eyes I recalled my love of horses, which I had tucked away in my mind years earlier—the sounds brought it back. We now have a small herd living here, and I love them deeply. Perhaps my relationship with them will deepen again through sound.

I like this general explanation from the Sound Healing Center's website:

> The basic concept that all Sound Healing is based upon states that a stronger vibration will tend to entrain a weaker vibration into the same vibration. There are a variety of types of resonant systems. There is resonance in

spaces (including chest, abdomen and head cavities, and organs), materials (including bones, muscles, tendons, skin, blood) and etheric (chakras, auras) and emotional fields (gratitude, joy, and love).

There is also resonance within each cell of the body. There is research that has found that each cell actually has its own resonant frequency that can be picked up with an extremely sensitive microphone. Diseased cells also have their own frequency.

The key to treatments is how we [resonate] a person's system into higher emotions of: gratitude, joy, love and compassion. We have discovered that when a person is resonating these higher states of emotion, symptoms disappear. It has also been shown through research that the whole human system enters a state of homeostasis. The heart functions better, the immune system works better, blood flows easier and cells regenerate more actively. The bonus is that these higher states are where most of us want to be most of the time anyway. The goal is to resonate people into these higher states of awareness often enough so that you are then able to hold the states on your own.

The vibrations of the very states we seek—gratitude, joy, love and compassion—can be reached through sound! Sound leads us to an entire world of healing quantum physics. The Sound Healing Center also says it has found that "the frequency of a cat's purr (around 45 hertz) regenerates bones!

Let's open the door, shall we?

✳ December 3

As I learn how important vibration is to our health and healing, I am also finding out that we each have our own resonant frequency. I went out to do morning chores, singing "om" to hear where my voice naturally lands.

Feeling happy to be outdoors and singing, I noticed the horses all standing away from their hay, facing the trees that were knocking icicles off each other, scaring the horses away from their food and shelter.

I went in to offer comfort, still singing. Then I stood in their three-sided shelter and sang a made-up song that went something like:

I am feeling so much joy today
I am here to offer you comfort while those trees sway
You are safe with me
I love you
I am sharing my joy with you, over and over again.

I could picture golden pink as the colour of my song, and I imagined sending that love over to each of the four horses. It was so cute to watch their ears turn as they listened to the song, coming closer. Soon, the bravest one was eating in front of me. I kept singing and sending love. Every one of them came over to greet me, to bless me, by sharing breath. They came up and breathed into my nose, and the sound of their breath was a medicine. Then they gave me an attunement, meaning that they sent a vibration to the part of my body that needed it to bring me into harmony.

It must have looked hilarious as one miniature horse gently turned her bum to rub back and forth against my left side, while the second rubbed the top of my head with his chin. Next, the giant unicorn horse rubbed her massive head up and down my back. What a start to the day!

We can use the vibration of song to access our joy and love any time we want. Joy doesn't need to wait for our sadness, anger or grief. It lives in harmony with the other feelings; that is so much of its gift to us. Our vibration of joy attracts others to us.

I sing made-up songs over and over again until I feel the vibration of joy and love come over me. Experiment with the power of song; feel it for yourself and then send the vibration to another and see what happens. This can be done in your mind, under your breath or out loud—it only matters that you feel it. And if other feelings come too, that is okay. Trust that your joy is welcoming to all.

❋ December 4

A book series I am reading has six volumes, one dedicated to each of six sisters, and then a seventh, final instalment that reveals a plot that weaves throughout all of the books. The storyline made me think of the seven chakra energy wheels along our spines, and the way energy flows between the crown of the head (the seventh chakra) to the base of the spine (the first), lifting us emotionally, spiritually and physically. How incredible. The more open the chakras, the more powerful the flow. Those of you who feel the flow of light, of kundalini energy, I envy you and honour your knowledge. I look forward to the day!

Jonathan Goodman's *Healing Sounds* explains the chakras nicely:

> The word *chakra* is a Sanskrit term meaning "wheel," for chakras are seen as spinning wheels of light by those with the ability to see subtle energy. The chakras are found in many traditions, including Hindu and Tibetan and their existence seems to be based, not upon religion, but upon awareness of energy. There is even scientific instrumentation that is beginning to record and validate them.
>
> There are seven main chakras. These chakras are

transduction points—places where subtle energy from higher planes begins to become denser. The energy from the chakras then becomes more dense as it comes into the body. It next becomes the acupuncture points and meridians and finally, this energy transduces into the density of the physical body. Imbalances in the physical body can be detected through the chakras. Frequently, healers who work with subtle energy can detect imbalances before they manifest in the physical body by feeling imbalances in the chakras. By balancing the chakras, imbalances in the physical body will often disappear.

Each chakra has its own colour, frequency, sound and spiritual significance. I recommend that we use our intuition to sense the degree of openness or clarity in each and have our attention directed for today. It will be different each time we ask.

There are three upper and three lower chakras, bridged by the fourth chakra (the heart). When we think about one chakra, we can also consider the flow from the first root chakra, all the way up to the chakra in question.

Deepak Chopra and the Chopra Centre are excellent sources of information about chakras and clearing. Here's a wonderful example about the fifth chakra (the throat):

The fifth chakra, Vishuddha, is the first of the three spiritual chakras. In the area of the throat, it governs the anatomical regions of the thyroid, parathyroid, jaw, neck, mouth, tongue, and larynx. To be open and aligned in the fifth chakra is to speak, listen, and express yourself from a higher form of communication. Faith and understanding combine the essence of the Vishuddha chakra.

The element corresponding to the fifth chakra is ether or space, and the sense is hearing.

When you align the first and second chakras, it helps with overcoming fear. Opening the third chakra helps you to feel your personal power and have the confidence to express yourself. Knowing what's in your heart comes when you align the fourth chakra. Then, when it comes to verbalizing your needs, desires, and opinions you're better able to determine how to be truthful to yourself and others.

Our whole being. Being whole. Recently, for the first time, I had an image of all three of my lower chakras—seeing yellow, orange and red, together like at sunset. I am excited because I have never pictured more than one chakra at a time.

Today I am thinking about the blending of chakra colours when they sit next to each other. The heart chakra has been tough for me to picture at times—the green or pink in my heart at the front, and across my back and shoulders, down my arms and hands as extensions of my heart. Today I imagine the green of the heart chakra sitting happily beside the yellow of the third chakra (the solar plexus) underneath. I feel light when I picture yellow and green together, as sunlight and forest, happy to be together.

Then I move higher up and imagine how happy the green of the heart is to sit next to the blue of the throat above, like the sun in the sky. I haven't visualized the entire flow yet, and I can feel a block in my base root chakra just now, but my crown chakra is tingling, as it does when I feel connected, knowing I am on the right track.

Imagine our own rainbow, from the base of our spine travelling upwards to the crown of our head: red, orange, yellow, green/pink, blue, indigo and finally violet. There is magic everywhere in life, starting with our own personal rainbow!

December 5

How wonderful to be in a month of light. Many, many celebrations will bubble around the world. Our natural state is light; our heart lives naturally in joy and love.

For many of us, December is also a difficult time, and I pray that we will feel the sweetness of paradox.

Loving another does not lessen the love for the one we have lost, it honours them. Feeling our light is a balm for our grief, pain and loneliness. We can laugh and cry at the same time. We can mourn and celebrate, as though we are at the best Irish wake.

We have great depth and endless light and love. Let's celebrate this.

December 6

There are parts of me that I don't want to express and let out, so I like to be around people who are less cautious with themselves. That way, I can bathe in their light. It rarely occurs to me that I might also be one of these people. Isn't this always the truth? What we seek the most is likely hiding in plain sight within us. We just don't see it.

I've been thinking about this lately in terms of what I look for from my partner and in my friendships—the pieces of them that I believe would make me feel complete. My partner has endless light energy, laughter and spontaneity and deeply feels the outside world—all a perfect counter to my intensity, seriousness and fear-based control. Likewise, many of my friends possess a type of joie de vivre and have larger-than-life personalities that can fill any room. Again, a nice complement to my introversion and cautiousness, allowing me to always be the listener and stay within a relatively risk-free bubble.

I know that what they all provide and add to our relationships is also within me, but I'm still reluctant in many ways to let these parts of me out. I'm also past the point of someone handing me some form of external validation—like the Scarecrow's diploma or the Cowardly Lion's medal in *The Wizard of Oz*. The truth at ground level is that I know I have to do it for myself. And I'm scared and doubtful of the work it will take to surface and express these parts of me.

So this is my quandary: stay in my comfort zone and continue to lean on others to help me feel complete, or open the doorways, surface these parts and go through the discomfort and awkwardness of completing myself.

Let's believe in ourselves and be who we are. Let's walk that road, brick by brick, to find ourselves.

❄ December 7

A young girl, explaining to her mother why it's not important for her to be polite to an AI home assistant, says, "It's a robot. It doesn't have feelings."

There was a fascinating discussion on our public radio station this morning about how we as human beings relate to the ever-increasing number of devices in our homes, workplaces and cars that are powered by artificial intelligence. There are two things about the discussion that I found enlightening. The first was a series of personal testimonials from people who were forced to take a hard look at themselves (or their loved ones) based on the way they treated or spoke to their AI devices. Inherent in their behaviour was a bias towards seeing the devices as less than human, therefore deserving of being treated with disrespect, rudeness and derision. Once, we saw dogs purely as work or farm animals—before they became pets and companions—and we felt justified in treating them with cruelty. Similarly, our relationships with our smart machines are revealing our dark side.

The second aspect of the discussion that came to me as a revelation was our creator-like relationship with these devices. We are literally designing and building them in our own image. Using ourselves as the templates for movement, functionality and intelligence, we constantly push the limits of our machines to be more and more like us. But instead of being open, benevolent creators, many of us are becoming judgmental, authoritarian parental figures to our machines.

What this suggests to me is that we have a very long way to go in becoming fully mature emotionally. We're dragging huge sacks of wounds, injustices, insecurities and hurts with us everywhere we go. In our politically correct societies, we've learned that we can't open these sacks and dump them on others (most of us can't, at least), so instead we wait until we're in the privacy of our own homes to unleash our darkness on our inanimate house servants.

In anthropomorphizing our AI devices, we expose our true selves. As in all relationships we enter, the other mirrors us back to ourselves. Kindness and compassion are not about how we see and treat others; rather, they are values and character traits that speak to the way we see ourselves and the way we choose to be in the world.

December 8

Everything we do is for ourselves. Everything.

I don't write this to be dramatic, and our egos will not like this message, but it is true. Doing for another is self-serving in some way; it can keep me employed or married or safe. Doing for another can make me look good to others and to myself. Even our higher aspirations—for world peace, for instance, or an end to cancer—are about our own wants, our desires to feel safe or to protect ourselves from suffering and grief. Being a great friend or parent can be about us experiencing unconditional love, being in the company of a light-filled child, sharing their magical journey.

We give gifts to see happiness, to feel good about enabling that moment. Our relationships are designed so that we can experience what we want: love, company, happiness or security.

We are here for our own experiences, and each level of experience has its own vibrational power. In his book *Power vs. Force*, David R. Hawkins writes about his map of the levels of consciousness. He says the highest vibration possible is associated with enlightenment, followed by peace, then joy, then love.

My twenty-year career was based upon motivating myself, having courage, taking pride in providing solutions and having the desire to be successful. Courage, pride, desire and fear are also levels on Hawkins's map of consciousness, though my successes felt empty. When I shifted my focus unconsciously to expressing myself, I experienced willingness, acceptance and sometimes self-love—all of which are higher-level vibrations on the map. It wasn't until I started aiming higher for myself, to experience love, joy and peace, that things started lightening up on the inside. I gave myself experiences I knew would serve the highest version of myself. I opened myself to children, to the chance to live in nature, to horses, and most recently to learning how to pray. I still have a long way to go, but I have moments now of joy, peace and love. I know what it feels like to be true to myself, and I know now how powerful and good I am.

For today, let's try to put our egos to the side, let go of the judgments and get clear about what we want for ourselves from our home life, our work and our relationships. Let's be honest with ourselves; that way, we can develop our understanding of our own unique journey. Ask yourself: Am I getting the highest vibrations possible? Am I getting peace, love and joy from life? If not, meditate, ask and pray: In this situation, what will give me true joy inside? What will bring me to feel true love inside, true peace inside?

We can all aim for higher vibrations and shift ourselves. These changes do not come from another; they come from within, from giving ourselves permission. We deserve to feel and experience love, joy and peace—it is why we are here.

❈ December 9

A recent survey of 2,500 American adults found that 48 percent had experienced a major stressful event in the last twelve months. These included such big life changes as loss of a loved one, loss of a job, separation or divorce, bankruptcy or a life-altering medical diagnosis. You and I know that daily living is also full of many stressful moments that can compound the stress we feel from these major events. While I have no control over whether a life-altering event will happen to me, I can control the stress I feel from these daily events—I can de-stress that daily buildup.

This is a good month to put a practice in place, either early in the morning or, as I like to do, nightly just before I go to bed, to unpack the stresses of that day. To be honest, no one method works for me all the time, so I've learned to be flexible and try a few approaches rather than be overly reliant on one. Some nights I will meditate, envisioning a calm, serene setting that I can put myself into, or do a simple breathing practice like the box breath. Other nights I will grab a pad of graph paper and jot down the stresses that arose that day in one column, while listing in an adjacent column all the actions I could take to resolve the issues that triggered those stresses.

When I lived in the city I would put my running gear on an hour before bedtime and go for a good run, doing my best to keep my head clear and my body present to the movement. I'd often come back from these runs peaceful, lightened with endorphins and ready to sleep. There have been other nights when the best daily stress relief was a great chat with a good friend. Talking out the stresses with a respectful, honest listener, rather than keeping them bottled up, is good, healthy mental medicine.

I've discovered that no two stresses are alike, and therefore no single form of stress relief can be effective all the time. Being adaptive and fluid in my approach is crucial to letting the stress flow out of my body, as is a single-minded focus on returning to my lightest possible self.

✿ December 10

When we put a thought or an idea out into the world or we take a step forward, there will be a reaction. The laws of physics require that there be a reaction to everything we generate in thought, feeling and action.

Today I feel a big reaction to the world's reaction! I didn't realize how attached I can be to gaining agreement and support. The other night I registered for a course I am interested in and when my partner asked questions about the time and cost involved, my defences were up in an instant. I pushed back hard, accusing my partner of being a saboteur and unsupportive. It felt as though a fuse had been lit and I exploded before I had a chance to realize I was holding dynamite. Yikes!

What I didn't realize at first was that my partner's questions echoed my own uncertainties, and when I heard them coming from outside of my head, I pushed hard against my partner and myself to shut them down.

I've apologized, but the anger is here still. I think I am angry at myself for not standing up for what I want, for not forging ahead with power, for lacking clarity and vision. Such judgments. No wonder I am like a powder keg. My anger is telling me my boundary has been crossed, but I am the one who has crossed it! I am judging and calling myself names, forcing myself forward, and my anger is waving the flag to stop.

So I take a breath and I stop. The healthy adult in me sees that this course is related to the path I am on, yet I'm not completely certain about taking it just now. I will take one class, and if it doesn't resonate strongly, I will ask for a refund. I tell myself I will then have enough information to know whether it is right for me.

Many times, the source of anger, anxiety or frustration is the way we are treating ourselves. The world is always pushing back, and when this happens, it gives us a chance to affirm that we are on the right path, get more information, strengthen our resolve or change course. Resistance helps us find our way.

❋ December 11

Millennials, the oft-judged generation, are leading the way in a long-overdue conversation about burnout. Threads in chat forums and in the comments of online publications are full of the causes for this burnout, including a lifetime of perfectionism, a "try harder" work ethic, an inherent expectation that effort impacts results, the fallout from the 2008 economic crisis, baby boomers clinging to their jobs, and shifts in the way the two genders work and divvy up household responsibilities.

I confess: there was a time when I looked at millennials and their complaints and expectations and judged them to be privileged, sheltered and whiny. I've changed that view considerably, simply because what I see now is that our society needs the kind of disruption millennials bring.

Besides, every previous generation has suffered its own form of burnout, and two things have kept this dysfunction from being exposed and changed: denial and complicit mediocrity.

As a late baby boomer born in 1963, I've been exposed to both the advantages that my generation enjoyed and the challenges that GenXers and millennials face. And I've done my fair share of complaining about what wasn't just or right. I can also relate to burnout, having seen friends go through bouts of chronic fatigue syndrome in the late '80s and having had my own episode in the early '90s, while in my early thirties. And none of us dared to talk about it for fear of being labelled weak or spoiled.

Burnout is not exhaustion—although we can feel exhausted, hopelessly so. For me it was chronic. The most difficult part of being burned out was the everyday passionless emptiness in my body, a growing apathy and a simmering belief that nothing ever felt completed; life seemed a long assembly line of repetitive, endless, pointless tasks and responsibilities. Being an adult sucked, and I began to feel the need for binge partying, drugs, dating—anything, just to feel something. I'm grateful that I hit rock bottom and, once there, that I had the support I needed to find my way out.

Finding my way back wasn't about more "to dos" of personal betterment or optimization. I had to rejig the whole paradigm. I had to find my wholeness—the place where I was confident, where I knew I was solid. A sense of worth based not on achievement but on meaning and connection. A sense of self released from any external standards and my own egocentric identity metrics. And from there, I had to build more moments of intimate meaning into my life.

Like today's millennials, I had to experience a disruption of my soul.

❄ December 12

Rabbi David Rosen knows what truly separates the pessimist from the optimist. "The pessimist is the unrealistic one," says Rosen. "He's coming from on top, expecting to see a full glass, and therefore he's disappointed with what's missing. The optimist comes from underneath. He knows the glass was originally empty, and therefore he can celebrate everything in it."

There it is again: when we expect life to be different or we have a strong attachment to people behaving in certain ways, we leave ourselves open to disappointment, then disillusionment, and finally we become pessimistic. Optimists live lightly because they hold few expectations and leave themselves open to surprise and gratitude. As a survivalist, I'm prone towards optimism because I know I can take care of my basic needs and I'm willing to be self-responsible and do whatever it takes to ensure my good health and contentment. Sure, I ask others for help along the way when I think I need it, but I'm not attached to them saying yes. I'll say, "No is an acceptable answer." And when people do offer me help and support, I feel deeply grateful.

But I know many do not see life this way. Almost daily, I see and hear people frustrated that one expectation or another hasn't been met to their liking.

"I won't date that guy; he isn't committed to working out!"

"I can't believe they've run out of decaf tea at this place!"

"I don't understand why this credit card company won't increase my limit!"

"I should have that promotion. I'm the most dedicated manager they have!"

"I've done everything my therapist said and I've read every self-help book there is—I don't get why my life is still shit. Nothing works out for me—ever!"

Intervening in these moments can be fruitless until people are willing to see for themselves that their pessimism and disillusionment are of their own creation. Often it goes something like this:

"It sounds like you were expecting this to be different."

"Of course I was. Anybody would! What can you do to help me, and can you fix this?"

"No, I can't fix this—it's not really what I do. I can help you, but I don't have any solution or Band-aids for this."

"What? How come? I came here thinking you would fix me and make me feel better."

"I know . . . you were expecting something different."

December 13

Fun. We really shouldn't need to describe what that is, right? Spontaneous, immediate, fulfilling, intriguing, lightening.

Aren't you amazed at how many adults have forgotten how to have fun? As we age, it seems that we can't or don't have fun without the aid of alcohol or drugs or some virtual, fantastical world. What happened to our sense of fun? Where did it go?

Is it locked away inside of our adult identity, waiting for a child, a puppy or a kitten to come into our lives and open the door? Is it sitting beneath a line of what is appropriate or acceptable behaviour, allowed to surface only during much-needed vacations, when we can be assured of our anonymity? Is it on a shelf, where we can see it every day, but because there's not enough time or the moment is never right, we never reach up to take it down? Isn't fun like air—available all around us, and at any time?

Today might be a great day to find our fun. We can dust it off by doodling with a pencil, playing our favourite game, singing at the top of our lungs to a catchy tune or maybe even learning how to use a yo-yo. We can make paper airplanes or origami animals, or just crumple the paper into balls and toss them into baskets. This is about play and flushing anything intense and serious out of our systems.

As Friedrich Nietsche put it, "A person's maturity consists in having found again the seriousness one had as a child, at play."

December 14

The surest way to become Tense, Awkward, and Confused is to develop a mind that tries too hard—one that thinks too much. —Benjamin Hoff, *The Tao of Pooh*

Perfectionism is a downward spiral.

I'm a former, recovering perfectionist. I came to it early in my childhood, and it was my way of connecting with and trying to be seen by my parents—trying to do things as well as they did. I grew up older than my years, exhibiting over-responsibility and people pleasing. The trap of perfectionism is that we can never be perfect; rather than celebrating each or every accomplishment, perfectionists tend to carry a powerful "not enough" story that we seek to unload or soften by trying harder. Perfectionists want to be perfect because we can't accept our imperfection. We think too hard, we think too much, we practise, practise, practise. And frankly, because of our restlessness and anxiety, we're really annoying to be around.

I describe myself as a "recovering" perfectionist because I'm still learning how to let go of the need to get things 100 percent right, to be in control. I'm still learning to trade angst for relaxation and calm. I'm doing my best to eliminate the word "perfect" from my vocabulary because it is often an exclamation point at the end of every achievement. I'm working to use "great" as a suitable replacement. It's a bumpy transition, though; while "perfect" feels like a fresh, crisp box, "great" feels like a crumpled paper bag.

I imagine it will take some time to accept what my eyes still see as sloppiness or chaos—which, I realize now, describes life as the rest of the world lives it. As I walk up and out of the downward spiral that is perfectionism, my goal is to feel a sense of relaxation more often in my body and an expansive opening in my mind that I believe is acceptance.

❈ December 15

We have brought a puppy home—a livestock guardian dog. He is a bundle of cuteness, and yet his breed is completely new to me. His purpose is to live with livestock and protect them from predatory intruders. This means he is smart enough to live on his own, make decisions on his own and be otherwise independent. It also means he will bond to me and take direction, but not obey me. And if I treat him like a cute puppy and cuddle him, he will bond to me instead of the animals and become territorial and defensive. This is a dog that needs me to set and respect boundaries. He needs me as his leader.

For the first twenty-four hours, he was inside the house and we were coddling him. He whined and bit, and his eyes had a checked-out marble stare. This morning, I brought him out with me without talking to him, walking slowly so that he could follow, and I went into the horse shelters to rake manure. The horses weren't there, so I knew it would be a safe way to introduce him to the herd. Watching this puppy, I saw him transform. His eyes went dark, he became calm and quiet, and he followed me. He walked lightly on the hay, smelling deeply and lying down, watching me intently, looking for cues as to what I might need from him.

I realized in that instant that he was in his purpose and in his bliss. He was so peaceful and joyful. I didn't say a word. He followed me as I walked towards the horses. I held the intention of connection and I kept present in the moment. The pup and I stood quietly at one end of a large snowy ring; the herd stood on the other side, quietly munching their hay. Then Shorna, the large Percheron, turned towards us and slowly approached. The dog sat down, locked eyes with her and didn't make a sound or a move. I stood by in case I needed to foster the introduction. Shorna stopped about ten feet away, greeted the pup and turned back. The next horse, the gelding, approached more intently. The pup lay down—not backing down, but making himself small. They went nose to nose and greeted each other. As he gets bigger, the livestock guardian dog will be out there alone with the herd, for protection and companionship. I said goodbye and walked away, the pup by my side, confident and with a bounce in his step. He didn't need me to tell him he had done well. We walked back to the house and I put my hand on his back lightly and said, "Good job."

When we land in our natural environment, our true nature takes over—easily, gracefully, as it has always been. Honouring a boundary of partnership is so beautiful—another is allowed to flourish, and we flourish ourselves in doing so. Can we be present in our relationships, honouring the other and giving them space to flourish on their own, while we stand by to witness and appreciate in silence? Our presence is our gift, greater than anything else we could give.

I am at a point on my journey where the longing I feel at times is, I believe, my yearning for God. Yes, I am saying the "G word" today. Please consider a word you might like to use—the divine, the creator, energy, essence, spirit, flow, universe, or whatever it may be.

I'm sharing this thought with you because our faith is a relationship that affects our overall health and well-being—as much as, if not more than, any other relationship we have broached together.

The more deeply I fall in love with nature and animals, and the more I still myself, the more I move towards a relationship with the creator. Yet I am not sure what my status is with God.

I've started a course to learn how to pray this week, with Grandmother Flordemayo. She is a member of the International Council of Thirteen Indigenous Grandmothers, and you can learn more by visiting grandmotherscouncil.org.

In the first class, Grandmother shared how she prays. She talked about surrendering to the Great Creator, giving it all up by asking for help, asking for what we need. She said that if we cry, we should cry loudly; if we scream, we should scream loudly and make all the noises necessary to be heard—because, she says, no one can do this for us.

I have never considered surrendering to God before. I've prayed, I've said thank you, staying at a safe distance. If I am to let myself believe that God is real, and believe I am loved as God's child, it would be a game changer for me. To surrender my heart completely and ask from my openness, and then be answered … the very idea leaves me speechless.

It is what I have always longed for, deep down. More than anything, I want to hear and feel God's presence. I want a conversation, the kind Neale Donald Walsch describes in his series *Conversations with God*. I want to pray and hear answers and guidance and messages. There, I've said it.

One of my dearest friends has developed her faith over the years, and she describes her life as a partnership with the divine. She lives a wonderful, ordinary, good life filled with miracles, coincidences and visions. She does not feel the loneliness I experience. She is in an active relationship with God and her guides. I believe because of her, and because I want rock-solid faith too.

To have faith is to have hope and meaning, to have love and support. Have you considered your relationship with God or a higher power? I can't think of a better path towards living lightly, and it's one I think I am finally ready to explore.

December 17

When we talk about our dreams and our journey, sharing a bit of ourselves, we send out a signal, a welcome invitation to connect with others who might be on the same path. Time to step into the invitation that "how are you?" offers.

Sharing about the good that is happening in our lives can be awkward at first. We may worry about sounding as though we're bragging or that people won't be interested. We need to feel good, right down into our bones, when it comes to sharing about ourselves. A wee bit of truth-telling goes a long way for our hearts!

Let me start: "I'm really excited to be writing this book with my partner. The feeling of words coming, the fact that I care so much and knowing that we have the opportunity to work together are really exciting."

It's important to sidestep the need for another to approve, agree or encourage. The good feelings come purely from sharing. And a short share is enough for us to feel our joy. The other feels it too, and that is our gift to them.

Neighbours and dear friends are starting to say, "I dream of having a really great partner too" or "I love hearing about your life. You are a bright light for me." What a special way to connect in a few minutes. Sharing our joy is honouring for ourselves and another.

✸ December 18

I spend time picking up threads in my life, noticing their colours and how long each thread runs. Some are from my childhood, like my best friend from Grade 1. Others are recent. These threads knit themselves together and a beautiful design is emerging.

Speaking with my best friend today, as she grieves her father's recent passing, she tells of the love and grace surrounding the last month of his life—the caregivers, her daughter, the people who love him, the stories of those who knew him, some of them from the town I live in today. As I listen to her and we share time, there is magic brewing between us; space seems to be opening for us to live near each other again in this second half of our lives.

We never invite loss into our life. I watch my friend go into a profound other place in her grief and I wait for her. I know one day she will wait for me, when it is my turn. I pray we all are this fortunate—to have another who is willing to wait for us while we are with the dark.

The threads of our healing journeys mix in with our laughter and friendship and start weaving the most beautiful rainbow, beyond what I could ever imagine. I am struck by the magic of this life; how heartbreaking loss can give birth to miraculous beginnings when we are willing to surrender to the flow of life. That which breaks our heart open makes space for light to shine through in ways that were not possible before. This is the transformative power of surrendering to life.

Where in our lives are we ready to surrender control and let down our defences so that life can love us to the moon and back? I promise we cannot make this up better than the universe does itself. The gifts, the plot twists, are truly incredible when we open our hearts and say, "Yes, I am ready to be loved, to have joy and to float in peace like I never have before. I want it so much that I am willing to surrender to the flow of life to have it."

❋ December 19

The Cambridge Dictionary tells us that "integrate" means "to combine two or more things in order to become more effective."

As we are learning to love ourselves, powerful moments will be happening frequently, even regularly. We may have a burning desire to bring these powerful moments into our everyday lives—to feel integrated. Some days, the level of miracles and blessings arriving—as we sip coffee, drive or do our laundry—is almost ludicrous. It is astounding, like watching a great movie. We want to be *in* the movie.

Life requires our participation; it demands that we star in this blockbuster film. There are other characters, settings, a whole backdrop that knit our plot together.

I remember a time when I integrated this way. I was single and fairly heartbroken, heading home from South Africa after my love story didn't happen. I had tried everything I knew to find love and it hadn't worked. So I returned home to the neighbourhood I loved most. The realization came to me one day that there were other things in my dream, along with a partner. That was when I thought about the scenery, the other characters. I knew there would be children and nature, yet I didn't feel sturdy enough to become a parent without having a partner. I realized there was also a dog in my story. In that moment, I knew I could adopt a dog. I met my partner two weeks after bringing my rescue dog home. We met under the moon one night at the church around the corner, where people brought their dogs to pee late at night. It turned out we were living around the corner from each other. That was fifteen years ago.

Some days are meant to be dedicated to the other parts of our film. Script, character development, voice coaching, costumes, location selection, makeup . . . so much depth and detail are required to support the main plot. What aspects of our film can we make real right now? What are some gentle steps we feel ready to take that maybe we hadn't considered because we've been watching or waiting for the main plot to unfold? I believe this is how integration happens: when we put ourselves into the movie.

December 20

Our creative dreams and yearnings come from a divine source. As we move toward our dreams, we move toward our divinity.
—Julia Cameron

I would be remiss if I didn't pay homage to Julia Cameron's *The Artist's Way*. This book is a precious tool for our journey. Julia has devised a most beautiful method to help give ourselves permission to be creative and follow our bliss.

I believe we know when we have connected with our creative selves. Some of us burst into tears, brimming with pent-up longing. Some of us start humming or become giddy. Let's not wait another day; let's pledge not to say no even one more time. Let's say yes to doorways that open and invitations that come because we have wished them into being. If we don't know how, let's ask. If we don't have the money, let's ask. We will be helped in amazing, surprising ways.

Expressing ourselves creatively is as important as oxygen. It doesn't mean that we have to change jobs, or that we are throwing our lives away. We can make peace with our defence mechanisms, promising them we will be careful and responsible. We also can remind ourselves how important creativity is to our joy and love and peace—in short, to our well-being. Our defences will bend for the sake of our well-being. Our defences will agree that our childhood criticisms and hurts are important, but they are not current threats to our safety. Closing the door on our creative soul, on the other hand, is a threat to our very existence.

If you are expressing yourself creatively in this life, way to go! I am imagining wonderful stories about how you gave yourself permission, how you found your way. Creativity is an expression of our sacred selves.

✖ December 21

"I don't trust people who try to talk circles around me," he said. "Keep it simple. And if you can't, then it's probably bullshit."

I was sitting beside this guy on a park bench, both of us enjoying a coffee as the first light of morning appeared above the horizon line of the lake. My father always counselled me to be "a man who can talk to princes and paupers alike," and I've taken his words to heart, seeing each person I meet as someone I can learn from. This particular fellow was wise and rough, with a lower jaw that jutted out from his face in an act of defiance. He was my angel of the day.

As I sat there sipping my coffee, I thought about what he had said. It rang true for me. I've learned that the more flowery and eloquent the speaker, the more likely it is that they're hiding behind their words. And it seems that we admire, value and reward people who can trowel words onto us like spackle. So let's have some simple honesty today, okay?

I think you know this deep down, but let me tell it to you straight: there's nothing wrong with you. There never was anything wrong with you. Somewhere in your life, you've been told by other people that you have something to apologize for or to get right in life. That's a lie. Somewhere along the line, some of you have been wounded by another wounded person, and that is horrible and painful. And while this may have shaped you, it is not you, and nothing that happens to us can ever affect who we are at our core.

We are drawn to drama. We are prone to justifying our fears. Denial will be our downfall. But we have the ability and responsibility to choose. We have a need to belong to each other—yes, even you introverts and loners.

We are love and life, and we are connected to every living other in our universe.

It's that simple.

✹ December 22

Have you learned the lessons only of those who admired you, and were tender with you, and stood aside for you? Have you not learned great lessons from those who braced themselves against you, and disputed passage with you?
—Walt Whitman

In elementary school, from about Grade 2 until the end of Grade 7, I had an arch-enemy. We argued almost every day and fought during so many recesses that our school principal, having given up on the strap, just had us separated; we had to spend every school break in different classrooms.

To be fair, I think we were both going through a lot at home. We were both first-generation immigrants in a new country. He had a very critical father who would beat him for any perceived weakness, and I had parents who were verbally and physically abusive with each other and sometimes with me. Our frustrations and fears about our dysfunctional home lives became our armour and weapons on the playground. Enraged by something the other had done or said, we would thump each other mercilessly.

I hated the version of me that my enemy poked and provoked out of me. I was reckless, out of control, menacing, hurtful and dishonest. I was an attention seeker, a people pleaser, a fickle friend and a thief. I would have preferred to be anonymous in elementary school and not be noticed for my differences, which came from my parents, who had no desire to fit into their new country. I looked different, sounded different, ate different things—all of which became fodder for my arch-enemy. As his differences became fodder for me.

My Grade 6 teacher, who would later become a life mentor, took me aside in the hallway one day after a really nasty fight with my enemy. Handing me paper towels for my bloody nose while tipping my head back, she offered me these words: "It's true, maybe the two of you do bring out the worst in each other. But that's not all. There are also good parts in both of you, and those are coming out too. You just have to learn to appreciate the bad as well as the good. Because you're helping each other."

Years later I understood what she really meant. My enemy and I were each other's best friend—and best therapist. Rather than have our darker feelings sit and fester inside of us, we punched and kicked them out of each other and left them in the dirt at school. In Grade 7 we stopped fighting, having nothing left to exorcise from our psyches. And though we never became great friends, we had trust and respect for each other. Thinking about it now, I believe my arch-enemy and I had the most honest relationship I have ever experienced. I really miss him.

🌸 December 23

When is it right to give up? That's an intriguing question, especially when we realize that our culture prides itself on mantras based on persistence, perseverance and determination. "Feel the burn" and "No pain, no gain" may be motivating in the gym, but are they useful as life mottos?

I've said many times that we are designed to grow and learn—it's simply wired into our DNA—and we benefit tremendously when we are willing to push our limits and limitations. But at what point does living our lives based solely on these ideals become harmful or toxic to us? I think it happens when we lose sight of when it is just right to surrender—when we lose touch with ourselves and tip the scale from being earnest to emotionally masochistic.

Emotional masochism means that although we say we want happiness and we're pursuing our best selves, in fact we relish the experience of struggling and misery. We aspire towards a vision of our best selves but deny that we have made any real-time progress or achieved any results. Let me be clear: if we are wallowing in a "not enough" story and holding out for an ideal us, we are locking ourselves in a state of suspended punishment. We are our own worst enemies because pain has become our only real pursuit.

This is when it is time to give up. When we pause to let our soul speak to us, then listen and reflect on what message it offers us—maybe we are trying too hard, maybe we are suffering because pain is all we are allowing ourselves to feel right now. Perhaps our soul is saying, "Why are you hurting me? Let go. I am enough. Heal me."

This is the time to give up, give in and truly surrender.

December 24

An altar is a place of non-ordinary reality held within ordinary reality. —Center for Shamanic Education

In essence, a ritual is about bringing sacredness into your life, and about honouring something greater than you and I. It is about honouring the mystery, and the bringer of life in all things, from the flowers, to the trees, to the birds, the tiny caterpillar glistening on a fresh leaf, or the waking sun, and the moonlight. There is a divine force that moves through all things, like a river, enlivening all of life. It is the same force that moves the plant to flower, the wolf to howl, or lights up a baby's face. As we become more aware of this higher force moving in our lives and express our gratitude for it, it expands and colours daily life with a radiance and light that connects us to all living things.
—Azriel ReShel, *Uplift*

I've created an altar for the first time. As I reflected on my intentions, it all came to me—the objects I would choose, even the placement on my bedside table. It was magical to allow the concept to flow simply and easily. There would be a plant to represent the growth and aliveness I want; an artificial candle for light; a seashell so that I can hear and be heard; and finally, a small pottery dish with fresh thyme, cilantro and a beautiful ripe raspberry—fresh and of the earth—that I will tend to show my care and nourishment.

Symbols are powerful outward expressions of our intentions, as well as a wonderful way to experience our intuition and creative selves.

✼ December 25

Some of us are in the midst, some of us are on our way up and out, and others are heading in and down—all of us are in or out of the deep waters of life.

Sometimes I can get caught up in my own process—I may start projecting my pain onto others, particularly those I love most—and I have learned that it doesn't help or heal me to do so. If I hear myself blaming, judging, worrying, fighting or snapping, I know I am acting out my pain. It's time to stop, take a breath and check in: "Am I okay? Can I wait until my therapist appointment this week? Do I need support? I am phoning a friend for support. I am going to yoga to relieve the tension. I am apologizing for my behaviour." These self-checks assure me that I am okay.

Once I know I am okay, I go into town and am kind at the grocery store or the coffee shop. Or I pet my dog lovingly. I am loving and kind to others, keeping it light.

My friend committed this year to speaking to all with love, kindness and compassion. What a powerful and simple promise—one I can keep, even when I am in my own "stuff." Taking it out on another can feel like a big step backwards. Let's be kind to ourselves. Use self-check questions to assess your level of upset and then go into a kindness promise that you can fulfill automatically on harder days.

Being loving, kind and compassionate is the best course for getting back on track.

And if you are concerned about your own safety and well-being, please tell someone. Ask them to stay with you while you call a professional—or ask them to go with you for an appointment. Please do this.

❋ December 26

Bronnie Ware is a name that has come up earlier in this book, and it is one you are going to want to remember. As a palliative caregiver for many years, Ware helped people during the final weeks of their time on earth. Her book *The Top Five Regrets of the Dying* is a must-read if you really want to gain insight into what death can teach us about living. As she explains:

> "I wish I'd had the courage to live a life true to myself, not the life others expected of me."
>
> This was the most common regret of all. When people realise that their life is almost over and look back clearly on it, it is easy to see how many dreams have gone unfulfilled. Most people had not honoured even a half of their dreams and had to die knowing that it was due to choices they had made, or not made. . . .
>
> From the moment that you lose your health, it is too late. Health brings a freedom very few realise, until they no longer have it.

Can we let that sink in just for a second or two? "From the moment that you lose your health." For some of us, I know this is already our reality—we're living with, and in spite of, health challenges. But for most people, their health and their perspective on time are rarely questioned illusions. They live as if both will always be available to them. And this is what Ware heard over and over again: the dreams we have for our life are delayed, put on hold or never realized because we won't choose them or because we choose something less for ourselves.

Our fear is the culprit here. It is like a cozy blanket that we won't let go of, or a warm fireplace we won't move away from. It keeps us lulled and addicted to being comfortable. Our fear keeps us in place, settling for a life of little or no challenge. Fear is what makes us trade the pursuit of our dreams, knowing our purpose and living a meaningful life for consuming goods.

To live lightly is to know that we are all vessels for our dreams, and the only way to release them and make them real is by lifting the lid.

🌸 December 27

Disgust is one of the most underrated emotions. It affects everything from your beliefs to who you like to spend time with. . . . Everyone has a different threshold for what triggers their disgust. The more disgustable you are, the more judgmental you are. . . . Psychologists call this the "disgust disposal effect," which, rational or not, causes us to try to get rid of things that disgust us. . . . [The experiments show that the] feeling of disgust is so powerful that it makes us want to remove ourselves from the situation whether it's by judging other people to psychologically distance ourselves from them or accepting poor deals in negotiations so we can end them sooner.
—Science of People

Universal to all human beings, the facial cues of disgust are a crinkled forehead, scrunched-up nose, narrowed eyes and pulled-back chin. We live in judgmental times—bullying, racism, perfectionism, intolerance and prejudice are prevalent. More subtle is our standoffishness—at work, in our relationships or in our community.

If you struggle with judging yourself and others—and I certainly do—it may be because of an inherent and unconscious moral code. If we were raised with many rules and consequences, if our parents experienced shame as children, if we experienced violence or abuse as children, then there is a very strong moral code embedded in our psyches that we developed so as to belong and help keep ourselves safe. While they serve as very important defence mechanisms when we are children, our moral codes need to be revealed and revised now that we are adults. Right and wrong, good and bad, heaven and hell, black and white is the language of judgment. Judgment is a defence, as is our Inner Critic, and every one of us has one.

Moving towards love, joy and peace will cause you to knock on your inner judge's door. Think of it as an overdue conversation between your adult self and a judge who was imagined and empowered by a small child many years ago. There is lots of catching up to do, and updating our judge's role may look more like using our intuition and good adult judgment based on experience, faith, observation and great listening.

December 28

A gift is a wonderful way to learn about attachment—and, more specifically, what it is that we are attached to. Gift giving for many of us becomes stressful because we embed within our gift a hope, and more often a need, for it to be received as an expression of our love and caring. "It must be the perfect gift," we say—one that truly connects with the other person and says to them, "I see you, and I love you." Gift giving is so powerful that Dr. Gary Chapman identifies it as one of the five pathways to intimacy in his book *The Five Love Languages*.

It's fine to give someone a gift if we know we have put some thought and consideration into it, making sure that it fits with our experience of them. Where I see things become tricky is when we look for the validation of our love in the other person's reaction and appreciation of our gift. It is as if our gifts have strings attached; we need to hear someone say, "I love it, it's perfect—and so thoughtful of you!" as confirmation of our love.

It may be that we get too attached to being seen as loving at the expense of being confident in our love. When we want to be seen as loving people who give meaningfully, we will frequently be disappointed by other people's reactions to our gifts and other acts of love. By contrast, when we are confident in our love, all our behaviour, including the giving of gifts, comes from a rock-solid benevolence and our own authentic generous nature. How others react or respond to our love doesn't have an impact on how much we love them.

You may be thinking about all of this today as you reflect on the gifts you have given others and the ones you have received from them. Did you get the reactions you were looking for, and did those moments of graciousness and love happen? Were you aware, as you opened gifts from others, that your honest and immediate reaction was being studied? Did you fake pleasure for anyone—or feel like you should have—so as not to hurt their feelings?

If you did—or if you suspect that someone did so that your feelings wouldn't be hurt—let's make an agreement right here, right now. Let's agree that you are better than this. You are a powerful force of connection, with free choice, and your love for someone is neither conditional nor dependent on how they receive your gifts. From this date forward, we can give gifts without any strings attached.

December 29

For a couple of years, we have had a new tradition in our family for New Year's Eve. Each of us writes a letter to ourselves on December 31, then we fold it, place it in an envelope and mail it to ourselves a year later. Every person's letter is slightly different, but we generally start by sharing love and then gratitude for what we have experienced or accomplished during the year.

It takes me a day or two to really think about the letter I want to write to myself. I try to be realistic about what I would like to happen in all parts of my life over the next fifty-two weeks—which experiences I would like to be deeper or richer, and what new experiences I am open to exploring. I ask myself to honestly list any uncompleted goals that need my attention, and then I whittle that list down to the one or two that I'm confident I can follow through on. I also think about the people I cherish in my life and reflect on whether there is anything I am withholding—things left unsaid or undone—and I work those into my letter as commitments for the year.

The very last part of my letter is an acknowledgement of what I know to be my deepest inner truth. It is who I know myself to be when I am grounded, open, connected and, of course, light.

When this last paragraph is complete, I sign my letter "with love," and then I draw a heart and sign my name.

And like a time capsule, my letter lies dormant in a drawer while its contents germinate and take root in my mind and grow into the things I say and do—awaiting that moment a year from now when I receive it in the mail.

December 30

Feeling safe in our primary relationship and feeling at peace in our life can open the way for our buried anger to surface. A part of finding our light is that we make it safe to show our beautiful vulnerability. Yet being vulnerable will trigger an automatic defence mechanism in us, particularly where and with whom we feel safest.

Big sigh. I have been having anger attacks that have been directed at my partner, and while I am able to maintain some boundary of appropriate behaviour and apologize, these outbursts hurt me and they hurt us. I feel the sting—that I am light in so many areas of my life but not at home. Knowing our children watch and learn, I want to model healthy anger, healthy love and healthy marriage for them. Most of all, I want my partner to feel the depth of my love and my joy and my gratitude, for them and our life together.

If traffic, criticism or dirty dishes set us off, provoking a reaction ten times as severe as the offence, this is an anger attack. Anger is an important defence when we think we are in danger or under attack. And being vulnerable can feel dangerous. Hurt and repressed anger from our childhood, and all that we have not allowed ourselves to release, culminate over our lifetime in explosive material, set off when we feel afraid, sad, lonely and ashamed.

It is tricky because exploding gives me my power back—chemically in my body and psychologically by creating distance from my partner—and thus, supposed safety. Then I feel sadness and shame right after, tipping me again into defending and protecting myself. It is a difficult loop to stop.

Self-love and self-soothing are the keys to breaking my dependence on anger. Admitting my insecurities and fears to myself and then loving myself unconditionally—not because I am perfect, but because I am lovable—will start to build my own resilience until I don't need others to validate my lovability and my quality as a human being.

There are many, many tools for self-soothing, from walks in the forest to petting our animals, journaling, creating art, meditating, using gravity blankets or receiving therapeutic touch. By acknowledging that I am self-soothing to build my ability to be vulnerable and intimate, I make the activity sacred, not a distraction.

I find Dr. Leon Seltzer's writings on the *Psychology Today* website on the topic of anger extremely hopeful. Here's an example:

Psychologically, accomplishing this feat of staying present and holding on to our emotional poise when it feels under siege may well be one of our greatest challenges in life. But if we can develop this ability, we'll likely discover a sense of personal power greater than any we've ever experienced. And in learning how to share our hurts—and our fears of being hurt—we may at last realize our potential for emotional intimacy, one of the greatest rewards.

🌸 December 31

An ode to you today,
a celebration of how far you've come,
and where you are going!

All your feelings inside flow,
building a new understanding of yourself,
that takes guts, heart and soul.

You are reading this page by no coincidence.
Thank you for leading the way.
Thank you for finding joy and contentment.
Thank you for looking for your truth.
Thank you for listening to yourself and another.
Thank you for being gentle, open and curious.
Thank you for communing with nature, animals and the world
   around you.
Thank you for living lightly.

Acknowledgements

We are truly grateful to those of our friends and family who journeyed with us and reached out to encourage both of us during the writing of *Living Lightly*. Thank you for your suggestions, your personal sharing, and mostly for your generous love.

Living Lightly would not be in your hands if not for the care and conscientious efforts of Brad Wilson, Noelle Zitzer, Lloyd Davis, and the many people at HarperCollins Canada who have held and supported this book in order to bring it to you. To Alan Jones, thank you for capturing the spirit of the book in the beautiful cover art.

A special thank you to Rick Broadhead for making this dream of ours possible.

And to you, now holding *Living Lightly* in your hands, we hope this book feels like a good friend.

Are you looking for more Living Lightly every day?

Want to be part of a growing online community of souls committed to living fully, exploring new experiences, making new discoveries in our inner and outer landscapes?

Are you curious about connecting with Kim and Dale directly or sharing your thoughts in an inspiring online discussion?

Are you searching for places that are magical, people who are full of life energy?

livinglightlytoday.com

Come join the journey—we are waiting for you!

Kim & Dale